D0769312

Lean Logistics

The Nuts and Bolts of Delivering Materials and Goods

by Michel Baudin

PRODUCTIVITY
productivity press

New York, New York

Most Productivity Press books are available at quantity discounts when purchased in bulk. For more information contact our Customer Service Department (888-319-5852).

Productivity Press
444 Park Avenue South, Suite 604
New York, NY 10016
United States of America
Telephone: 212-686-5900
FAX: 212-686-5411
E-mail: info@productivitypress.com

Library of Congress Cataloguing-in-Publication Data

Baudin, Michel.
  Lean logistics : the nuts and bolts of delivering materials and goods
/ by Michel Baudin.
    p. cm.
  Includes bibliographical references and index.
  ISBN 1-56327-296-2 (alk. paper)
1. Business logistics. 2. Materials management.
3. Warehouses--Management. 4. Physical distribution of goods--
Management.
I. Title.

  HD38.5.B376 2004
  658.7--dc22

                                        2004027226

08 07 06 05   5 4 3 2 1

Acknowledgments

This book is the distillation of many projects, and was made possible by the contributions from colleagues, clients, and friends.

Again, thanks are first due to Kei Abe, for sharing his vast experience of the subject and helping me tell what works from what doesn't. I would also like to acknowledge Kevin Hop, Jim Ayers, Crispin Vincenti-Brown, Jean-Marie Dol, Gerard Poulet, and Gerald Gregoire as fellow consultants with whom I have had the honor to collaborate on projects and who have shared valuable ideas.

Thanks are also due to Carol Shaw, Cash Powell, and Jean Steele, from the University of Dayton, for helping me structure, organize, and present this material to its target audience in short courses.

By bringing up real problems and opportunities, clients have helped me focus this book and, I hope, make it broadly relevant. Among them, thanks are due in particular to Dale Bayley from Parker Hannifin's Racor Division, Tom Berghan from Korry Electronics, Hormoz Mogharei from Injex, Pierre Choussat from Sofanou, and Christian Thomas, formerly from MetalEurop.

Finally, I would like to acknowledge professionals who have helped me as friends, including Bob Shroer, Charles Parks, and Mike Conti, as well as, collectively, the members of the NWLEAN and gateway2lean internet discussion groups on Yahoo! for spirited and substanitive debates. For streamlining the book and making it easier to navigate, thanks to editor Ruth Mills, and for its production to Bob Cooper and his staff at Productivity Press.

Contents

A guided tour 1

PART I *Overview of lean logistics* 7

CHAPTER 1 What is logistics? 9

    Logistics in general and in manufacturing 10

    Alternative definitions of logistics 23

    Military logistics 25

CHAPTER 2 The lean approach to logistics 27

    What is "lean logistics"? 28

    Objectives of lean logistics 28

    Material flow concepts of lean logistics 31

    Information flow concepts of lean logistics 35

    Collaborative supplier/customer relationships 45

PART II *Dock-to-dock material flows inside the plant* 47

CHAPTER 3 Transportation inside the plant 49

    Measuring transportation system performance 50

Types of vehicles 51

Structuring the transportation system 55

In-plant milk runs 67

CHAPTER 4 Warehousing strategies and devices..73

What are warehouses needed for? 74

Selecting storage devices for different needs.. 77

Types of warehouse storage devices.. 82

CHAPTER 5 Warehouse management 89

Six ways to improve warehouse visibility 90

Slot allocation and indexing... 96

Determining how full a warehouse should be... 101

Tracking inventory 104

Security and access control... 106

CHAPTER 6 Warehousing materials, WIP, and finished goods 109

Incoming materials stores inside the plant.. 110

Stores for work in process and semi-finished goods............................... 117

Finished goods stores.. 121

PART III *Material flow in the supply chain* 129

CHAPTER 7 Supplier milk runs...131

The supplier milk run concept... 132

The advantages of milk runs 133

Where milk runs don't work... 136

Using milk runs and remote suppliers 137

Details of supplier milk run operations 142

CHAPTER 8 Consolidation centers near the plant...159

Definition of a consolidation center and motivation for using one................ 160

How a consolidation center works 162

CHAPTER 9 Packaging and returnable containers..171

Assessing packaging needs.. 172

Choosing between disposable and returnable containers....................... 175

Economics of returnable and disposable containers 178

Types of returnable containers 179

Factors affecting customer–supplier collaboration on returnables 183

Scope of use of returnable containers..190

Sizing the containers 193

Preparation of shipping containers 194

PART IV *Logistics information systems* 197

CHAPTER 10 Pull systems 199

How pull systems differ from push systems 200

Pull systems: A counterintuitive approach 201

Issuing pull signals..204

Pull signals in dedicated versus mixed-flow lines 207

Sizing and simulating pull loops..208

Relationship between pull systems and market mechanisms.........................213

How pull systems work within production control 218

Pull signals need simple protocols 220

CHAPTER 11 Manual pull signals 223

Using fixed devices...224

Using mobile devices you already have..227

Using physical tokens..230

CHAPTER 12 Hybrid and electronic pull signals............................249

Kanbans and information technology 250

Toyota's e-kanban system 252

Using kanbans with suppliers who don't...253

The body-on-sequence system 255

Vendor managed inventory (VMI) 257

Dynamic replenishment 259

Other technology-based methods...261

CHAPTER 13 Kanban operating policies 265

When should a kanban be pulled? 266

Kanban rules for operators and materials handlers......................................267

Rules for production and materials/logistics managers 268

Other lists of kanban rules 269

CHAPTER 14 Scheduling principles 271
    Decentralized scheduling 272
    Leveled sequencing and its purpose 273
    Rate work and response work 274
    Order shuffling 274
    Don't build cripples! 275
    Late pegging of goods to orders 277
    Emergency response 278

CHAPTER 15 Scheduling lines with setups between products 281
    What are the true constraints generated by setups? 283
    Using a fixed repeating sequence 287
    Scheduling with timetables 287
    Using kanban boards 290
    Scheduling a Flexible Manufacturing System (FMS) 296

CHAPTER 16 Leveled sequencing of mixed-flow assembly 303
    How leveled sequencing works with the pull system 304
    Leveled sequencing method #1 305
    Leveled sequencing method #2 309

CHAPTER 17 Production planning and forecasting 311
    Planning objectives 312
    Drilling down from monthly to daily planning 316
    Forecasting 320
    Involvement of sales and customer service 328

PART V *Business relationships in a supply network* 331

CHAPTER 18 Third-party logistics 333
    Defining third-party logistics (3PL) 334
    How 3PL affects lean logistics 335
    3PL: special case of outsourcing 336
    Where to use 3PL 338

CHAPTER 19 Supplier–customer relationships.................................341

    Supplier–customer relationships versus in-plant logistics...................342

    Two ways to run a supplier–customer relationship...........................342

    Transition to and stability of the collaborative mode.......................348

    Conclusions...350

CHAPTER 20 Supplier support..353

    The different types of supplier support..354

    Toyota's supplier support system..355

    Supplier support outside of Toyota...358

    Supplier quality assurance...363

    Recommendations on providing supplier support.............................366

    Recommendations on receiving supplier support..............................368

Where should you go from here?...371

Bibliography 373

    Books in English..373

    Books in Japanese..376

    Books in German..376

    Books in French...376

    Books in Spanish..377

Index 379

A guided tour

While this book is the second installment in the "nuts and bolts" series, it is targeted at a different audience than the first one, *Lean Assembly*. Production lines and operations are assumed to be in place and this book examines the details of physical distribution, customer-supplier relationships, and production control information flows. As a comprehensive treatment of lean logistics, it fills a gap between books on lean manufacturing that provide overviews of logistics among other topics and books on logistics that ignore or underrate the lean approach.

The best designed factory will produce nothing unless it is told what to make and a system is in place to bring in materials and ship out goods. This book is meant for the people in charge of these activities, in materials management, shipping and receiving, warehouse management, production control, purchasing, customer service, or supplier support. Its goal is to give them ideas they can use to help their companies realize the benefits of lean.

It can be read cover to cover, but it is also intended as a resource for professionals who need to zoom in on details as needed for project work, for example in setting up milk runs, converting to returnable containers, improving warehouse operations, or implementing kanbans. It has several features designed to achieve this result with a minimum of effort by the reader, including the following:

1. Even though this book picks up where *Lean Assembly* left off, *Lean Assembly* is *not* required reading in order to understand this book—it stands alone.

2. Multiple ways are provided to help the reader find specific information. In addition to a detailed table of contents and index, each chapter is preceded by a summary providing as much of the information in the chapter as can fit within a few paragraphs. The summaries provide the gist of what is in the chapter and allow the reader to dig into the body selectively to find details, justifications, clarifications, and examples.

This book is the distillation of many projects that always involved client employees and often other consultants, many of whom are listed in the acknowledgments. The ideas presented were always the result of a collective thought process, and are given in the spirit of experience sharing, rather than laying down laws for the reader to follow. The book shows problems encountered and solutions used, and it leaves the readers free to decide whether and how to adapt these solutions to their own circumstances.

Assembly line design and logistics are commonly viewed as distinct specialties, with experts in each viewing their own area as much more essential than the other. To the logistician, production is straightforward as soon as all the parts are available. To the manufacturing engineer, the production process is central, and keeping the parts available is considered a support role. In 17 years of consulting, this author has been on both sides of this fence. In fact, he has worked on aspects of lean operations ranging from the details of work station designs to logistics, organization issues, and business strategy; and has developed a sense of how they fit together.

This book has four parts. Part I describes logistics in general and lean logistics in particular. A reader opening a book on logistics may encounter instructions on filling out bills of lading, a description of the order fulfillment process in electronic commerce, or a philosophy of business relationships between suppliers and customers. Given the breadth of topics covered under this label, an explanation of what it means in this book is in order. Chapter 1 gives a definition of logistics, explores its consequences, compares it with alternatives and with the perspective on the subject held by the military, who created it as a discipline, and who coined the word. Chapter 2 provides an overview of the lean approach to meeting the challenges described in the first chapter, emphasizing the interdependence of the concepts.

The remaining four parts explore each of the features of lean logistics introduced in the overview. They are organized *bottom-up*, in the sense that the physical organization of movements of materials around production lines inside a plant are discussed first, followed by movements between plants, consolidation and distribution centers, and customers in supply networks, followed by the information systems used to drive, control, and monitor these movements, leading finally into the types of business arrangements among participants in a supply network. This approach presents building blocks first, and then the way they work together in a coherent system.

Inside the plant, materials move from Receiving to Shipping through production lines with possible stopovers in various forms of storage. Consequently, Part II of the book covers in-plant transportation, warehousing, and materials handling. Because the plant is a controlled environment, it affords opportunities for improving transportation performance that are not available between plants, such as selectively collocating operations. There are also many types of means of transportation that can be tailored to the activity of the plant and used either for on-request deliveries or regular milk runs. These issues are discussed in Chapter 3.

Chapters 4 to 6 are devoted to warehousing, a topic that is much maligned in the lean manufacturing literature. But there are almost no plants where *all* materials go straight from Receiving to Production and Shipping without any storage and retrieval. In the leanest plant, stores may hold only a few hours' worth of raw materials, works in process, and finished goods; but that is not zero, and this performance is due in part to the way the decisions are made as to which materials to store where, in what kind of devices, and by what process.

Part III leaves the confines of the plant and examines issues that come up in inbound and outbound logistics. Chapter 7 starts with the far-reaching idea of organizing milk runs to collect matching quantities of parts from multiple suppliers at scheduled intervals and then shows how this concept, initially applied to the local area only, can be extended to remote suppliers. Then it examines the details of milk run operations, from truck selection to route planning.

While supplier milk runs are often organized around a remote consolidation center, or crossdocks, located at the center of gravity of a cluster of remote suppliers, Chapter 8 examines the different role played by consolidation centers near the plant, whose function is to allow plants to work with remote or overseas suppliers as if they were local.

Chapter 9 addresses returnable containers, their advantages, and the challenges of converting from disposables. In Japan, the use of returnables has been the norm for decades; in the United States, the automobile industry is leading the way by converting to the use of returnable containers, and other industries are beginning to follow.

If lean logistics were a human body, Parts II and III would describe muscles and bones; Part IV, the nervous system. The production control information systems operate on top of the transportation, handling, and warehouse infrastructure inside the plant and within the supply network. Without the infrastructure, management cannot make the lean concepts work; without a superstructure providing appropriate direction, it cannot take full advantage of the infrastructure. Topics in Part IV are presented in the same bottom-up sequence that was used earlier in the book. The functions that are in the nature of reflexes come first, followed by the higher-level decision support and decision-making processes.

A lean logistics organization's response to events is different from that of other systems. Chapter 10 describes the characteristics of pull systems that are independent of the type of signals used to trigger actions, introduces analytical tools to anticipate the performance of a pull system, highlights distinctions between pull systems and market mechanisms that tend to be blurred in the literature, and shows where the pull system fits within production control as a whole.

When new to pull systems, companies should start with manual signals, such as are described in Chapter 11. Manual pull signals range from marked locations to a variety of recirculating cards, or kanbans. In many cases, there is no need to go beyond a manual approach. In large-scale implementations, however, even Toyota's e-kanban system replaces cards with electronic signals for parts of the circulation loops.

Chapter 12 shows how the pull system can not only be a hybrid using both manual and electronic signals, but can also take advantage of Electronic Data Interchange (EDI) technology, use the body-on-sequence system, or take the form of Vendor-Managed Inventory (VMI). Chapter 13 covers the operating policies on which the success of the system hinges. Operators, materials handlers, and production supervisors must not only learn the rules but assimilate them to the point that they become second nature.

Chapter 14 moves from the realm of flow regulation through pull signals to that of locally sequencing and scheduling the work to be done in response to the flow of incoming pull signals. Chapter 14 explains when this is needed and the principles on which it is based in a lean environment.

Chapter 15 applies these principles to production lines that are constrained by setups to have production runs larger than the quantities associated with a single pull signal, and describes a variety of solutions that range from publishing timetables to placing kanbans on boards and using simulations. Setups are easier to engineer away from mixed-flow assembly lines than from processes that require heavy machinery. Chapter 16 describes two methods for sequencing products through such lines with one-piece production runs, respectively applicable when products have no common components and when they do.

Finally, Chapter 17 addresses the way Sales, Forecasting, Production Control, and Purchasing cooperate to turn the flow of orders and market intelligence into a master schedule for the plant as a whole. Even though the requirements on this activity vary widely between industries and companies, there are principles and approaches with broad applicability.

Whereas Parts II, III and IV are about the mode of operation of a supply network already constituted, Part V goes one more level higher and examines issues related to its structure itself, such as whether inbound and outbound logistics are handled internally or outsourced and what kind of business relationships should be established between suppliers and customers.

Manufacturers have been increasingly willing to turn over inbound and outbound logistics to third parties, and many trucking companies are now advertising themselves as "third-party logistics" (3PL) providers. Chapter 18 describes the services offered under the 3PL label, how they can be integrated with lean logistics, the economics of this special case of outsourcing, and the appropriate scope of 3PL for a manufacturer considering it.

It is well known that lean manufacturers prefer long-term, collaborative relationships with few suppliers to transaction-based relationships with many. They cannot, however, set up such relationships unilaterally, and the management of the supplier companies must also want it. Chapter 19 examines what it takes to establish and sustain them when both sides can gain short-term advantages from turning adversarial.

Supplier support is one form of collaboration that has brought Toyota success, and this success has recently been emulated in the United States not only by other car makers but by aerospace, defense, and electronics companies. Chapter 20 describes Toyota's system and explains the right timing for starting such a program as well as the challenges faced both on the side of the customer providing support and the suppliers receiving it.

PART I   *Overview of lean logistics*

Where the field of logistics is defined, as understood within this book, and where the key concepts of the lean approach are outlined.

CHAPTER 1

What is logistics?

Summary

Logistics is comprised of all the operations needed to deliver goods or services, except making the goods or performing the services. In manufacturing, it covers the material flows between plants and between production lines within a plant. It also includes the information flows generated by the processing of transactions associated with the material flows, the analysis of past activity, forecasting, and the planning and scheduling of future activity, as well as the funds flows triggered by the movements of goods and information.

On the other hand, it does not include the transformation of materials through machining, fabrication, or assembly. In-plant logistics is under the control of one organization, but inbound and outbound logistics practices evolve through the interplay of independent economic agents, each of whom acts based on assumptions about the others. This often results in dysfunctional but stable patterns, such as volume fluctuations being amplified upstream in a multi-tiered supply chain. Resolving such issues requires not only technically workable solutions but also the means of persuading players that the game has changed.

Information and funds flow can be further broken down into protocol and decision layers, where protocols are preplanned event responses. Setting the boundary between these layers is a key issue in designing a logistics system. Parts spend more time in the custody of Logistics than in Production, but improving Production is often the easiest way to reduce the waiting time in Logistics.

The literature contains many other definitions of logistics, which we fault with failing to clearly state both what kind of a thing it is and how it differs from other things of the same kind. The term "Logistics" comes from the military, and civilian and military logistics have influenced each other.

Logistics in general and in manufacturing

Defining logistics

The following definition emerged from numerous discussions of the subject with practitioners. It is short but followed by examples illustrating its use. At the end of this chapter are also described alternative definitions found in the literature.

> **Definition:** Logistics is comprised of all the operations needed to deliver goods or services, except making the goods or performing the services.

The word "deliver" characterizes the activity by its outcome. "All the operations" then refers to everything that has to be done with goods, information and money in order to effect this outcome. Without the "except" clause in the definition, it would encompass all of business, and we know logistics doesn't.

Here are examples of what logistics, with this definition, covers and doesn't cover:

- *In machining:* Bringing workpieces, fixtures, and tools to a machine is logistical, but cutting metal isn't.
- *In assembly:* Bringing parts to the line is logistical, but applying fasteners isn't.
- *In aviation:* Logistics includes bringing the plane to the gate, getting passengers on and off, arranging for a crew to be available, loading and unloading luggage, etc., but not piloting the plane.
- *In the car rental business:* Normal operations in the car rental business are all logistical, because it is the customer who drives the car. The only non-logistical aspect is cleaning and repairing the cars.

Recognizing the boundary between logistics and production

In manufacturing, logistics includes the following:

- *Material flows:* Shipping, transportation, receiving, and storage and retrieval between plants and between production lines within a plant.

- *Information flows:* Transaction processing associated with the material flows, analysis of past activity, forecasting, planning, and scheduling future activity.
- *Funds flows:* Payments triggered by the movements of goods and information.

On the other hand, extracting ore, smelting, fabricating, machining, and assembly operations are not part of logistics. Any activity that transforms materials in any way is *production*, not logistics. Because this book is about manufacturing logistics, the boundary between production and logistics needs to be sharper than it might otherwise appear.

Logistics encompasses everything that happens outside the factory walls, as seen in Figure 1-1. The plant sees materials come in from a network of suppliers and products go out to a distribution network. What happens inside each of these networks affects the plant, but is often not visible to its management beyond the first tier. Allowing each plant to know more about both its suppliers' suppliers and its customers' customers is a stated objective of supply chain management, but is not yet commonly achieved.

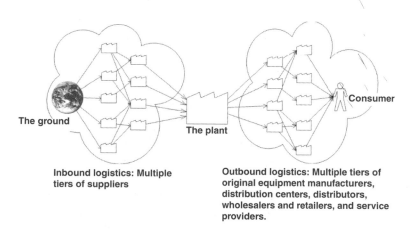

Inbound logistics: Multiple tiers of suppliers

Outbound logistics: Multiple tiers of original equipment manufacturers, distribution centers, distributors, wholesalers and retailers, and service providers.

FIGURE 1-1. Inbound and outbound logistics

Inside the plant, the logistics/production boundary is in fact between organizations. Production does not only run machines and assembly stations; it also conveys workpieces between contiguous stations. Even though these transfers do not transform the workpieces, this activity is still considered to be production, because it is run by the Production Department.

Conversely, palletizing goods in shipping might be construed as transforming them, but it is still considered part of logistics because it is done by an organization called "materials handling," "materials management," or "physical distribution."

Where the boundary is placed between logistics and production is a managerial decision. Technically, part preparation by Logistics overlaps with materials handling by Production and the handover can take place at many points. The extent and boundaries of the logistics space in manufacturing are shown in Figure 1-2. While logistics activities take up more space than production, they usually employ an order of magnitude fewer people.

At some locations, materials handlers deliver open bins of parts to flow racks directly behind the assembly line; at other locations, to a supermarket from which a special operator called a "water spider" working for Production prepares the parts, picks kits, and delivers them to assembly. In the first case, the boundary between Logistics and Production is right behind the assembly station; in the second case, one step removed from it.

In-bound, out-bound, and in-plant logistics: how they differ

Another key boundary is that between the plant and the rest of the world, which is usually materialized in the form of docks for receiving and shipping. *In-plant logistics* is often called *dock-to-dock logistics*. Besides the obvious differences in distances, quantities, and vehicles, in-plant logistics differs from the *in-bound logistics* of getting parts from suppliers and the *out-bound logistics* of distributing finished goods in the way it is managed. In-plant logistics is under the control of one organization. In- and out-bound logistics, on the other hand, are ruled by the interaction of multiple independent economic agents—including multiple tiers of suppliers and distributors, trucking companies, railroads, and air and sea freight companies—making their own decisions.

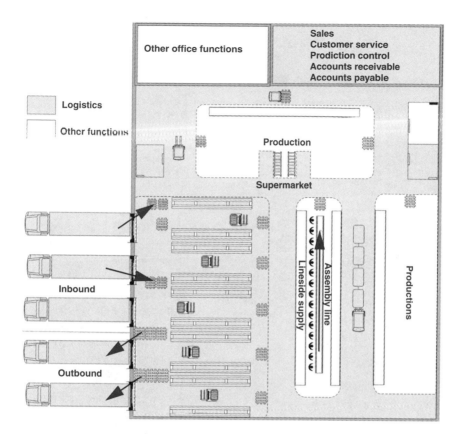

FIGURE 1-2. In-plant logistics

It is a widely held belief that an invisible hand steers all these agents striving to get the best deal for themselves towards a mode of interaction that is best for society as a whole. To say the least, there are many examples, in logistics as well as in other domains, where it results instead in stable but clearly less than optimal patterns, as shown in Table 1.

This kind of situation arises as a result of each agent not just pursuing the best deals in isolation, but doing so based on knowledge or assumptions about what the *other* agents will do. This is known as a Nash equilibrium, after mathematician John Nash. It can be a desirable or an undesirable state of affairs, but moving away from it requires a change not only in each agent's perception of what "the best deal" is but also in the expectations each agent has of the others.

TABLE 1. Examples of dysfunctional outcomes of free interactions

	Long, inefficient commute in private car	Los Angeles is the dysfunctional result of the interplay between developers, residents, city planners, and others.[a]
	Window-mounted air conditioners in every unit	Hong Kong laissez-faire produces residential buildings with window-mounted air conditioners in every unit, which are ugly, noisy, less effective, and more expensive than a central system for the building.
	Unprofitable, polluting plant stays open	This unprofitable, polluting plant remains open because, to the owners, the cost of shutting it down and the risk of litigation exceeds that of taking the operating losses.

a. Photo courtesy of Richard Risemberg, rickrise@earthlink.net.

The business people who run the companies involved in a supply network are trained to focus on *customers*, not suppliers. They feel that, unless they keep customers happy, they will lose them to the competition. On the other hand, they are not trained to show concern for the convenience of their *suppliers*, except for suppliers that are in a position of strength from control of a scarce resource or a unique technology. They do not argue with their customers' ordering pattern, no matter how erratic it may be, and, in turn, expect no backtalk from their suppliers. This is how they play the game.

The amplification of fluctuations in the flow of orders as you move upstream through a multi-tiered network of suppliers was called the *bull-whip effect* by researcher Hau Lee at Stanford Business School. This phenomenon is beginning to be known and understood by suppliers, and you increasingly hear managers talk about "riding the bullwhip," and describe their positions as shown in Figure 1-3.

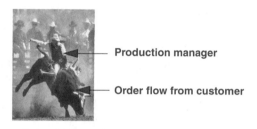

Production manager

Order flow from customer

FIGURE 1-3. Riding the bull, if not the bullwhip

In *Lean Assembly*,[1] we described the bullwhip effect as generated by the ordering logic used by the participants. At a deeper level, however, the reason managers choose to use this logic is that they don't think it is their job to make life easier for suppliers. Changing this perception among participants in multiple tiers is a prerequisite to applying known strategies that can be used to reduce or eliminate the demand fluctuations that are generated inside a supply network.

Leveled sequencing in final assembly is one such strategy introduced by Toyota, and it is one of the most misunderstood tools of lean manufacturing. Its explicit goal is to sequence products so as to smooth the flow of materials to mixed-flow assembly operations, and thereby make the workload more even and more predictable both for inside and outside suppli-

---

1. Lean Assembly, Productivity Press, 2002, pp. 37–40

ers. In the car industry, the time horizon of the sequencing is one shift, which means that it has no direct impact on customer experience. Because of this, the value of leveled sequencing escapes those lean manufacturing implementers who have been taught to respond to "the pull of the customer" and to focus exclusively on tasks the customer is willing to pay for.

To apply this concept, managers at multiple nodes in the supply network have to stop thinking their relationships with customers are like those of retailers with consumers. That consumers are sometimes fickle and capricious can't be helped and they must be kept satisfied, but it does not mean that the same applies upstream from that point.

Other types of logistics

Business Logistics. T. Tanimoto[1] calls "business logistics" the efforts of a company to organize packaging, handling, transportation, storage and retrieval of all types of materials and goods, and related information, to improve its overall performance and competitiveness.

Supply Chain Logistics. Tanimoto then uses the term "supply chain logistics" to designate the expansion of these efforts to multiple tiers of suppliers and customers or distributors. Most companies, however, have little or no access to suppliers' suppliers or customer's customers: whatever influence they may have is limited to companies they directly buy from or sell to. Companies' actions in supply chain logistics often consist of reinforcing the tier structure to *reduce* the number of suppliers or customers they must interact with.

---

1. T. Tanimoto, Butsuryu-Logistics no riron to jittai (Theory and Practice of Physical Distribution and Logistics), Hakutoshobo, (2000)

Social Logistics. Tanimoto also identifies "social logistics" as the setting, maintenance, regulation, and taxation by governments of the infrastructure within which companies operate, including the following:

- *Transportation:* Roads, railroads, canals, ports and airports.
- *Communications:* Voice and data communication networks.
- *Controls and law enforcement:* Inspections of goods at border crossings and verification of regulatory compliance.
- *Taxation:* Tolls, taxes, duties, as well as incentives and subsidies designed to influence the behavior of independent economic agents towards such common goods as preservation of the environment.
- *Emergency response:* Restoration of services after earthquakes, floods, fires or other natural or human-made disasters.

Social logistics is a matter of public policy and subject to debates that are outside the scope of this book.

Another perspective on the logistics domain

That Logistics is comprised of flows of materials, information, and money is clear. The information and money layers, however, can be organized into "protocol layers" and "decision layers." The distinction between the two is illustrated in Table 2.

TABLE 2. Examples of protocol and decision layers

	Information	Money
Decision layer	Giving priority to a customer	Contracts with suppliers
Protocol layer	Issuing an order based on reorder point	Invoice processing

A *protocol* is a set of rules that governs interactions in a preplanned manner such that no decision is required of the participants. For example, in a reorder point system, the issuance of a replenishment order is a *planned response* to the on-hand level crossing a given threshold. Whether done manually or automatically, it requires no decision. On the other hand, giving priority to one customer's orders over anothers is a *human decision* based on commercial considerations and would be difficult to automate. Likewise, in the financial domain, the routine processing of invoices is protocol execution, but negotiations on pricing and conditions are decision-making processes.

The allocation activities to the protocol or the decision layer determines which kind of information system—computer-based or not—it requires. Protocols for normal transaction processing should be as simple as possible, but the more exception handling they provide for, the less management intervention their application will require. Exception handling may, for example, consist of "escalation procedures" posted at Receiving to resolve shortages with suppliers. Activities involving human decisions, on the other hand, need decision support systems to present the decision maker with relevant but concise information.

Misallocations are commonplace. Following are two examples of activities that respectively require human decisions but shouldn't and, conversely, are protocol-driven but should involve human decisions:

Selecting what to work on next. Rather than actually scheduling production, ERP systems usually issue dispatch lists giving lists of tasks in priority order to shop floor operators, with the understanding that they do not *have* to follow the priority sequence. They can, for example choose to run a less than top priority job in order to avoid a setup or because needed parts are more easily accessible. In effect such systems leave the choice of what to work on next to shop floor operators who do not have all the information needed to make decisions that are most beneficial to the company. In this situation, the operators should have a protocol to follow that *tells* them what to work on next with no decision making required, such as picking the next job from a flow rack.

Order shuffling is a legitimate activity based on business needs, requiring decisions, but it should take place *before* the orders are released to the shop floor for production, with the logistics and production process set up to make the production lead time so short as to remove any incentive for playing priority games with the work in process. This, of course, is not easy to accomplish, but it is how lean manufacturing works.

Forecasting. Many companies' idea of forecasting demand is to apply an algorithm, usually quite simple, to extrapolate from the recent past. Producing a forecast, however, should not be reduced to executing a protocol. This is an area where human decision is called for to take into account not only past sales but inputs from the sales force, customers, trade publications, and leading economic indicators. Forecasts are then used in sales and operations planning, which is a negotiation among managers in charge of sales, production, and finance.

How production performance affects logistics

Regardless of where exactly this boundary is set, parts usually spend weeks in the custody of a Logistics organization but only a few hours in Production. As a consequence, many ask why so much effort should be directed to improving Production when there is so much more at stake in Logistics. This question, however, is predicated on the mistaken assumption that the two are unrelated.

The operations of our neighborhood warehouse club illustrate this point. Whenever we visited it at first, there were long lines at all checkstands, as shown in Figure 1-4, which customers accepted as what they had to go through to enjoy low prices.

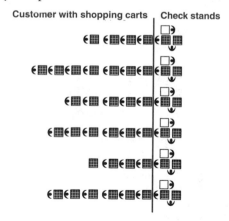

FIGURE 1-4. Lines at warehouse club checkstands

A checkstand transaction that might last 5 minutes was inevitably pre-ceded by a 25-minute wait. To improve on this, one might be tempted to focus on the organization of the waiting lines, using one or more of the following strategies:

- Dedicate "express lanes" for customers with fewer than 12 items, as is commonly done in grocery supermarkets, as shown in Figure 1-5.

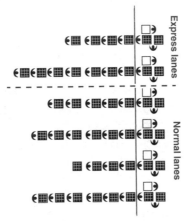

FIGURE 1-5. Express lanes

- Merge lines into a generic queue with the next customer going to the next available checkstand in the row, as at banks, post offices, and air-port counters, as shown in Figure 1-6.

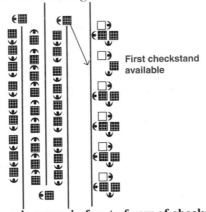

FIGURE 1-6. Generic queue in front of row of checkstands

- Have customers take a ticket with a number and post a display of the number currently being served, as is done at many government offices and deli counters, as shown in Figure 1-7.

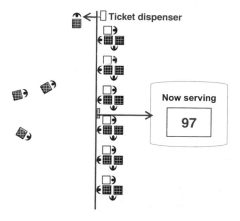

FIGURE 1-7. "Now serving" ticket system

Any of these might have improved the customer experience somewhat and possibly reduced the average waiting time by 10%. The store, however, eventually reduced the waiting time to no more than 5 minutes without applying *any* of them.

The key was the way customer transactions were handled during the few minutes spent *at the checkstand*. The checkout procedure involved one clerk reading along the item numbers from the customer's shopping cart while transferring them to a new cart, while a second clerk typed that number into the point-of-sale system. What the warehouse club did was invest in new checkstands, with conveyor belts and barcode scanners, that were oversized versions of the ones used in grocery supermarkets, as shown in Figure 1-8, and the long waiting lines melted away.

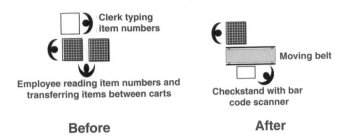

Before   **After**

FIGURE 1-8. Checkstand upgrade

What happened at the checkstand was saturation. The row of checkstands, on the average, must be able to process customers faster than they arrive, or the line will grow indefinitely. The ratio of the time used to process transactions to the time available is the utilization of the row of checkstands and, as that utilization approaches 100%, the waiting time in line grows to infinity, as shown in Figure 1-9.

Improving the organization of the waiting lines can slightly lower the curve and reduce the total time in line by maybe 15%, but increasing the checkstand capacity by 25% through a barcode system moved the limit to the right and yielded a 50% reduction.

In this everyday life situation, as in manufacturing, *logistics* performance is largely determined by what happens in *production*, even if logistics accounts for most of the manufacturing lead time. This is not to imply that improvements in logistics are negligible. They are not, and they need to be pursued in conjunction and coordinated with improvements in production.

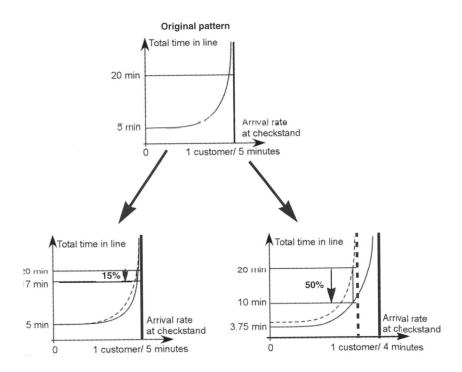

FIGURE 1-9. Saturation of warehouse club checkstands

Alternative definitions of logistics

Many other definitions of logistics have been proposed, but they don't clearly state both what kind of a thing it is and how it differs from other things of the same kind. Originally, it is a military term, first used in the Napoleonic era. According to Webster's encyclopedic dictionary, it designates

"the branch of military science and operations dealing with the procurement, supply, and maintenance of equipment, and hospitalization of personnel, with the provision of facilities and services, and with related matters."

The reference to *related matters* unfortunately opens this definition to multiple interpretations.

In business, the term has become popular since the Gulf War of 1991, particularly since the publication in November, 1992 of an interview with William Pagonis, the general who had been in charge of logistics in that war. A commonly used definition for logistics in business is that given by the Council for Logistics Management (http://www.clm1.org/aboutus/aboutus_clmdef.asp):

> "Logistics is that part of the supply chain process that plans, implements, and controls the efficient, effective forward and reverse flow and storage of goods, services, and related information between the point of origin and the point of consumption in order to meet customers' requirements."

While this definition carries the authority of a professional society, it is difficult to use for the following reasons:

- If logistics is defined as "part of the supply chain process," then the "supply chain process" also needs to be defined.
- This definition appears to exclude the possibility that logistics could be done in an ineffective or inefficient manner.
- Listing goods, services, and related information appears to exclude flows of money from consideration.
- The emphasis placed on meeting customers' requirements in the definition is unnecessary and may lead the reader away from the many possible improvements in logistics that are not *directly* related to customers.

In "Supply Chain Strategy," p. 5, Frazelle gives the following definition:

> "Logistics is the flow of material, information and money between consumers and suppliers."

While his definition is crisper and clearer than the CLM's, it has the following shortcomings:

- It is too broad in that it appears to encompass production itself. Workpieces flow through milling machines, but, as discussed above, cutting metal is not part of logistics.

- It is too narrow in that it does not include services. Getting passengers on and off a plane, for example, does not fit this definition, unless you agree that people are a special case of materials.

- The reference to consumers, as opposed to customers, is puzzling, because it restricts the discussion to consumer goods, to the exclusion of capital goods, whose end users, by definition, are not consumers.

Military logistics

Logistics, as a military term, is defined by Martin Van Creveld as

> "the art of moving armies and keeping them supplied."

William Pagonis defines it as

> "the integration of transportation, supply, warehousing, mainte-
> nance, procurement, contracting and automation into a single
> function that ensures no suboptimization in any of those areas, to
> allow the overall accomplishment or a particular strategy, objec-
> tive, or mission."

While Pagonis's accomplishments in the field deserve the highest respect, his definition is similar to the CLM's in that it mixes the description of *what* a function is with *how* it should be performed. Without integration and automation, and with suboptimization, his list of functions would still presumably comprise logistics, albeit badly done. On the other hand, Van Creveld's definition, while short and crisp, does not encompass all the functions Pagonis sees as part of logistics. "Maintenance," for example, does not readily come to mind as a part of keeping armies supplied. In essence, what all these functions add up to is *all* military operations except combat.

Military logistics differs from *manufacturing* logistics in so many ways that there is less crossover of ideas than one might expect.

1. Unlike armies, the nodes in a manufacturing logistics network don't move. Suppliers, consolidation centers, factories, distribution centers, and wholesale and retail outlets are in fixed locations. One of the key challenges of military logistics, delivering supplies to moving destinations, is therefore not present in manufacturing.

2. While manufacturing companies do face surprises from competitors, it is not on the same level and does not unfold as fast as enemy action in war. The demands placed on a manufacturing logistics system are therefore more predictable than on military logistics.

3. Delivering ammunition, fuel, and food to soldiers in combat is not obvious, and the dominant objective in military logistics is getting the job done *at all*. Optimization issues only come to the fore in logistics efforts that on a large scale and prolonged, such as the support of the Pacific War for four years. In manufacturing, by contrast, facilities are always located within easy reach of trucks, railroads, ships, or airplanes, and the ability to deliver is never in question. The focus is therefore always on doing it cheaply. As Pagonis puts it, "The military focus on life and death, whereas business measures profits."

For decades, civilian businesses, manufacturing in particular, looked to the military for ideas and concepts, but the tables are now turned. It is now the military logisticians who borrow best practices from the private sector. Not only is this acknowledged by Pagonis, but the U.S. Air Force has a strategy called *Lean Logistics*. It openly borrows its name from a civilian development which is the subject of this book and is outlined in the next chapter.

CHAPTER 2

The lean approach to logistics

Summary

Lean logistics is the logistics dimension of lean manufacturing. The logistics organization is the pit crew to Production's race car driver. Its first objective is to deliver the right materials to the right locations, in the right quantities, and in the right presentation; its second, to do all of it efficiently. Outbound logistics is organized to serve as a source of market intelligence. Shortages are prevented by vigilance rather than inventory.

Lean logistics tailors approaches to the demand structures of different items, as opposed to one-size-fits-all. It is a pull system: materials move when the destination signals that it is ready for them. Moving small quantities of many items between and within plants with short, predictable lead times requires pickups and deliveries at fixed times along fixed routes called "milk runs." In turn, this supports the use of returnable containers.

Information systems for lean logistics combine visible management with computer systems. Toyota uses a worldwide network for logistics and markets in Japan through an internet portal. Production planning/scheduling involves leveled sequencing and pull systems, and uses the capabilities engineered into the shop floor. MRP provides suppliers with forecasts, EDI and kanbans are used to issue orders, and auto-ID helps maintain inventory accuracy.

Option-specific components are ordered through the body-on-sequence system, and responsibility for commodities is delegated to suppliers through vendor-managed inventory or consignment. Suppliers are organized in tiers, and used as single sources. Customer/supplier collaboration extends from product design to emergency response, and suppliers organize mutual support in improvement efforts.

What is "lean logistics"?

In this book, *lean logistics* is the logistics dimension of lean manufacturing. The term could and has been applied to services, but we focus on manufacturing as a domain that is rich in logistics concepts, approaches, and techniques that can be called "lean" because either they are part of the Toyota production system or were adapted from it for application in different contexts.

Objectives of lean logistics

The objectives of any business organization can be summarized in different ways from different perspectives. For manufacturing logistics, the most relevant may be what we call "the two F's": effectiveness and efficiency.

Being effective, as Peter Drucker[1] put it, means getting the right things done, being efficient, and doing them without wasting resources. Effectiveness is about the "what"; efficiency, about the "how." Obviously, effectiveness takes priority, and efficiency at doing the wrong things is not an objective worth pursuing. Yet this is what most materials managers in manufacturing companies are doing when they worry more about keeping trucks full and forklift operators busy than about delivering the right parts in the right quantities at the right time and in the right presentation to production.

On the outbound side, a customer who orders a case is not usually forced to accept a truckload, but in production, an operation that needs a small bin of parts—or even one that is fully stocked—sees full pallets arrive still shrinkwrapped, simply because it is convenient for the forklift driver to deliver them at that time and in that form.

By definition, logistics does not transform materials. Many lean manufacturing authors conclude from this that there is no value added in logistics. Logistics authors counter that logistics provides the value of time and

---

1. *The Effective Executive*, by Peter Drucker, Harper Business Essentials, New York, N.Y. (1967)

place. In addition, we also see value in *presentation*. These three types of logistics value added are dramatized with extreme examples in Figure 2-1:

- A beautiful maternity ward ready six months from now is no use if you are in labor today.

- Your bicycle is worth more in your hands at the start of the race than 50 miles away.

- Bullets in a sealed box offer no protection against a pouncing lion.

The value of time

The value of place

The value of presentation

FIGURE 2-1. The value of time, place, and presentation

For the manufacturing organization as a whole, there is much more at stake in the quality of the service provided by the logistics organization than in the productivity of its members or the utilization of its equipment and facilities. Logistics operations occupy more space than production and are therefore highly visible, but production operators outnumber logistics personnel about 10 to 1, and production machinery and its supporting facilities also represent an investment that is an order of magnitude larger than that used for transportation, storage, and retrieval.

If there is one forklift driver too many, the cost to the organization is in the tens of thousands of dollars per year, but shortages of parts can cost millions. Yet, in his analysis of logistics performance, Frazelle[1] proposes measures of logistics performance covering costs, productivity, quality, and responsiveness without ever suggesting that quality and responsiveness, which measure effectiveness, should be addressed before even addressing costs and productivity, which relate to efficiency.

In lean logistics, the functions of Materials Supply and Production are not treated at the same level. As discussed in *Lean Assembly*,[2] materials supply is the pit crew to production's race car driver. Adopting this perspective does not mean neglecting efficiency, only putting it where it belongs, to be addressed *after* effectiveness.

The objectives of lean logistics can therefore be stated as follows:

1. Delivering the materials needed, when needed, in the exact quantity needed, and conveniently presented, to production for inbound logistics and to customers for outbound logistics.
2. Without degrading delivery, pursue the elimination of waste in the logistics process.

Inbound logistics is production's pit crew, and its emphasis is on the level of materials service as opposed to the efficiency with which it is provided. This is a key driver of lean logistics and the rationale behind many of its features.

---

1. Supply Chain Strategy, pp. 38–67
2. pp. 172–173

Material flow concepts of lean logistics

The following paragraphs provide an overview of the key concepts that make the flows of materials in lean logistics different from earlier approaches.

Outbound logistics is a source of market intelligence

Since outbound logistics is the tail end of the order fulfillment process and deliveries trigger the collection of revenue, there is generally no confusion within the company regarding the importance of this activity. There is however one aspect of it that makes it different from a mirror image of inbound logistics, and that is its role as a source of market intelligence.

Many companies, and not just lean manufacturers, mine their sales data. What is, however, specific to lean manufacturing is the realization that the physical organization of distribution can act as a screen blocking access to market information and the design of creative ways to remove or work around these screens.

Lean logistics prevents shortages through vigilance, not inventory

Whether raw materials, work in process, or finished goods, the rationale for keeping inventory is shortage prevention. While keeping large stocks of coal, iron ore, or petroleum may work for this purpose, this approach breaks down as the product mix and the variety of materials and components used increase. Instead of a secure supply, the result, known as "the paradox of stock," is warehouses that are full and contain ample supplies of all but one of the items needed for a product, and from which, therefore, not a single unit can be assembled and shipped.

The lean approach is instead to hold the minimum needed to support production but monitor it closely, plan production to smooth the consumption rate of each item over time, organize inbound logistics to make replenishment lead times more predictable, and respond with countermeasures at the first sign of problems. Spectacular examples of this approach include how Toyota was able to maintain supply of parts from the Midwest to NUMMI throughout the Mississippi flood of 1993 and to restore full production in six weeks after the Aisin Seiki fire of 1997 cut off 99% of the supply of proportioning valves in Japan.[1]

Logistics must be tailored to specific needs, not one-size-fits-all

Most manufacturing organizations have only one way to do the work of logistics. One common pattern for inbound operations inside the plant is as follows:

1. Parts come in full truckloads from one supplier in each truck.

2. Operators use forklifts to unload the truck one pallet at a time.

3. After Receiving, forklift operators put away pallets into single-deep pallet racks into any available slot, and log the location with a radio terminal.

4. The computer system issues work orders or routing slips.

5. The forklift operators retrieve full pallets from the warehouse and log this operation with a radio terminal.

6. They deliver full pallets wherever they can find space to set them down near the destination production area.

The same pattern is applied to all items, regardless of required quantities or frequency of use. The logistics organization is attached to this one-size-fits-all approach, and its management is particularly concerned that its members would not be able to deal with the complexity associated with a different approach for each category of items.

The lean logistics perspective is the opposite. Regardless of which single approach is chosen, it will be effective and efficient for some items and neither for others. If an assembly line consumes a pallet of an item every 20 minutes, then it makes sense to deliver this item by the pallet load. If, for a different item, a pallet holds twelve boxes and one box lasts a week, then deliveries should be for no more than one box. And since it makes no sense to use a forklift to deliver one box, other means of transportation should be used, such as a cart that can hold a mixed load of boxes of dif-

---

1. *Toyota Motor Shows Its Mettle After Fire Destroys Parts Plant*, Wall Street Journal, 5/8/97, p. A-1

ferent items. Of course tailoring the approach to the needs results in a more complicated system, and the logistics organization may need more training to cope with it.

Milk runs smooth the flows

The need to move small quantities of a large number of items both between and within plants with short, predictable lead times and without multiplying transportation costs has driven lean manufacturers to organize pickups and deliveries at fixed times along fixed routes called "milk runs." The term is a reference to the system used for home delivery of milk in the United States until the 1960s. It is in fact not the standard meaning of "milk run," which is aviation slang for an easy trip, similar to a "cake walk." As shown in Figure 2-2, the milk run concept applies in different forms to inbound, outbound, and in-plant logistics, at least for some of the items consumed or produced.

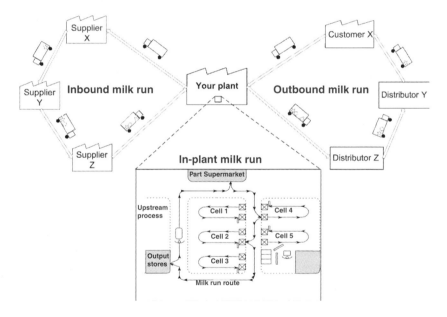

FIGURE 2-2. Inbound, outbound, and in-plant milk runs

Other metaphors could have been used to describe this approach. Inside a plant, dispatching forklifts on request to pick up locations can be viewed as a taxi system, in opposition to which milk runs can be viewed as buses, picking up and dropping off passengers at a series of stops at fixed intervals on regular routes. In Japan, this system is known as "junkai" which means "tour."

The milk run concept is largely ignored in the logistics literature, and barely mentioned even in the literature on lean manufacturing in English. In Japan, it is described in Kojo Kanri articles and special issues.

Returnable containers improve part protection and cut costs

Until the 1960s, such foods as milk, yogurt, or beer were sold to consumers primarily in returnable bottles or jars, but the trend since then has been towards disposable containers. While some local breweries in Germany may still use returnable bottles, the closest most companies get to reusing packages is recycling the materials they are made of.

In this context, it comes as a surprise that lean manufacturers are going in the opposite direction and favoring returnable over disposable containers for packaging parts in transit. In automobile plants, returnable plastic bins now dominate, even for shipments from overseas, and cartons are a vanishing minority. In other industries, one also sees plants where suppliers' disposable containers do not make it past Receiving or past a consolidation center, and where parts are transferred to returnable bins at the point of entry.

There are many reasons for this:

1. Provided returnable containers are handled with sufficient care to make 20 round trips or more and they are cheaper to use than single-use containers that must be disposed of in an environmentally acceptable way.

2. Returnable containers can be fitted with item-specific dunnage that effectively protects the parts from one another, prevents operators from inserting wrong items, and makes the parts easier to count. But item-specific dunnage is too expensive to be used only once.

3. Collecting returnable containers from industrial customers is easier than from consumers, because there are fewer of them, and milk runs provide an infrastructure for the return flow of empties.

4. The number of returnable containers in circulation for an item is controlled and caps the number of parts in the pipeline.

Like milk runs, however, returnable containers have yet to receive any attention in the literature on lean manufacturing and logistics, in spite of the numerous practical challenges implementers face.

Information flow concepts of lean logistics

The material flow systems provides the muscles; the information flow system, the nerves. This section outlines the key concepts of the information systems that are part of lean logistics.

Lean logistics is a pull system

Lean manufacturing is often described as a "pull system," as opposed to the "push system" it replaces. This distinction is only relevant in the logistics domain. It is no more applicable to conveyance within a production line than to water flow within a pipe, but it is applicable to the transportation of parts between plants or between lines within a plant.

The distinction between a pull and a push system is then simple (See Figure 2-3):

• In a pull system, parts do not move until the destination plant or production line signals that it is ready for them.

• In a push system, parts move as soon as they are ready, regardless of the conditions in the destination plant or line.

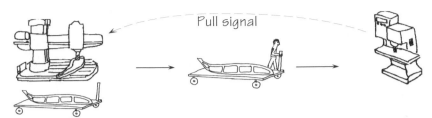

Pull: Part/Lot moves when next operation is ready

Push: Part/Lot moves to next operation when ready

FIGURE 2-3. **Push and pull concepts**

Many managers fail to work out the logical consequences of the pull concept. They *want* parts to move on as soon as they are ready, because they assume it will get them out the door in finished goods faster, but, in a pull system, this is not supposed to happen. Instead, the parts stay in the output buffer of the line until a pull signal arrives, and this output buffer is located right at the end of the line where it is *visible*, not in a separate room. If the line's production runs are for pallets and the pull signals for individual boxes, then boxes are what moves, as shown in Figure 2-4. The output buffer works like a retail store, from which the next line "buys" parts by issuing pull signals, and in which the parts that have not been bought yet remain on the shelves.

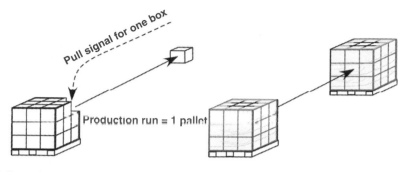

Pull: partial pallet stays   Push: entire shrinkwrapped pallet moves

FIGURE 2-4. Quantities moved in pull versus push system

The pull system is an adaptation of commercial market mechanisms, where money is the pull signal. The move to a pull system on the shop floor is a partial reversal of the trend observed from the 1840s to the 1970s, away from market mechanisms and toward what Alfred Chandler[1] called "the visible hand" of management to allocate resources and work within companies and industries. The attempt to use MRP to plan and schedule the shop floor can be seen as the extreme of the visible hand reaching into operational details and prescribing from a central location which parts should be run when through each machine.

Pull systems allow local decisions to be made locally, using a logic that makes these decisions naturally consistent with global business needs. The concept is simple; making it work on the ground, with actual products, processes, people, and equipment, is not.

Pull signals can take on a variety of forms, from empty containers or fixtures to cards called "kanbans" and electronic signals. We will discuss the selection of appropriate types for each application.

---

1. *The Visible Hand,* Alfred Chandler, Harvard University Press (1977)

Information system = Visible management + Computer systems

In most businesses today, "information system" is synonymous with "computer system," but, in lean manufacturing, the information system combines visible management with computer systems. Successful "5S" projects make plants not only clean but easy to navigate. A first-time visitor to a well-lit, clearly marked neighborhood supermarket can find butter without asking for help, but the challenge of locating an item in an uncharted warehouse makes the maintenance of an accurate inventory database all but impossible. The difference is highlighted in Figure 2-5.

| Unmarked aisle | Marked aisle |

FIGURE 2-5. **Visible management in a supermarket**

The computers available when lean manufacturing pioneer Taiichi Ohno was professionally active could not do much that was useful in a factory. If you tried to use them, the care and feeding of the computer systems became your full time occupation, and applications that could justify their costs never materialized. It is little wonder that Taiichi Ohno had little use for these machines. Many current practitioners of lean manufacturing retain an anti-computer bias to this day. While it is possible even for today's tools to become time sinks and money pits, they can be productivity boosters.

Meanwhile, as a company, Toyota has not been shy of computer systems. Figure 2-6 is a diagram from a 1994 Japanese book entitled "Toyota network bible," outlining a large-scale application of computer technology to production control and supply chain management.

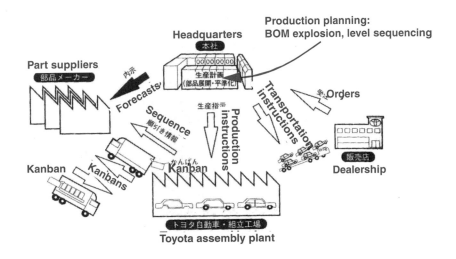

FIGURE 2-6. Toyota's logistics information system (1994)

In 2000, Toyota launched its own Internet portal named "Gazoo," with the goal of getting its fingers on the pulse of the market again. In its early days, Toyota sold cars in Japan door to door. This method was later abandoned as too expensive, but it had the advantage of providing better market intelligence than dealers. Gazoo aims to restore this market visibility by allowing car users to communicate with Toyota through their navigation clicks.

Production planning and scheduling

The order fulfillment process is industry-specific, and there is therefore no single approach that can be called "lean planning and scheduling." Instead, there are common principles that are applied in different ways depending on circumstances. Toyota's production planning and scheduling methods blend a flow of consumer orders aggregated through dealers into a leveled sequence for final assembly whose execution pulls parts in and triggers the production of thousands of items up the supply chain. This works for cars. To make injection-molded plastic parts from a single resin, there is also a lean way to plan and schedule production, but most of the specific features used for car assembly are irrelevant. The following paragraphs describe underlying principles that can be used across industries.

Separate rate work and response work. In telling the plant what to make, when to make it, and with what resources, the lean approach is also tailored to the different types of demands the plant faces. One key distinction is between items made on a routine basis, which we call "rate work," and items made irregularly, on request, which we call "response work." It is based on the Product–Quantity (P-Q) and seasonality analysis described in *Lean Assembly*.[1] We recall that it leads to the classification of both products and their components and materials into A, B, and C categories, and the rate work is comprised of the A products with their dedicated production lines and the B products with dedicated lines by product family. Together, the A and B products usually account for more than 90% of the total volume. The C products are the low-volume–high-mix response work.

Scheduling A products is then simply a matter of adjusting the volume. For B products, it means sequencing the items through the production line with goals that may be maximizing output, minimizing WIP, or smoothing the flow of incoming materials. Orders for C products are treated like individual projects and made from scratch.

Don't play priority games with WIP in rate work. Even rate work first comes in in the form of customer orders, which can be shuffled every which way *until they are released to production*. Past this point, materials are committed and the work proceeds first-in–first-out until the complete

---

1. *Lean Assembly: The Nuts and Bolts of Making Assembly Operations Flow*, Michel Baudin, Productivity Press (2002), Chapters 2 and 3

order emerges from production. This is possible because lean engineering of the production process and the use of a pull system have made production lead times short for *all* orders. If the plant is fully booked, *order* lead times may be extended, but the waiting happens *before* production starts, not in mid-stream. Exception handling, by definition, is response work, done on resources or in time allocated for this purpose, and is not allowed to interfere with rate work.

Don't build cripples. "Making cripples" means performing partial assembly of goods with missing components, which creates stocks of units that are "99% complete" but cannot be shipped, and often results in complicated, error-prone catch-up operations. Short production lead times also enable the manufacturer, if not to terminate this practice altogether, at least to restrict it to brief shortages of non-safety-related parts that can be installed in an otherwise complete unit. On a car, a trunk lock satisfies these conditions, but a proportioning valve doesn't: it distributes brake fluid to the wheels, which is related to safety, and, as shown in Figure 2-7 is mounted in a location that is not easily accessible. And indeed, when the Aisin Seiki plant in Kariya burned on 2/1/97, depriving Toyota of 99% of its supply of proportioning valves in Japan, the Toyota assembly plants shut down within four hours rather than attempt to build cars without this part.

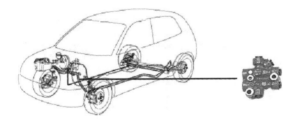

FIGURE 2-7. **Proportioning valve inside a car (Aisin Seiki)**

Of course, validating a sequence of product units to build during a shift against available stock is technically feasible given an accurate database but, oddly, is not done by ERP systems but by Advanced Planning and Scheduling (APS) systems. This validation, however, is insufficient, because product units may be built during the shift using parts that are not yet available at the time of the planning run. The parts delivered on a 10:00 AM milk run, for example, can be assumed available for production by 12:00 PM but are not in-hand at 6:30 AM when the schedule is generated. To the best of our knowledge, this level of complexity is not handled by the software available as of this writing.

Integrate production planning and scheduling with the pull system. With a pull system, explicit scheduling of the work is needed only at the top of the supply chain—the start of final assembly in car making—with pull signals conveying the required information upstream. To the recipients of the pull signals, however, they constitute a demand, to which they may respond by explicitly scheduling their own production resources.

The net result is not the elimination of the need to schedule but its decentralization. Not only is the problem of scheduling a cell of five workstations intrinsically easier than that of scheduling a plant with hundreds of machines and thousands of part items, but the detailed structure of a cell and the information about operator skills, process, and setup times can be better handled locally by a cell leader or a scheduler attached to a supervisor than globally by a central computer system.

To the extent its discipline is followed, the pull system prevents local scheduling from pursuing goals that are not in the best interest of the plant as a whole, and the use of various forms of leveled sequencing, where applicable, dampens the bullwhip effect.

Exchanging information with suppliers

In lean logistics, supplier communications go far beyond commercial transactions. The following paragraphs explain the key additional elements.

Use of MRP for forecasting. MRP, in the original sense of Materials Requirements Planning, is performed in lean manufacturing as well as everywhere else. The difference is in the use of the output. In lean manufacturing, MRP is used strictly to translate forecasts of finished goods demand into forecasts of materials requirements, for suppliers to act upon as they see fit. While these forecasts are not orders, the agreements with suppliers usually include compensation for suppliers when consistently optimistic forecasts make them buy excess materials.

EDI and kanbans. Kanbans are recirculating physical tokens, most often cards, that serve as pull signals and have been used by Toyota as a means of issuing orders to suppliers for some items since 1949. Fifty-four years later, while most manufacturing companies have yet to master the logic of the kanban system, its implementers are challenged to take advantage of increasingly effective computer and communication technology. Human-readable tokens still need to be attached to containers but they must also be machine-readable through barcodes or RFID tags, and the pull signals issued based on the kanban system's replenishment logic using Electronic Data Interchange (EDI) technology.

Body-on-sequence. In the automobile industry, some model and option-dependent components made by local suppliers are ordered by electronically feeding them the exact start sequence of cars started on the first station of final assembly. The supplier then starts making the components, knowing that they must be delivered to the required station on the final assembly line within, say, 214 minutes. "Body-on-sequence" is the term used for this system at Toyota and NUMMI; Ford calls it "In-Line Vehicle Sequencing."

Vendor-managed inventory and consignment/pay-per-build. At the opposite end of the parts spectrum are commodities like nuts, bolts, and washers, for which customers like to delegate as much responsibility as possible to suppliers. In vendor-managed inventory, the supplier is given access to the customer's inventory database and is allowed to initiate shipments when reorder points are crossed. Consignment arrangements delegate more responsibility by letting the supplier own the stocks in the customer's plant until the parts are used, and in the pay-per-build scheme, suppliers are paid based on the quantities of their parts incorporated in finished goods leaving the production line, per the bill of materials.

The role of Manufacturing Execution Systems (MES) in lean logistics

Lean manufacturing makes materials easier to track through the plant and through the supplier network, but it also makes it vital as a tool to exercise the vigilance to prevent shortages.

In flow lines and cells, there is a visible mapping from physical location to process status. Since there is no backtracking or eddy flow, just seeing where a part is enables you to tell exactly which operations it has already undergone, and which remain to be done. Also, since parts through the line move one at a time, first-in–first-out, the time at which a part completed an operation can be inferred from data about the complete production run. If moves between lines are triggered by kanbans, then the "traveler" documents that accompany parts in job shops can be eliminated for all standard products and survive only in the form of "build manifests" for products with options or customization. The MES is then used to print the kanbans and build manifests.

While visibility on the shop floor eliminates WIP tracking transactions through every operation in the computer system, the need remains for materials to be checked in and out of warehouse locations, or else it is impossible to maintain accurate inventory data.

The MES also should have a key role in preventing shortages but in most plants does not. Knowing how much of an item is on hand, the rate at which it is consumed, and the delivery schedule, it should be able to anticipate shortages and issue warnings to managers in a position to launch countermeasures. Yet even in factories with multimillion-dollar information systems budgets, shortages are not discovered until an operator reaches for a part and can't find one.

Monitoring supplier performance

The history of transactions with each supplier is summarized into supplier performance metrics that are used to certify some suppliers as trustworthy, others as needing help and guidance to achieve this certification, and yet others as candidates for replacement. While Purchasing traditionally pays the most attention to what suppliers charge because price data is the most readily available, collecting performance data on delivery and quality is also necessary to keep the company from hurting itself by always choosing the lowest bidder.

Collaborative supplier/customer relationships

The relationships between suppliers and customers have received more attention in the press[1] and the literature[2] than the more technical aspects of lean logistics outlined above. The lean approaches to managing supplier/customer relations, however, goes hand in hand with milk runs, pull systems, and the other approaches described above.

A lean supplier network has the following characteristics:

1. *A small number of direct suppliers with a tier structure.* Lean manufacturers rely on a tier structure allowing each large supplier to manage a group of smaller ones.

2. *Single-sourcing.* Lean manufacturers do not use the strategy of sourcing the same item from multiple suppliers to assure supply. The single-source suppliers may make their own second-sourcing agreements but they retain sole responsibility for the supply of the item.

3. *Collaboration in product design.* The more complex a manufactured product is, the less sense it makes to treat its components like commodities. Instead, they are specific to the product and designed for it; and better, cheaper, and more manufacturable designs result when the engineering teams of supplier and customer collaborate during design in target costing, value engineering, and Design For Manufacturing and Assembly (DFMA).

4. *Collaboration in cost reduction during production.* During production, supplier and customer work together to reduce costs through a process called "Kaizen costing," in which the customer provides technical assistance in exchange for price breaks.

---

1. *How Chrysler Created an American Keiretsu*, J. Dyer, HBR, 7–8/96, reprint 96403

2. *Supply Chain Development for the Lean Enterprise*, Cooper & Slagmulder, Productivity Press (1999)

---

5. *Collaboration in problem-solving and emergency response.* Lean manufacturers do not look for suppliers who "never have any problems" but for suppliers who don't hide them and are diligent about solving them, particularly when they are emergencies. If a key piece of equipment breaks down and cannot be repaired right away, the supplier notifies the customer immediately. If the breakdown was due to human error, a mistake-proofing device is implemented within a week.

6. *A community.* The suppliers of a lean manufacturer are an organized community. Suppliers to NUMMI participate in the Golden State Automotive Manufacturers Association (GAMA); suppliers to Toyota in Kentucky, in the Bluegrass Automotive Manufacturers Association (BAMA); suppliers to Applied Materials, in its Lean Suppliers Association (LSA). These groups hold conferences, visit each other's plants, and, in the case of Toyota, contribute to each other's improvement projects through activities called "jishuken."

This approach originated in the automobile industry, in which leadership and initiative rest with the car makers who assemble the final product. This is not a universal pattern. Computer industry companies, by contrast, follow the lead of software and chip suppliers for product design, and of chip suppliers—particularly microprocessors and memories—in logistics.

This chapter has shown lean logistics as seen from a sufficient altitude to grasp it as a whole, see what its main components are, and see how they interact and depend on each other. It has shown the forest. The following chapters zoom in on the trees.

PART II   *Dock-to-dock material flows inside the plant*

Which describes the physical infrastructure of transportation, storage, and retrieval needed within the factory to support lean manufacturing.

CHAPTER 3

Transportation inside the plant

Summary

A close look at the transportation system inside the plant often reveals that production is dissatisfied with its performance, that it is not as safe as it could be around people, that it uses the wrong vehicles or methods for specific needs, and that it consumes more resources than it should. In-plant transportation differs from inbound and outbound in that the greatest improvements are achieved by eliminating trips rather than by reducing distances.

The identification of the most heavily traveled routes, and the tabulation along these routes of such parameters as the number of times the materials are touched or the number of times they move vertically and horizontally reveals improvement opportunities that are obvious in hindsight.

Restricting forklifts to marked aisles may be the key to increasing the manufacturing density of a shop floor by 70%. Relocating a heavily used item may be enough to go change its handling from a $40,000 forklift with a certified driver to a $400 pallet jack anyone can use. Changing the minimum in-plant transportation quantity from a pallet to a small bin may enable you to eliminate the returns of partial pallets to the warehouse for incoming materials, while simplifying and accelerating the movement of finished goods.

The analysis may also reveal that decentralized manual palletizing with semi-automation retrofits may be more economic and reliable than one central automatic palletizer fed through a network of conveyors. The solutions frequently include moving from using forklifts dispatched like radio taxis to milk runs of pushcarts or trains of tow carts working like buses and subways.

Measuring transportation system performance

For inbound and outbound logistics, distance may vary from a few miles to thousands, and of course is a central consideration. Inside the plant, by contrast, whether you are moving parts 50 ft or 500 ft does not make much difference. Regardless of distance, the following needs to happen:

1. The minimum transportation quantity must accumulate at the point of origin.

2. The parts need to be prepared for transportation, which may entail, for example, placing them in bins and palletizing the bins.

3. A vehicle needs to come and pick up the parts, for example a forklift with a driver.

4. At the destination, the parts must be prepared for production—that is, removed from pallets and bins and possibly placed on lineside shelves.

Cutting the distance between two lines in half will make little difference, but integrating the two lines and eliminating the transportation step will.

The first step in analyzing in-plant transportation is of course to measure the volume of traffic between destinations. If one pallet is transported by forklift from point A to point B every 20 minutes, then it is probably a good idea to find a better solution, which may involve changing the plant layout to bring points A and B closer together and eliminating the transportation step. On the other hand, if that route is only traveled by one box every month, then it is not a promising target for improvement.

Having identified a heavily traveled route, the next step is to follow a shipment and observe what happens to it. One way to do this is to count the number of times a part is touched along the way, as an individual unit, in a tote, and in a pallet.

In a plant where production occurs on multiple floors—a pattern that is rare in the United States but common in other parts of the world—then vertical movements between floors, requires more resources than horizontal movements within a floor, and it makes sense to count the occurrences of both.

Even where production is on a single floor, there may be vertical movements to store and retrieve parts in the upper reaches of pallet racks, requiring more expensive equipment and more skills than movements at ground level only.

A common pattern in the United States is to have manufacturing spread through multiple buildings in one campus. Then the relevant distinction is between transfers within a building and transfers between buildings.

Types of vehicles

Most plants do not take advantage of the full range of vehicle types available to meet their various needs. For example, they may use only forklifts or only conveyors for all tasks, which is unnecessarily expensive and gives inadequate service where these devices are a poor fit. The following paragraphs review the most common options and their range of applicability.

Forklifts

Forklifts are such common devices that they immediately come to mind in any discussion of in-plant transportation. They are versatile and powerful, but they are not without disadvantages:

1. They cost tens of thousands of dollars.
2. They can only be operated by specially trained drivers.
3. They are a safety hazard and must be constrained to run in designated areas.
4. As shown in Figure 3-1, they are appropriate for moving pallet-sized loads but not smaller quantities.

The common forklift that travels throughout the plant has relatives like narrow aisle trucks that are specialized for storage and retrieval or picking operations in warehouses, but these are not *transportation* vehicles per se.

Forklifts move large bins   Not economical for one small bin

FIGURE 3-1. Forklift for large and small bins

Pallet jacks

The manual and powered pallet jacks shown in Figure 3-2 are a one to two orders of magnitude cheaper alternative to forklifts for short, *horizontal* movements, and don't require special training. They are not commonly used for long carries, but the only job they absolutely cannot do is access stacks of pallets, the upper shelves of pallet racks,or the top of pallet stacks.

FIGURE 3-2. Manual and powered pallet jacks

Push carts

When moving parts in boxes or totes rather than pallet loads, the simple push cart shown in Figure 3-3 is cheap, safe, and can be operated by any-one on narrower aisles than forklifts. They are easiest to steer when only the front wheels swivel, but models with all four wheels swiveling can be useful in tight corners. Many baby strollers have four-wheel steering, but allow parents to lock the back wheels in line for easier steering in open spaces.

In another variation, carts have hinged shelves that rise when empty to facilitate access to the lower shelves. The hinged cart is an effective device for transportation but not for line side presentation, because it uses up too much space for a single item.

Mix-loaded manual push cart

Cart with hinged shelves

FIGURE 3-3. **Mix-loaded manual push cart**

Tuggers and trains of tow carts

Neither the forklift nor the individual push cart is adequate to deliver thousands of items in box quantities at multiple locations every half hour, as is commonly needed in the automobile industry. The solution then is to hook up carts into a train and pull them around designated routes with a tugging engine whose driver also loads and unloads the boxes along the way.

Mix-loaded train of tow carts

FIGURE 3-4. **Mix-loaded train of tow carts**

Networks of conveyors

Networks of powered conveyors play a central role in the non-lean approach to automation. They are much less in favor in the lean manufacturing world, which may be surprising, because they offer a model of continuous flow in small quantities, as opposed to the accumulation of discrete loads for transportation by vehicles. The examples shown in Figure 3-5 is for check sorting at First Tennessee Bank at Memphis Airport.

FIGURE 3-5. Conveyor network, courtesy of Engineering Handling Systems

Conveyors are in fact not excluded from lean manufacturing plants, but they are used more for transferring parts *within* a line than *between* production lines. If a transportation route between production lines has a sufficient high and stable volume to justify a conveyor between them, they should be collocated with the conveyor correspondingly shortened and made a part of the resulting integrated line. Dell uses conveyors with automatic controls to move kits from picking to assembly and systems to testing and boxing. As these operations are contiguous, it can be argued that this is in fact movement within the production line.

Belt conveyors in various forms and other devices that work like pipelines are commonly used also to move bulk materials, such as foundry sand, pellets of resins in plastic molding, or molten aluminum in high-volume diecasting shops. Provided the consumption of the materials is high and stable enough, this method is used in lean manufacturing plants as well as in others.

Automatic Guided Vehicles (AGVs)

Automatic Guided Vehicles (AGVs) have been around since the 1980s, but are still not a common sight, and are not common in lean manufacturing plants. The problem with AGVs is that the part of the transportation process that they automate is the movement itself, which, as discussed earlier, is less of a concern than preparing and loading the materials at the origin, and unloading and presenting them at destination.

One typical application of AGVs was to shuttle boxes of silicon wafers between bays in a wafer fabrication facility in the late 1980s. But the AGVs were manually loaded and unloaded in each bay, and one company that tried this method dropped it in its following generation of wafer fabs, as too expensive for too little benefit.

Structuring the transportation system

Based on the above discussion of the fitness of different vehicle types for different tasks, the following paragraphs discuss their deployment in a plant through examples.

Inside the plant, structuring the transportation system is the key to many improvements. The principle illustrated in Figure 3-6 may be obvious, but it is routinely violated in factories. Each transportation task should be carried out using methods that are tailored to its load and frequency. Just as you use a train between towns, a car within a town, and a dolly inside a house, you should use appropriate vehicles and an appropriate network of transportation aisles within a plant. In the following sections, a few examples will show what is at stake in this simple idea.

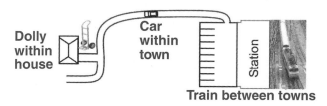

FIGURE 3-6. A transportation method for each need

Example 1: Marking transportation aisles

Many shop floors, as the one shown in Figure 3-7, have no marked transportation aisles. This has two main consequences:

1. Extra materials, pallets, fixtures, surplus equipment, and other items encroach upon and eventually block transportation aisles.

2. There are no restrictions on where vehicles are allowed to go, and production operators must keep looking over their shoulders to avoid accidents.

Unmarked aisle   **Marked aisle**

FIGURE 3-7. Marking transportation aisles

Figure 3-8 shows how the shop floor needs to be organized into manufacturing islands—where only production personnel may work and where vehicles from the materials or logistics group are prohibited. Specific transportation aisles are reserved for vehicles, and operators must exercise the same caution when crossing these aisles as do pedestrians on a public roadway.

All aisle markings must be kept current and must be enforced. A few markings that are inaccurate, obsolete or ignored are sufficient to destroy the credibility of all markings with production operators and transporters alike.

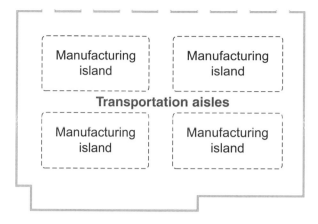

FIGURE 3-8. Network of transportation aisles

Example 2: Packing dried foods

This example shows how structuring the transportation system can allow a plant to increase productivity, reduce floor space requirements, and improve safety at the same time. Figure 3-9 shows packaging lines for dried foods running at a takt time on the order of 1 sec. The filler fills and seals paper pouches, which the following operations aggregate into larger and larger groups, resulting in a shrink-wrapped pallet ready to load onto a truck. This type of line is fully automatic and the primary job of operators is to keep the machine hoppers full of packaging materials. The machines occasionally jam, and the operators are also expected to clear the jams and restart the lines.

In the "before" condition, forklifts brought full pallets of packaging materials right between the lines. In fact, there were no restrictions at all as to where forklifts might go, and no marked transportation aisles. This forced the lines too far apart for one operator to attend to two of them. In addition, the coexistence of people and forklifts in the same environment was uneasy and unsafe, with operators being constantly on the lookout for forklifts.

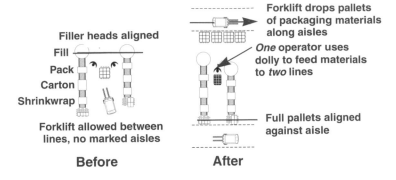

FIGURE 3-9. Example of packing lines for dried foods

This came to a head when a sister plant closed and this plant was asked to wedge in five more packaging lines within the same hall. There was no way density could be increased in the current mode of operations. On the other hand, it could if we did the following:

1. Constrain forklifts to marked transportation aisles.

2. Assign drop-off and pickup locations along the transportation aisles. One result was aligning the *ends* of the lines rather than their *beginnings*. Staggering the fillers actually helped locate more lines in the same floor space, while lining up the full pallets along the transportation aisles.

3. Supply the operator with a dolly/push cart to bring packaging materials from the drop-off location behind the fillers. The filling lines are now much closer together, allowing one operator to attend to two at one time.

Example 3: Storing frequently used raw materials

This example shows how the use of simple analytical tools such as outlined above can bring to light opportunities to simplify transportation operations. Following the movements of the two most frequently used raw materials revealed that they were systematically stored in the upper floors of a pallet rack, as shown in Figure 3-10, while the bottom floor was used for janitorial supplies. As a result, every 20 minutes, when production needed a new pallet of these raw materials, the operators had to call in a forklift with a certified driver to bring it across the aisle.

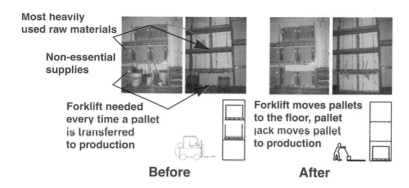

FIGURE 3-10. **Retrieving raw materials with pallet jacks versus forklifts**

The team analyzing this flow immediately realized that it was wrong. Yet they had lived with this approach for years without noticing it. In this case the value of counting vertical moves versus horizontal moves was not in the ratio that came out, but in what it suddenly made the team see that they had missed before.

In the "after" picture, the forklift is not completely eliminated, but its role is changed to repopulating the bottom row of the rack every few hours, which is less constraining. The production equipment is automated, and the operators have the spare time to cross the aisle with a pallet jack to fetch pallets as needed.

Example 4: Delivering car batteries to assembly

This example shows how quantities that are easy to move around the plant are frequently not convenient for production. These issues were discussed in Chapter 11 of *Lean Assembly* from the perspective of production. We are now considering the logistics implications.

In the "before" picture, forklifts deliver whole pallets of batteries to the line side. To install the right battery on the car, the operator must walk to the pallet, and hand-carry it up 25 feet to the car. In addition to the problem of hand-carrying heavy objects like batteries over long distances, picking batteries from pallets requires inconsistent times and too much physical effort.

The picking times vary because picking from the near corner on a full pallet does not take the same amount of time as walking to the far corner, squatting, and picking up a battery from a near-empty pallet. Within a takt time of 1 minute, a range of times of 10 seconds is not negligible. The problem of picking from pallets can be alleviated by using "pallet pals," rotating tables mounted on a scissor lift with springs. Pallet pals allow operators to turn the pallet to the current picking position, and the springs push the pallet pal higher as the load becomes lighter. But pallet pals would not solve the problem of having to walk back and forth between the right pallet and the car.

The solution shown in the "after" picture of Figure 3-11 relies on a picker using a manipulator to load the batteries from pallets to a single piece presentation flow-rack presenting each of all five battery types at always the same location within 4 linear feet of the "ocean-front property" facing the assembly line.

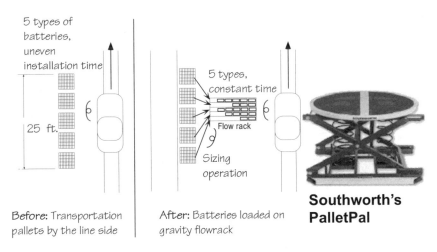

FIGURE 3-11. Example of battery supply to car line

Example 5: Using small, mix-loaded carts versus forklifts

This example shows how the transportation system can be organized so that movements from the warehouse to production are strictly one-way. Figure 3-12 shows a mode of operation in which forklifts bring full pallets of parts to a flexible assembly cell.

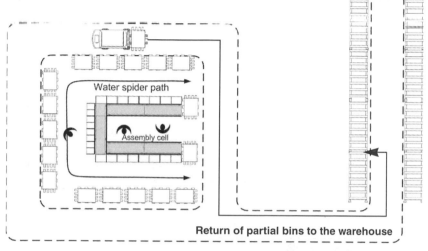

FIGURE 3-12. Full bin delivery with return of partial bins

The space around the cell is too small to hold pallets of all the components needed for all products. As a consequence, materials handlers must return partial bins to the warehouse when changing the line over between products. Tolerating the partial use of bins or pallets, as in the practice of many plants, has the following consequences:

- It adds handling work, causing the same parts to take multiple trips between the warehouse and production.

- It destroys the visibility of the flow of materials. A one-way flow of materials is easy to follow, and the physical location of materials conveys information. The "eddy flows" of partial bins blur the picture.

- It compromises the accuracy of inventory data. When assemblers encounter a defective part or accidentally damage a good part, they set the bad part aside and pick another one, usually without recording that action. When materials handlers return partial bins to the warehouse, they do not know exactly how many parts are in them, and counting the parts in each bin would take too long.

- It complicates warehouse operations. Partial bins are usually kept apart from full bins, but then the inventory of any item may be split between the warehouses containing full and partial bins. In addition, if an item is consumed at more than one location, there may be multiple partial bins for this item.

There are many ways to avoid this, and one of them is shown in Figure 3-13, mix-loading carts with all items required for a product in the warehouse using an order picker and delivering individual box quantities to the cell.

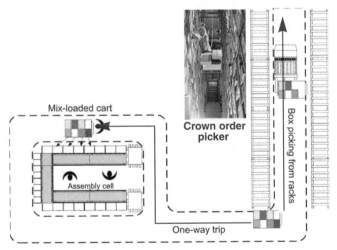

FIGURE 3-13. Using small, mix-loaded carts instead of forklifts

Example 6: Adapting the transportation system to the bin size

Figure 3-14 shows two ways of handling the flow of finished goods from a set of parallel production lines to shipping. In the top part, the operator palletizes the finished goods at the end of the production line, and they are handled on pallets with a forklift thereafter. The boxes receive a generic label identifying the product and production run at the end of the line, and a customer specific label prior to shipment. The pallets are stored in first-in–first-out (FIFO) lanes with their generic labels, and then moved to the production control office to receive their customer labels.

Customer orders, however, are usually for a number of boxes, not pallets, which causes the handlers to split one pallet for almost every order and store a partial pallet on a rack for this purpose until the next order for this product comes. Then they shrink wrap, stage, and ship the order.

These procedures are clearly more complicated, error-prone, and labor intensive than they should be. The treatment of partial pallets is particularly cumbersome, because customers do not like to receive more than one partial pallet in a shipment, and therefore the boxes on partial pallets have to be recombined into full pallets, which, in addition to generating more handling work, violates the company's policy of shipping FIFO for traceability.

The cause of these problems is that the goods are handled in pallets while ordered in boxes, and the solution is to postpone palatalization until shipping, as shown on the bottom of Figure 3-14. An operator with a bread cart makes the rounds of the production lines and picks up *boxes* of goods rather than pallets and delivers them to a gravity flow rack with one lane for each product. On the opposite side, the handler picks the boxes FIFO to fill the orders, affixes customer-specific labels, palletizes the boxes, shrink wraps the pallets and ships them.

The number of people and resources affected by this simplification of course varies with production volume and product mix, and the different components must be sized accordingly, but the key idea is valid regardless. The sole purpose of pallets in this facility is to hold boxes during transportation to the customer site. Pallet loads are not a meaningful unit of volume *inside* the plant, and therefore should not be used.

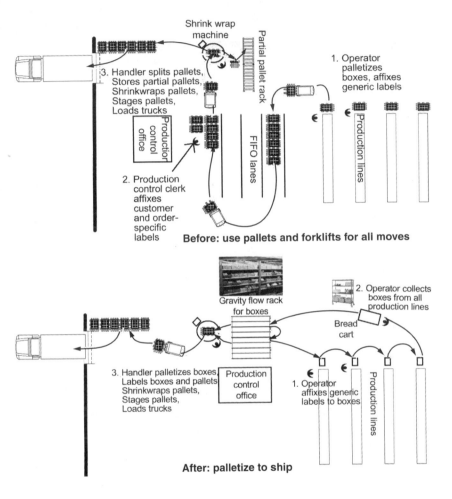

FIGURE 3-14. **Handling parts in boxes versus pallets**

Example 7: Using a network of conveyors to automate palletizing

Figure 3-15 shows two options for palletizing boxes and conveying them to Shipping in a high-volume–low-mix plant making products like detergents or toothpaste. Retail units are filled at a rate higher than one per second, and aggregated in multiple stages into supermarket display cases and cardboard shipping boxes, which are then themselves loaded on pallets in configurations that vary with the shape of the box.

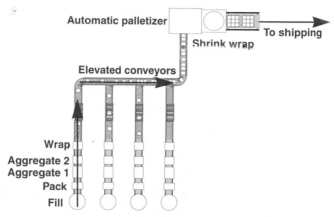

(A) Full automation with conveyor network

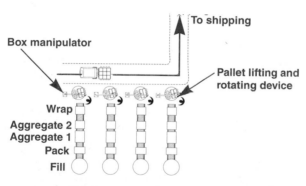

(B) Semi-automation with forklifts

FIGURE 3-15. Conveyor networks versus semi-automation

Figure 3-15A shows this done with no human intervention, using a central automatic palletizer, to which boxes come through a network of conveyors; and Figure 3-15B, with one palletizing station for each line and manual loading assisted with devices to lift and rotate pallets and manipulators with suction cups to relieve operators from the weight of boxes.

Both solutions are technically feasible and are in use in different plants. Full automation, in principle, should save labor, reduce inventory and eliminate human error. In reality, however, it raises the following concerns:

1. It is an order of magnitude more expensive to implement.

2. While it saves labor in forklift operations, the labor savings in palletizing may not materialize. Operators are needed to feed the machines along the lines with packaging materials anyway, and the elimination of manual palletizing may not reduce their number.

3. Automation *adds* labor in maintenance and in control system programming /configuration. Once programmed correctly, it should palletize all different types of boxes correctly and reliably. The debugging of this software, however, is usually expensive and drawn out, and so is the process for changing or enhancing it as new needs arise.

4. Reliance on one single automatic palletizer and one conveyor network makes the entire plant vulnerable to failure in either one. In such plants, the core technology is compounding, mixing, or spray drying, and the automated system diverts engineering attention away from these processes.

5. Layout changes are more difficult than with the manual system, as there is more to moving conveyors than to changing aisle marks on the floor.

The approach shown in Figure 3-15B avoids creating such "monuments" by keeping palletizing decentralized, and the use of various devices to make manual palletizing easier, reducing the risks associated with operator fatigue. On the other hand, this approach relies on operators to know the pallet configurations applicable to boxes of varying sizes. This means that they must be trained and that human error *will* occur.

It is possible here to say that one solution is always better than the other, but one where a rational choice can only be made for a plant on a case-by-case basis, considering such issues as its labor costs, the skill level of its work force, and the availability of engineering support services in its neighborhood. Figure 3-15B is consistent with the lean approach to automation, which stresses incremental steps focused on making the work easier for people to perform consistently, eventually leading to full automation.

In-plant milk runs

Forklifts moving pallets is a common sight in many plants, and probably the most common method of transportation, both where it is appropriate and where other methods would work better. The next questions are who orders the forklifts to take action and how a forklift is assigned to a task.

In one project on the shop floor of a household product plant, the team cleared an area destined to hold an assembly cell and marked its boundary with colored tape. Within minutes, a forklift came by and dropped a pallet of unrelated materials inside the reserved boundary. The team stopped the driver and made him take the parts elsewhere. Over the next few hours, multiple forklift drivers attempted to occupy this space about every 20 minutes, incredulous that a team of people could demand that space remain empty while they needed it to store parts.

These "denial of space attacks" abated only after the team raised the issue with the materials manager, but, even then, they did not completely stop. Clearly, the forklift drivers were under orders to deliver materials to the floor that had not been requested and for which no storage space was prepared, and the materials management organization had the authority to issue such orders. This is the essence of a "push" system, to which the alternative is the "pull" system described in Chapter 10.

Once the decision to move materials has been made, a forklift is assigned to the task by a method that is similar to the dispatching of radio taxis. The person requesting a transport calls a central dispatcher who communicates by radio with the fleet of forklifts and sends the next available one. Unless money is no object, however, city dwellers only use taxis occasionally, to go to an airport or to return home from a party, but not for commuting everyday between two fixed locations. Instead, they use buses and trains that run at regular intervals along fixed routes, picking up and dropping off passengers at scheduled stops. It is an order of magnitude cheaper, and the duration of the trip is predictable.

The first issue with using a taxi dispatching model on the shop floor is the time it takes for a forklift to become available. If a taxi company in a city has 100 cars, each occupied 90% of the time, then they will never be all occupied simultaneously. The probability of this ever happening is

$$\text{Probability (all taxis occupied)} = (90\%)^{100} = 26 \text{ ppm}$$

but if a shop floor has 10 forklifts occupied 90% of the time, then

$$\text{Probability (all forklifts occupied)} = (90\%)^{10} = 35\%$$

which means that 1/3 of the time, none will be available and the transportation operation will have to wait. If we need 9 full-time equivalents in forklifts and one forklift available 99% of the time, then we need to have 13 forklifts each busy 70% of the time. Given that forklifts cost tens of thousands of dollars a piece, then holding an average of four idle at any time is an unattractive proposition. Nevertheless, anything less will cause transportation operations to be queued.

The second issue is that the forklift and pallet model is a poor fit to the repeatable flow of items between the same locations. Pushcarts or trains of tow carts traveling on fixed routes at fixed intervals, like city buses and subways, picking up and dropping off quantities of materials that are usually less than full pallet loads, provide a cheaper, more reliable, and more predictable service.

This is the in-plant version of the "milk run" concept, whose application to inbound logistics is discussed in Chapter 7, and is illustrated in the example of Figure 3-16. The U-shaped cells shown comprise the area of responsibility of one supervisor and have their input and output buffers facing a transportation aisle. The milk run operator from the materials department deposits full bins and picks up empties on the racks lining the edges of the manufacturing islands. These may be flow racks feeding the cells directly, or the parts may be kitted for assembly by a water spider from the production department. The milk run operator goes through the figure eight pattern shown once every 30 minutes.

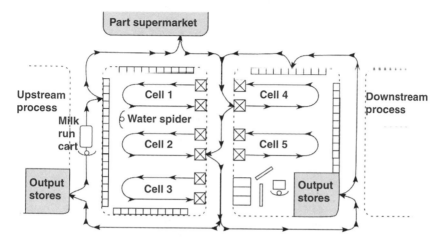

FIGURE 3-16. **In-plant milk run**

Compared with supplier milk runs, in-plant milk runs have the following characteristics:

- Their recurrence period is in tens of minutes rather than hours.
- The pickup and delivery quantities range from single pieces to bins, as opposed to pallets.
- They are managed within a single department of a single company, as opposed to one customer company, multiple suppliers, and possibly a 3rd party logistics provider.
- Milk runs in the controlled environment of the shop floor are not affected by weather or traffic conditions, and their schedules are correspondingly more reliable.

There are many possible variations of in-plant milk runs. Figure 3-17 shows a design for low-volume modular assembly of military electronic systems. The modules are printed circuit boards assembled and encased in cells. Final assembly consists of inserting the modules into a chassis and closing the chassis with a front panel on one side and a battery compartment on the other. After final assembly, the units undergo extensive test-ing, after which many of the units need troubleshooting and repair. While the engineers and managers recognize that "troubleshooting and repair" is not a normal part of a manufacturing process, they are not in a position to get rid of it now, and, by the time they may be able to eliminate this need, the product will have been replaced by a new one, with a process that still needs debugging.

Forklifts deliver parts to a supermarket behind the lines. One forklift deliv-ers parts in weekly quantities to a flow-through rack and takes finished units to Shipping.

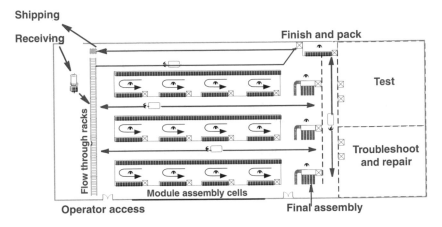

FIGURE 3-17. Variation in modular electronics assembly

On the opposite side of the rack, milk run operators load parts onto push-carts that they shuttle up and down the aisles between rows of assembly cells. Overall, milk run operators move the following:

- Parts from the rack to the module cells.
- Finished modules to final assembly.
- Assembled units to testing.
- Defective units to troubleshoot and repair.
- Repaired units to testing.
- Good tested units to finish and pack.

- Packed units to the output buffer.

The need for milk run operators varies with the production volume, and the idea is for one operator to take care of multiple shuttles. Also note the strict separation between areas accessible to forklifts and to people.

The key message about in-plant transportation is that the system needs to be customized to the needs of the plant, using a variety of methods. Using only one, as most plants do, is easiest to set up, but it results in using vehicles that are suited for the most *demanding* tasks for *every* task , which is wasteful and ineffective. This chapter considered transportation independently of the origin or destination, which may be production lines, or stores/warehouses, whose design and operation are discussed in the coming chapters.

CHAPTER 4

Warehousing strategies and devices

Summary

While excess *inventory is waste, some stocks are necessary for production. Storage and retrieval in warehouses is needed when incoming and outgoing flow patterns differ—such as when truckloads need to be broken down into pallets or totes aggregated into pallets and truckloads—and as protection against commonly occurring small disruptions. The elimination of inventory beyond what is obviously excessive in current operating conditions is pursued in conjunction with—not in anticipation of—the solution of the problems that cause the inventory to be needed.*

Warehouses should use multiple types of storage devices and strategies in different zones, based on item volume, frequency of use, destination, or origin. Block stacking, single-deep pallet racks, and gravity flow racks are by far the most common devices, even in lean manufacturing plants. Because block stacking requires the least investment, it is often the right choice during plant startup, but, as the plant ramps up, its long-term use is restricted to high-volume–low-mix situations with entire truckloads withdrawn daily.

Flow racks are effective at providing dedicated storage with strict first-in–first-out (FIFO) retrieval for items used by the pallet load every day. Single-deep pallet racks provide dedicated slots for items that are frequently used in low volumes and dynamically allocated slots for infrequently used items. Double-deep, pushback, and drive-in racks are much less common, and automated systems like AS/RS's or carrousels are rarely cost-justified.

What are warehouses needed for?

The word "inventory" figures prominently in Taiichi Ohno's list of seven types of waste. As a consequence, when discussions of inventory or warehouse management arise, several participants immediately say that, since "inventory is waste," it should just be disposed of. But Ohno never said that *all* inventory was waste, only that *excess* inventory was a type of waste that should be targeted for elimination. His point was to draw attention to the improvement opportunities lying in factories' tendency to hoard more than they need.

Some stocks of raw materials, work in process and finished goods are as necessary to production as blood is to the human body. When walking through a shop floor, a rack full of materials is not by itself an unmistakable sign of waste. If, however, there is no sign indicating its purpose, and operators, managers and engineers cannot explain why it is there, then chances are it is not needed and you have found inventory waste. Other telltale signs include paperwork indicating that the material has been in that location too long, or thick dust over the containers.

The need to store and retrieve materials arises first where there is a mismatch between incoming and outgoing quantities, as in the following cases:

- **Trucks in, pallets out.** An item is delivered from a supplier by the full truckload and consumed in production one pallet at a time at a regular rate. This pattern generates up to one full truckload of inventory for this item, with an average of half a truckload.

- **Totes in, pallets out.** A production line makes one unit of product at a time, accumulating the finished units into a tote at the end, and the totes are palletized for shipment. As above, there is an average of half a tote at the end of the line and half a pallet in stores.

- **Pallets in, trucks out.** Up to one truckload of pallets of finished goods accumulates in the shipping staging area.

- **Single-item trucks in, mixed-loads out.** In crossdocking operations, full truckloads from different sources are rearranged and shipped out by destination. While crossdocks don't hold parts any longer than it takes to transship them, they do contain a small float of inventory at all times.

- **Fixed-rate production to fluctuating demand.** A production line may make consumer goods whose demand fluctuates. Or it may make components for industrial customers whose own lines work at a steady pace but who use ordering software that introduces artificial fluctuations. In either case, producing at a steady pace and using finished goods stocks to absorb fluctuations is sometimes preferable to maintaining the capacity to handle peak demand at all times.

- **Fixed-rate production from fluctuating supplies.** Most production organizations are unable to deal exclusively with suppliers who always deliver perfect quality parts, in the right quantities and right on time. And even perfect suppliers can be delayed by snow storms, floods, or traffic accidents. Safety stock is impossible to hold for custom items and too expensive to protect against events like the supplier's plant burning to the ground or even going on strike. On the other hand, it would be unreasonable not to protect production against the possibility of a 30-minute delay in truck arrivals.

- **Shipping to a steady demand from an unstable production line.** While this is a situation that lean manufacturing is intended to avoid, it is not achieved instantly, even when diligently pursued. In the meantime, stocks of finished goods may be needed to protect shipments against failures of the plant's own ability to produce, be they due to component shortages or internal process problems. As shown in Figure 4-1, one of the best known metaphors in lean manufacturing is that of inventory as water covering up problems in the form of rocks on the bottom. Lower inventory, or the water level, and you expose the rocks and cause the problems to be solved.

It is true that mass producers have used high levels of inventory as a means of working around problems they had no plans to solve. However, if all you do is lower the water level, as shown on the left side of Figure 4-1, the rocks come closer to the surface and wreck your ships. Since this is easy to do, many companies have tried this and missed shipments as a consequence. The right approach is to dovetail the reduction in inventory with the solution of the problems. No matter how diligently pursued, the elimination of shortages and the improvement of internal processes are not instantaneous, and therefore the reduction or elimination of finished goods stocks should not be either.

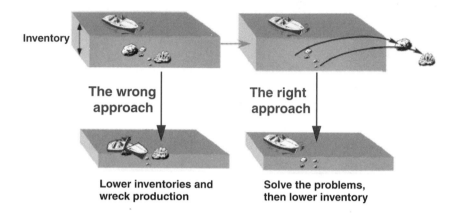

FIGURE 4-1. Lowering inventory to expose problems

The lot size adjustment buffers described above are inevitable, but they are small, and of sizes that can be calculated easily. Sizing safety stocks is a more difficult challenge. As pointed out in Chapter 4, the lean approach is based not on attempting to maintain large stocks of all needed items but on vigilance, detecting anomalies early, and responding quickly.

Again, prudence is required in determining what is *excess* inventory. If a plant consumes small quantities of an alloy with a single supplier world-wide, then management has no choice but to accept the supplier's terms, which may include a 6-month order lead time and a minimum order quantity that covers two years of consumption. On the other hand, if an item is a commodity that can be delivered overnight from a local supplier, then it is difficult to justify holding a week's worth of it.

In addition to materials that go into products the plant also needs to store and retrieve the following:

- **Spare parts for facilities and equipment maintenance.** Like production materials, most spare parts make a one-way trip to where they are used, but their flow is irregular. A steel mill may keep a spare pump in stock for years, as insurance against emergencies. The management of such stores involves periodically testing such devices.

- **Tools, fixtures, jigs, dies, reticles, etc.** Such devices are mounted on machines during setups, then cleaned and returned to stores after use, periodically refurbished, and eventually replaced. They are checked out and returned like library books rather than consumed like parts. Being managed directly by Production, these stores are outside the scope of this discussion.

- **Returnable containers.** Like tools and dies, they are recirculating resources, but, unlike them, they are managed by Logistics. Returnable containers are discussed in detail in Chapter 9.

Selecting storage devices for different needs

As in many other aspects of manufacturing and logistics, underperformance in storage and retrieval is often due to the one-size-fits-all approach: one type of warehouse is used for all items, regardless of volume or frequency of use. What characterizes a lean plant is not that a particular type of warehouse is used but that different types are used to meet different needs.

The most common type of warehouse is the single-deep pallet rack shown in Figure 4-2. It provides random access to slots, meaning that every pallet can be retrieved without moving anything out of the way first. All levels are accessible through forklifts, narrow-aisle trucks, or order pickers, but the bottom level is more easily accessible, using pallet jacks to retrieve whole pallets or carts to retrieve boxes from pallets.

Many plants use this concept and nothing else. Within this structure, however, there are still options on how items are stored. Items can be permanent residents with dedicated slots, or "hotel guests," with slots allocated to pallets as they arrive. Again, many plants have either dedicated slots for all items, or dynamically allocated slots for all items.

Random access to slots

Bottom level accessible to pallet jacks

FIGURE 4-2. Single-deep pallet racks

Figure 4-3 shows the storage and retrieval traffic generated by the use of dynamically allocated slots for a heavily used item in an off-site warehouse. The item arrives in sea containers and is transferred to the production plant in full trailers. In between, the pallets are spread throughout the warehouse only to be collected again. Figure 4-4 shows the simplification of the flows for this item brought about simply by dedicating a zone to it. Incidentally, by eliminating the traffic for this item in the rest of the warehouse, this also makes the work of storage and retrieval of *other* items easier.

The approach in Figure 4-4, of course, is only the first step of improvement. Since the item arrives in sea container loads and leaves in trailer loads, there is no real need to put away the pallets onto racks. By clearing up space for it, it should be possible to crossdock the pallets directly from sea container to trailer. The final step would be to eliminate the item's visit to the warehouse altogether and find a way to receive it at the production plant directly from sea containers.

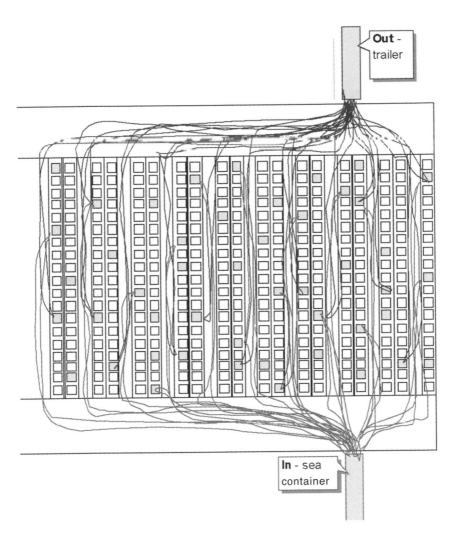

FIGURE 4-3. Dynamic allocation of slots to a high-volume item

This warehouse was designed to be flow-through, with materials coming in on one side and leaving on the opposite side. Figure 4-4 violates this principle, by having the outgoing trailer next to the incoming sea container. This, however, is a small price to pay to eliminate the unnecessary traffic.

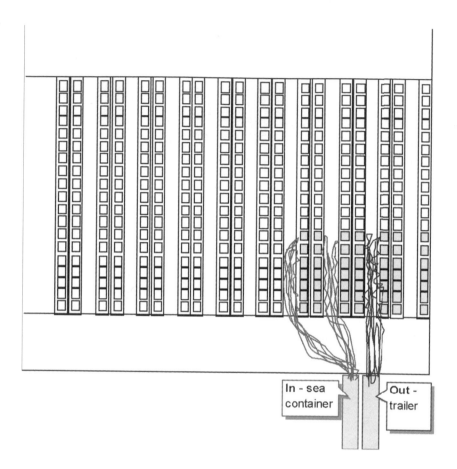

FIGURE 4-4. Dedicated zone for high-volume item

If an item is used frequently but in small quantities, the concept of having dedicated space remains valid, albeit on a small scale. The dedicated space may be no more than a slot holding one bin on a plain shelf. Where the concept of dedicated space is not valid, however, is for infrequently used items. Figure 4-5 shows a finished goods warehouse layout designed to accommodate both high-volume items shipped daily and infrequently needed items

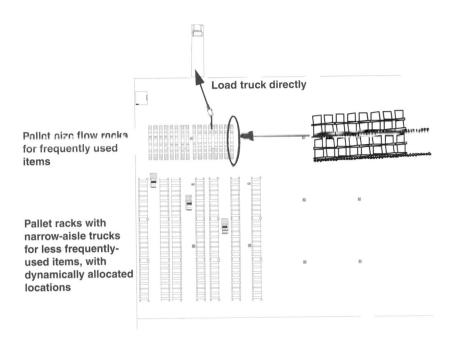

Load truck directly

Pallet size flow racks for frequently used items

Pallet racks with narrow-aisle trucks for less frequently-used items, with dynamically allocated locations

FIGURE 4-5. Warehouse for both frequently and infrequently used items

The motivations for using only one storage methods when the combination of several would work better vary. A common one is familiarity. In his or her professional life, the warehouse manager has only been exposed to one approach and is uncomfortable with any other. Another one is the limitations of the Warehouse Management System (WMS) in place: since it only supports one method of storage and retrieval, then no other method can coexist with it. This is a reversal of normal roles, with the people as servants of the computer system rather than the other way around. Lack of support by the WMS should not be allowed to prevent the use a method, with the information it generates handled manually until the WMS is enhanced or replaced.

Types of warehouse storage devices

Manual systems

The above discussion only considered single-deep pallet racks—also known as "selective"—and flow racks, which, while common, are not the only options, whether for pallets or for smaller units. Figure 4-6, based on sketches from Siemens Dematic, shows a few of these options.

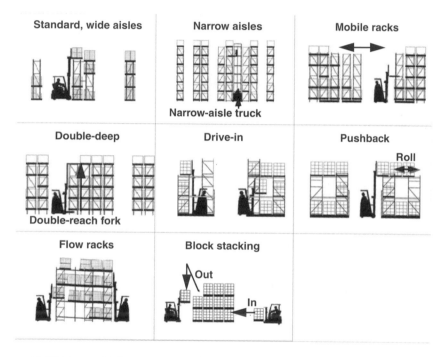

FIGURE 4-6. Pallet storage options

For different applications, these devices stack up as follows:

- *Narrow aisles* or *mobile racks* are variations on single-deep pallet racks that support a higher storage density, at the cost of requiring special equipment. The investment in equipment for narrow aisles may be easier to justify if it consists of order pickers, as in Figure 3-13, which allow the handler to ride up into the higher levels and pick individual boxes from pallets.

- *Double-deep, drive-in,* and *pushback racks* also increase storage density, also require special equipment, and allocate storage in multiple pallet units with *last-in–first-out* (LIFO) retrieval. Storage and retrieval requires less labor than for single-deep racks.

- *Flow racks* are for items with dedicated storage space. They support *first-in–first-out* (FIFO) retrieval at the pallet level, and require the least labor of all the approaches listed.

- Besides single-deep racks and flow racks, *block stacking* is the only approach in Figure 4-6 to be widely used. The main attraction of block stacking is that it requires no investment in racking and relies on the same forklifts the plant uses for other purposes. It requires pallets to be stackable, which means that the container walls must be sturdy enough to bear the weight of several pallets. For a labor point of view, it is the polar opposite of flow racks, which rely on gravity to move pallets.

Block stacking is the most labor-intensive method, because nothing moves unless a forklift moves it. As shown in Figure 4-7, stacks of pallets are arranged in "FIFO lanes," but retrieval from each stack is on a LIFO basis. Since one entire lane is used for a single item, it supports, on the same floor space, an order of magnitude fewer items than systems that rely on racking to store different items at different levels over the same real estate. These characteristics make block stacking appropriate for high-volume–low-mix applications, with items shipped by the truckload every day. Because of its low setup cost, it tends to be used when a plant first starts up, even where it does not fit long-term requirements.

Automatic Storage and Retrieval Systems (AS/RS)

None of the approaches in Figure 4-6 involves automation. All movements are power-assisted, but all actions are taken by people. With automatic storage and retrieval systems (AS/RS), as shown in Figure 4-8, operator action consists of either (1) entering materials into a loading station and the loading transaction on the control system, or (2) requesting materials from the control system and unloading on delivery. The selection of a slot and the movements of the materials to and from that slot are controlled and executed without human intervention, and faster than in the manual systems.

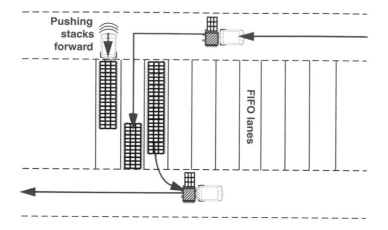

FIGURE 4-7. Storage and retrieval with block stacking in FIFO lanes

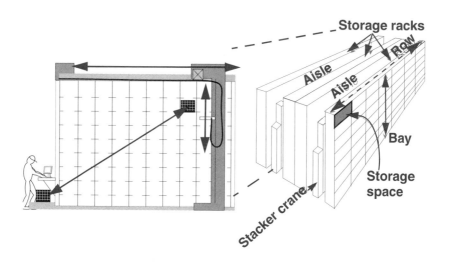

FIGURE 4-8. Working with an AS/RS

Like AGVs, AS/RS's have existed since at least the 1980s, yet they are far from common in manufacturing warehouses, and, where found, their users express buyer's remorse more frequently than enthusiasm. We have yet to encounter a case where an AS/RS was installed as part of lean manufacturing implementation. However, it is one decision to acquire an AS/RS when you don't have one, and another to dispose of one that is already bought, paid for, and in use.

Much of the dissatisfaction users experience with AS/RS's can be traced back to the acquisition procedure. When ramping up a new plant or a new production line, a rational approach could be to start with block stacking, which requires no investment, migrate to flow racks and pallet racks with manual operation as you outgrow block stacking, and finally, once operations are well established and the benefits of automation can be assessed, invest in AS/RS technology as needed.

The budgeting process of many companies, however, causes plant designers to include AS/RS's in the initial capital acquisition request. As a $5M line item in a $300M project, it will be more easily approved than as a stand-alone $5M project two years after plant startup, when management is more focused on having the plant make money than on spending to set it up.

As a consequence AS/RS's are designed *before* the organization has an opportunity to understand and specify its requirements, and this often results in discovering a mismatch after the fact, as in the following two examples:

- **Control system.** One plant bought an AS/RS with a control system that could only store and retrieve *full* pallets, while the plant operations required picking individual boxes from pallets. The plant had to set up a manual warehouse for partial pallets next to the AS/RS, which largely erased the benefits expected from it.
- **System sizing.** A machine shop sized an AS/RS for cutting tools based on the assumption that all tools would be stored away after each use in a machining center. After the plant started up, users found it more convenient to cache frequently used tool sets outside of the

AS/RS than to separate and store each tool individually, leaving the AS/RS three quarters empty.

More generally, AS/RS's have the following problems:

- **Lack of visibility.** Inventory in an AS/RS is only visible through its control system, and AS/RS's have been denounced as black holes where unnecessary inventory disappears from view.

- **Lack of flexibility.** The operating policies that can be used with an AS/RS are limited to what its control software will support. Manufacturing organizations often find that it does not meet their needs and don't have the resources to modify it.

- **Impact on manual storage and retrieval operations.** An AS/RS can spoil its users into not using the normal visible controls in the manual stores they still need to maintain.

- **Focus of attention.** In plants that have an AS/RS, its effective use becomes the focus of all debates about materials management. That it is more expensive than all other materials handling resources together makes it difficult for managers and engineers to think about any other issue.

Carrousels

Carrousels are simpler and cheaper than AS/RS's, primarily because they move along only one axis, as shown in Figure 4-9 in both a horizontal and a vertical version. The vertical carrousel is a more complex machine but uses less floor space. The movement of a carrousel may be controlled by the operator or by a control system that "knows" which items are stored where.

Like AS/RS's, they are found on manufacturing shop floors, but not often. In everyday life, they are most commonly found in dry cleaning stores— where they allow one attendant to retrieve a customer's garments while remaining by the cash register—and in airport baggage claim areas— where they allow luggage loaded at a single point to be unloaded by passengers distributed along the entire perimeter (See Figure 4-10).

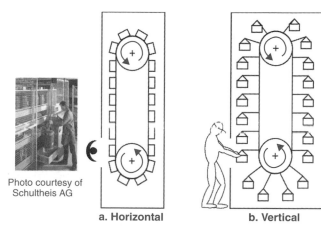

Photo courtesy of
Schultheis AG

Photo courtesy of
Electroclass SA

a. Horizontal   **b. Vertical**

FIGURE 4-9. Horizontal and vertical carrousel concepts

Carrousel delivers
customer's garments

Single loading point
behind the wall

Attendant remains
at cash register

Distribution along
entire perimeter

FIGURE 4-10. Carrousels in everyday life

In both examples, the advantages of carrousels are such that it is difficult
to imagine any alternative. There are, however, few *manufacturing* situations
where the case for carrousels is so compelling. In most storage and
retrieval operations, the *sequential* access provided by a carrousel is a seri-
ous drawback, since, in order to reach a target item, it may have to scan

through many others, leaving the operator waiting almost as long as it would have taken him or her to retrieve the item by other means.

Lean Assembly[1] showed vertical and horizontal carrousels as lineside presentation devices to prevent picking errors on an assembly line. But, even for this purpose, it has limitations. If the line assembles batches of different products in a fixed sequence, then bins can be placed in the carrousel in a matching sequence, so that the carrousel only has to move by one slot to set up for the next product. If, on the other hand, the line builds single units in a leveled sequence that is recalculated every shift, then the carrousel would have to switch bins with every unit, and the bin for the next unit may be arbitrarily far from the current one.

Like transportation vehicles, storage and retrieval devices come in a variety of shapes and modes of operation, and, there again, tailoring the choices to the different needs results in a cheaper system that can perform better than one-size-fits-all. Whether it does perform better, of course, depends on how it is used and managed, which is the subject of the next chapter.

---

1. Lean Assembly, p. 232-235

CHAPTER 5

Warehouse management

Summary

Warehouse visibility includes labels on the grid of columns supporting the ceiling, dock numbers that remain visible when docks are open, three-sided overhead zone identification signs, aisle/column/level labels on each slot in a pallet rack, and separators between slots as needed. Rack aisles must also be oriented to avoid blocking the view.

The most frequently used items have the most easily accessible, dedicated locations and use storage devices corresponding to their volume. Infrequently used items are dynamically assigned slots like hotel guests. Items from trusted suppliers exclusively bound for the same destination should be collocated.

Items from problem suppliers, on the other hand, are easier to monitor if collocated by source. Maps of dynamically allocated stores are needed for retrieval, preferably in a database updated by scanning barcodes or RFID tags. Performance degrades catastrophically when a warehouse is too full. An 85% maximum occupancy is recommended in the literature, but the saturation point varies with the design and mode of operation of each warehouse.

Tracking materials into and out of a warehouse is essential to inventory accuracy. Parts in the warehouse should be touched only by materials handlers, withdrawn only with a pull signal from production, and the item and quantity withdrawn recorded, preferably automatically through auto-ID technology. Parts should be in containers that make quantities visible and inventory accuracy enhanced by cycle counting. Security must not interfere with work and must treat employees with respect. It requires management communication, warehouse visibility, flow tracking, and, where applicable, employee stores.

This chapter covers issues of warehouse management that are independent of the nature of the materials contained, and its recommendations apply to a distribution center as well as a warehouse in a manufacturing plant.

Six ways to improve warehouse visibility

1. Location labeling on the warehouse floor

In the management of warehouse visibility, many issues are so basic that they should not need to be said, but it is obvious when walking through plant warehouse areas that they are often left unattended. One example is shown in Figure 5-1. Most warehouses are large rooms supported by a grid of columns, and simply affixing grid location labels on all sides of these columns makes it much easier to communicate with forklift drivers.

2. Dock identification

Even more common than warehouses without column grid labels are now-you-see-it-now-you-don't dock numbers. These numbers are mostly useful when the docks are open, as a means of helping forklift drivers avoid mistakes, yet most docks are labeled as in Figure 5-2, with the number hidden by the open door. Numbers printed on a roll-up door itself are also common. Numbers written to the *side* of the dock, where they can be seen at all times, are rare.

3. Zone identification

For zone identification, particularly where block stacking is used, it is easiest to simply paint or tape a name on the floor. It is, however, ineffective because the name of the zone is then only visible a few feet away, and only for a few weeks until it is erased or torn away by traffic. A common solution then is to hang a shingle from the rafters above the zone itself, but it is not visible from every direction, and is also subject to rocking if in the way of the ventilation system. A less common but much more effective

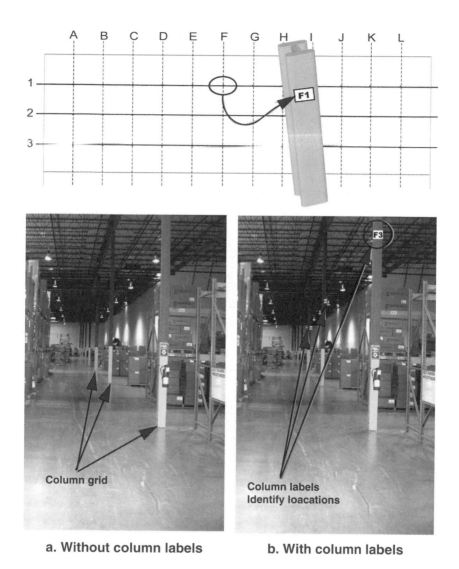

a. Without column labels

b. With column labels

FIGURE 5-1. Column grid labeling

solution is to use triangular signs and mount them rigidly either on the rafters or above the racks. It stays in place and is visible from all directions. (See Figure 5-3)

Now you see it   Now you don't

FIGURE 5-2. **Dock numbers hidden by door**

Each zone should be named after its purpose. "ACME" in Figure 5-3 could refer to a customer, with the zone holding finished goods pegged for this customer. On the materials side, ACME could be a supplier on probation, and the zone hold all the items received from it. Or the zone could hold semi-finished goods awaiting customization, with a sign saying "Customization Center."

X Not visible from afar, insufficient contrast, torn up by forklifts

X Visible from two directions only, moved by wind from fans

√ Visible everywhere, held rigidly in place

FIGURE 5-3. **Zone identification signs**

4. Rack identification

A standard, effective, and self-explanatory method for identifying locations in pallet racks is by three coordinates for aisle, column within the aisle, and level within the column. In factories, however, we encounter warehouses with the following problems:

- The location addressing scheme is not used and the racks are uncharted space.

- Location addresses are inconsistent. In some aisles, the ground floor is level 0; in others, level 1. In some aisles, level numbers go up from bottom to top; in others, down from top to bottom.

- Location addresses are not adequately displayed. They should be printed on labels with large bold characters for human readability, and include barcodes or RFID tags for automatic identification (auto-ID).

Figure 5-4 shows how this is done effectively in an IKEA warehouse store. Note how the color and the shape of the aisle signs enhances their visibility.

FIGURE 5-4. Aisle markings at IKEA

5. Slot separation

Marking a slot identification on a shelf is not always sufficient to ensure that the intended items remain aligned with it. As shown in Figure 5-5, while there is little risk of pallets becoming misaligned within a 3-pallet rack section, this can easily happen on a plain shelf holding small bags or bin quantities of many different items, but it can be prevented by materializing slots through separators.

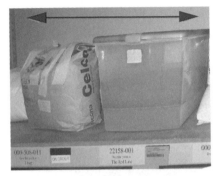

No slot separation: items can shift out of alignment with labels

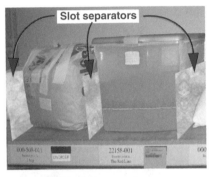

With slot separators: items are kept in place

Slot separators not needed: pallets cannot shift around

FIGURE 5-5. Shelves with and without slot separators

6. Rack orientation

Multi-level racks block the view! If single-deep pallet racks are oriented as in Figure 5-6 (A), then not only are the distances traveled to put away pallets longer than in Figure 5-6 (B), but the inside of the warehouse is hidden from view to all receiving personnel.

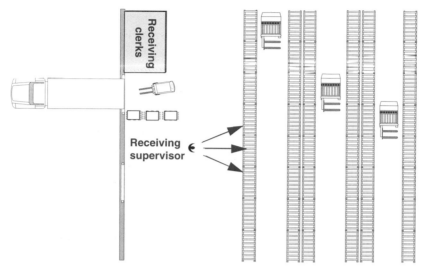

(A) Rack orientation hides the warehouse

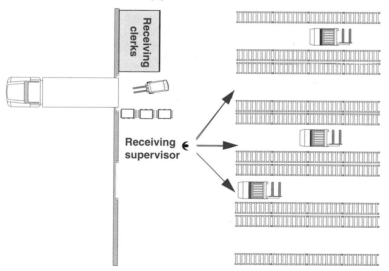

(B) Rack orientation makes the warehouse visible

FIGURE 5-6. **Rack orientation for warehouse visibility**

Slot allocation and indexing

We have defined several ways of identifying locations in the warehouse and the materials that go in them:

- **Column grid location.** The column labels identify geographical location regardless of the use of the room. It is as useful on a production floor as in a warehouse.

- **Zone signs.** These describe a category of items stored in a zone within the warehouse.

- **Aisle-column-level.** This is a three-dimensional identification of a rack location. It allows a materials handler to find this location, regardless of where it is on the floor or what is stored in it.

- **Item number or stock-keeping unit (sku) number.** Unique identifier of an item in the warehouse.

With all these elements in hand, we need to decide what to store where. Some plants, as in Figure 5-7, store items left to right and top to bottom in order of their item numbers, like books in a library.

FIGURE 5-7. **Example of shelving by item number**

Since it is easy to understand and provides a systematic way to find any item, it might seem a good idea. In general, however, it isn't. Since frequency of use or destinations for any item are subject to change, they cannot be encoded in item numbers. Organizing by item number therefore has the following consequences:

1. The most frequently used items may be in hard-to-reach places.

2. Items that go into the same product may be located far from each other.

3. If item characteristics are encoded in item numbers, similar items have similar item numbers and are located next to each other, even if they do go into different products. As a result, it is easy for pickers to confuse items.

4. Introducing a new item requires shifting all the items that are after it in the item number sequence.

Instead, we should use the classification criteria we have identified, which include the following:

- **Frequency of use.** Frequently used items have easily accessible, dedicated locations; infrequently used items, dynamically allocated slots.

- **Volume.** High-volume frequently used items may use flowracks; low-volume frequently used items, dedicated slots in racks or shelves.

- **Destination.** Items from reliable suppliers used only in one area of the production floor should be collocated, as should items shipped exclusively to one customer.

- **Source.** Items from a supplier with quality or delivery problems may be collocated for easier monitoring. This does not apply only to inbound materials, but also to internally made products about which customers have issued quality or delivery problem reports.

Depending on such circumstances as the size of the warehouse, the commonality of the items, or quality and delivery performance, these different criteria may be applied in different sequences. In addition, physical characteristics may also cause some items to be treated differently. As previously discussed in the section titled "Network of conveyors," liquids or powders used frequently and in high volume may have dedicated silos and automatic transportation to points of use.

Flow racks for high-volume frequently used items can be arranged by order of their item numbers, but it will not make much difference. If there are 5 to 10 of them, stored or retrieved hourly, materials handlers promptly memorize where they are. Ordering by item number is useful for the 50 or 100 items that have dedicated slots in a pallet rack, but it is not usable at all for the thousands of items that use dynamically allocated slots. They must be assigned whatever slot is available when they arrive, and the handlers must register these "hotel guests" for later retrieval. In the example of Figure 5-8, Ikea directs consumers to aisles from a list of item families in alphabetical order.

FIGURE 5-8. IKEA's item location guide

The assignments in Figure 5-8 are semi-permanent. They may change once a season but not everyday. The map is needed because customers cannot be expected to know this information.

Figure 5-9 shows an approach for manual tracking of dynamically allocated slots. Each slot has a "key" attached to it when it is empty. When loading a pallet into the slot, the materials handler takes away the key, detaches a duplicate identification tag from the pallet, and places both in the corresponding position on the map at the front of the aisle. Conversely, when retrieving the pallet, the handler takes along the key and the tag.

This approach avoids having to write anything down by hand, but it is still quite vulnerable to employees being distracted or not properly trained. Also, while it allows you to find easily what is in location 3b-4-2, this is not the most relevant question. Instead, what handlers most frequently need to know is "Where do I find item 52103?" With only the information in Figure 5-9, the handler has to visually scan the maps of all the aisles. With

10 aisles, this would be prohibitively time consuming. If, however, zoning is used to reduce the allowable storage areas for an item to one or two aisles, it may be manageable. Alternatively, a clerk could periodically scan the maps and maintain a catalog of item locations.

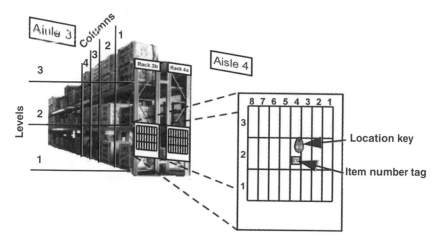

FIGURE 5-9. Manual mapping of a pallet rack

The labor required and the vulnerability of the manual systems for tracking dynamically allocated slots may explain why computer-based Warehouse Management Systems (WMS), as shown in Figure 5-10, are possibly the most successful application of information technology to manufacturing. Unlike ERP or Manufacturing Execution Systems (MES), WMS's do not generate much controversy. It is the consensus of materials managers that these systems pay for themselves through reductions in data collection labor, higher accuracy, faster retrieval, and support for cycle counting and data mining.

In many warehouses, barcode scanning is already in use, for functions like matching serial numbers to customer purchase orders (PO), and the hardware and communication infrastructure to support a WMS is already in place. In the example shown in Figure 5-10, the materials handler scans barcodes for both location and item number when loading a pallet. The WMS stores the pair of codes in an item-location cross-reference table, which can then be queried for the location of any item number. Barcode scanning is not perfect, and is in fact being superseded as an auto-ID technology by radio-frequency ID tags (RFID).

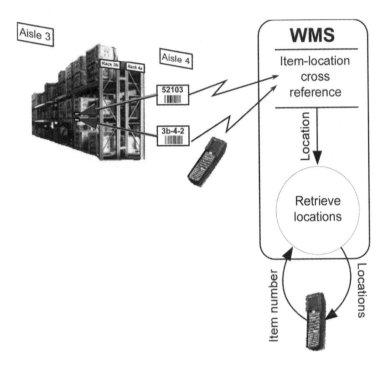

FIGURE 5-10. **Mapping of a pallet rack with a WMS**

Determining how full a warehouse should be

Many managers are uncomfortable at the sight of a warehouse that is not full. They feel that it is wasting space and should be shrunk. As a result, most factory warehouses are almost full all the time. But this is not in fact a desirable situation. The service warehouses provide is storage and retrieval, and you cannot *store* materials in an already full warehouse anymore than you can *retrieve* materials from an empty one.

Let us assume the plant consumes one truckload per day of an item and has a dedicated location for this item in the warehouse, then, assuming 10% of a day's consumption in safety stock to protect against traffic delays, the amount of the item in storage will be as shown in Figure 5-11, with an average occupancy of 60%.

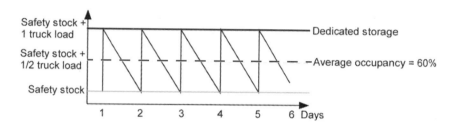

FIGURE 5-11. Storage of a heavily used item over time

Higher occupancy rates can be achieved when storage locations are dynamically allocated, because any space freed up by the retrieval of one item can immediately be used for the storage of another. Frazelle, in his discussion of warehouse space requirements planning,[1] says in general that productivity and safety "trail off dramatically" as occupancy exceeds 85% to 90%. There is no general formula for when storage and retrieval performance begins to degrade but specific designs can be simulated. The phenomenon itself is commonly experienced when accessing computer hard disks or parking at a shopping mall, as follows:

---

1. *World Class Warehousing and Material Handling*, Ed Frazelle, McGraw Hill, (2001) ISBN 0-07-137600-3, pp. 189–194.

- To store files on a hard disk that is nearly full, computer operating systems fragment them into pieces that are small enough to fit in available slots, and puts the pieces back together when retrieving them. The time needed for these operations is perceptibly longer than storing and retrieving contiguous blocks of data from a half-empty disk.

- While parking does not involve fragmentation, it still requires hunting for a spot and returning to that spot afterwards. The best, most convenient spots go first, and only the most remote remain available when the parking lot is nearly full.

Assume a single-deep pallet rack warehouse, to which one item arrives by the truckload and leaves in multi-pallet loads while other items arrive and leave in varying quantities. Then both of the phenomena described above occur. When the warehouse is empty, truckloads can be stored in contiguous slots on the ground floor. When it is nearly full, they are fragmented into single pallet units wherever a slot is available, and this will tend to be in the highest reaches of the racks that are farthest from the entrance, and multiple pallets need to be retrieved and assembled from different slots.

For illustration purposes, a simple formula can be obtained if we make the following assumptions:

1. As a result of on-going storage and retrieval activity in a single-deep pallet rack, all slots have an equal probability of being occupied, independently of one another.

2. The warehouse is large enough so that the occupancy is significantly unchanged as a result of storing an additional truckload. For example, if the warehouse has 5,000 slots and is 90% full, then 4,500 slots are occupied. If we store another 20 pallets, then occupancy rate rises by $20/5000 = 0.4\%$, which we can neglect.

The average number of slots that need to be visited in order to store a number of pallets is then like the average number of attempts needed to win a given number of times in a lottery where the odds are determined by the occupancy rate. This is given by the formula

$$\text{Number of slots} = \text{Number of pallets} \times \left[1 + \frac{\text{Occupancy rate}}{(1 - \text{Occupancy rate})} \right]$$

which we plot in Figure 5-12.

Any real situation is of course more complex and not amenable to such a formula. For example, if a WMS provides directed putaway, then the forklift operator is told where to store each pallet and doesn't have to hunt for a slot. This formula also says nothing about retrieval of multiple pallets from a fragmented warehouse or about the fact that some of the open slots in a crowded warehouse are in hard-to-reach places.

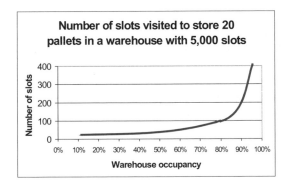

FIGURE 5-12. **Simplified warehouse saturation model**

What we do know is that we can expect storage and retrieval performance to fall catastrophically as the warehouse saturates. *A priori*, we don't know where to draw the line, but we know we should expect this phenomenon as occupancy rises, and we can watch for it.

Tracking inventory

Some plants, sometimes in the name of lean manufacturing, have allowed production operators to withdraw parts from the materials warehouse without any tracking transactions, on the grounds that record keeping was non-value added work, and that these actions could be accounted for through backflushing on finished goods.

There are two problems with this approach:

1. Short of doing a complete physical count everyday, the only way to know what is *inside* a warehouse is to record what goes in and what comes out. Not tracking withdrawals destroys inventory accuracy and prevents the generation of any realistic production schedule.

2. Just because a part is needed for one assembly operation does not mean that it is not also needed for *another*. The policy of letting production operators help themselves to materials resolves such conflicts by giving priority to whoever grabs the parts first, which isn't necessarily appropriate.

Where tracking transactions can be overkill is not in the warehouse but on the production line. If production is organized so that parts issued from the materials warehouse leave the line within hours, whether mounted into finished goods or scrapped as defective, there is no need to maintain a database of how many of which type of parts are where *within* the production line. There may, however, be a need to attach the serial numbers of parts to the serial number of the product for traceability.

Withdrawals of parts from a warehouse should be based on the following principles:

1. Parts in a warehouse should be touched only by materials handlers. Production operators or team leaders should not need or be allowed to fetch parts directly from the warehouse, and they shouldn't have the time to do it anyway. Delivering parts to production is the purpose of the materials organization.

2. Parts should not be withdrawn from the warehouse without some authorization signal from Production. This is the pull system described

in Chapter 10 applied to the warehouse. Materials handlers should not take the initiative of delivering unsolicited parts, and should not be instructed to do so by their supervisors.

3. Materials handlers should never take parts out of the warehouse without recording item number and quantity. Most warehouses have WMS's that reduce the transaction work to scanning a barcode. The move to RFID technology should completely automate the transaction and relieve the materials handlers of the need to enter data in any form.

4. In addition to the *warehouse* visibility features described in the beginning of this chapter, part count visibility should be enhanced by the use of appropriate containers, as described in Chapter 9.

5. The accuracy of inventory records should be enhanced by *cycle counting*,[1] a practice in which materials handlers make physical counts of a few items every day on a rotating basis. Cycle counts are to tracking as a satellite position fix is to dead reckoning. Starting from a known position, you can deduce the position of an airplane from its direction and speed over time. Likewise, from a snapshot of the content of a warehouse, you can infer what it contains over time from in and out transactions. As in dead reckoning, however, errors accumulate over time and eventually make the numbers wrong, which is why cycle counting is inevitable. The amount of it may drop over time as warehouse operations improve, but it cannot be expected to vanish altogether.

---

1. *Inventory Accuracy*, David J. Piasecki, OPS Publishing (2003), pp. 81–33.

Security and access control

Lead ingots may not need extensive warehouse security but diamonds do. More generally, whenever items are light, easy to conceal, and saleable on the outside, warehouses need to be protected. The challenge is to provide the appropriate level of security without interfering with the flow of work, while treating employees with the trust and respect that is an integral part of managing in a lean environment.

Most of the methods used to provide security generate more work or waiting time both for production operators and for materials handlers, as in the following examples:

- Entering the shop floor of some computer assembly plants requires going through metal detectors, in front of which there are long lines of employees at the beginning and the end of each shift.

- Some warehouse sections are surrounded by chicken wire fences and accessed by opening a lock.

- Some items are distributed through vending machine-like dispensers that scan and validate users' badges, and track the quantities withdrawn.

Like safety or mistake-proofing, however, security should *not* add labor. The concern here is not just day-to-day productivity but vulnerability in a crunch. Any procedure that adds labor is likely to be bypassed under pressure. Only if a security procedure adds *no* labor can management be assured that it will be followed at all times, even when the workload is exceptionally high.

Following are a few approaches that management can use:

1. The need for security must be communicated to all employees through the management chain, from plantwide all-hands meetings to the daily start-of-shift meetings of every team.

2. Visible management in the warehouse reduces the likelihood of pilferage. Another way to see it is that the *lack* of visible management makes it unlikely that disappearances will be noticed.

3. Security procedures must be designed not only to prevent unauthorized actions but also to make sure that authorized, legitimate actions

proceed unimpeded. This is also an area where auto-ID technology has a key role to play: On parts or bins, RFID tags can be used to detect unauthorized movements; on badges, to automatically open doors to authorized work areas for employees who previously had to key in a code, place a magnetic key on a reader, or use a key on a padlock.

4. Where feasible, company products should be offered at deep discounts in employee stores. In a prestige cosmetics plant, for example, employees can buy obsolete promotional goods at prices that go a long way towards eliminating any temptation to steal.

As announced at the beginning, this chapter recommends practices that are of value regardless of the nature and role of the materials in a warehouse. The next chapter digs one level deeper, into the specifics of warehousing incoming materials, work in process, and finished goods.

CHAPTER 6

Warehousing materials, WIP, and finished goods

Summary

Materials inside the plant are comprised of incoming raw materials/components, work in process (WIP), and finished goods. Product-specific parts built by the body-on-sequence method and standard items managed by vendors on consignment go to production without being stored and retrieved in a warehouse. Other items are stored either in a central warehouse or in supermarkets near the production lines, for water spiders to distribute to workstations.

Since there are no economies of scale in warehouses, the central warehouse does not perform better than local supermarkets, but the central warehouse is still needed for items delivered in quantities that are too large for supermarkets, items used in multiple products made on multiple lines, and items that need safety stocks due to delivery problems, or are collocated by source to monitor quality problems.

As in warehouse club stores, levels in pallet racks can be specialized, with handlers picking bins or totes from the easily accessible low levels, while the upper levels hold reserves that forklifts bring down as needed. A lean plant keeps WIP visible on the shop floor, and limits handler tasks to transportation between production lines. Warehouse storage and retrieval is only for semi-finished goods awaiting customization.

Before shipping, "finished goods" often still requires boxing, shrinkwrapping, pallet shuffling, labeling, and final inspection. After shipping, there is often further customization, in service centers or at dealers, which blurs the distinction between logistics and production, limits the use of 3rd party logistics, and constrain product designs to mistake-proof field customization. Finished goods do not occupy the same volume as the materials they are built from, which impacts warehouse sizing, dock configuration, and even plant location.

Incoming materials stores inside the plant

Central warehouses, local supermarkets, and direct delivery to the production line

Frazelle[1] reports a benchmarking study of warehouse performance in multiple dimensions, including productivity, storage density, inventory accuracy, shipping accuracy, dock-to-stock time, warehouse order lead time, and safety that he and S. Hackman conducted. They used a technique called *data envelopment analysis* (DEA) to define multidimensional equivalents to an efficiency measure and concluded that large warehouses did not perform any better than small ones. This has far reaching implications for the design of warehouses inside the plant. We may need a central warehouse because of the way parts are received and consumed, but we should not expect this warehouse to perform better than small satellite warehouses spread throughout the plant.

In car assembly, some items go straight from the receiving dock to production and are never stored by the materials organization. In the system called "body-on-sequence" described in Chapter 12, some model and option-specific components are ordered when final assembly of the car starts. The supplier immediately makes and delivers them sequenced in truckloads that are immediately conveyed to production without being put away in storage, as shown in Figure 6-1.

---

1. *World Class Warehousing & Material Handling*, E. Frazelle, McGraw Hill (2002) pp. 61–62

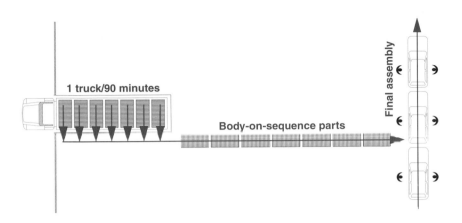

FIGURE 6-1. Body-on-sequence parts delivered straight to assembly

At the opposite end of the bill of materials are generic commodity items like nuts, bolts, and washers, that are provided on a consignment or pay-per-build basis (see Chapter 12) by suppliers who not only manage the inventory but deliver the parts to the line side, so that the plant's materials organization never touches them.

Most items, however, particularly in industries *other* than car assembly, are neither managed by the body-on-sequence method nor by consignment. They arrive in quantities that the materials organization must receive, put away, and distribute to production.

The semiconductor equipment industry makes machines that sell for millions of dollars a piece and a high rate is one unit per day. These machines contain custom-engineered mechanical parts as well as electronic controls that are delivered by courier services in box quantities. It is then feasible to split the content of these boxes right at Receiving into plastic bins and immediately distribute these bins to small stores spread through the production area and referred to as "supermarkets," for picking by operators nicknamed " water spiders." The disposable containers then do not make it past Receiving.

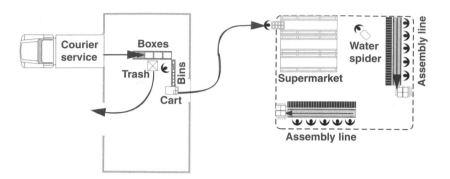

FIGURE 6-2. Delivery to a supermarket

With the higher volumes characteristic of the automobile industry, a similar situation can be achieved through the supplier milk runs described in Chapter 7, with parts arriving in trucks that contain a mixed load from multiple suppliers with balanced quantities. It may then be possible to sort these items into quantities that can be directly delivered to supermarkets on the floor.

The supermarket is the interface between materials handlers and water spiders. The distinctions between these two roles is not always clearly understood, particularly among managers. A materials handler does the following:

- Move, store, and retrieve parts in boxes or bins.
- Rearrange boxes or bins.
- Switch parts between types of containers.
- Prepare containers for transportation by taping, shrinkwrapping, fastening belts around pallets, etc.
- Print and attach labels, scan barcodes, and enter tracking data.

None of these tasks require any product knowledge. Materials handlers do not need to know anything about the product other than outer dimensions and weight of its containers, full and empty. They don't need to know its bill of materials or manufacturing process. Water spiders, by contrast, don't have to drive forklifts, but what they do requires product knowledge and they are recruited among the most senior, most skilled production operators. Their job is to prepare parts for immediate use in production, and includes the following:

- Removing any remaining packaging, plugs, or other protective hardware from parts.
- Feeding parts down narrow flow racks or other single piece presentation devices, as described in Chapter 11 of *Lean Assembly*.
- Picking kits or matching sets of parts and delivering them to the line.

Clearly, the likelihood of having a kit with the wrong parts, too few parts, too many parts, or defective parts is substantially reduced when the picker knows the product and has experience assembling it.

The term "water spider" is a mistranslation of "mizusumashi," the water *strider* commonly seen darting about the surface of ponds. Toyota called these employees "mizusumashi," based on the similarity of their motions between supermarkets and production lines with those of the insect. The term "water spider" has gained currency in lean manufacturing plants in the United States, even though actual water *spiders* are simply spiders that live in water and have nothing to do with mizusumashi. (See Figure 6-3.)

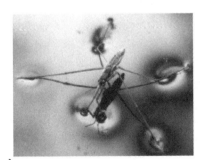

√ **Water strider or "mizusumashi"**
(courtesy of larvalbug.com)

✗ **A real water spider**

FIGURE 6-3. **Water strider versus water spider**

Before or instead of going to supermarkets, items with the following characteristics have to be stored in an incoming materials warehouse:

- They arrive in minimum quantities that far exceed daily consumption, be it in the form of full truckloads consumed by the pallet or full pallets consumed by the bin.

- They are used in multiple products whose demand volume and mix may change. Storing the items in a central warehouse postpones their pegging to a product—or family—and makes it easier to respond to changes.

- The supplier's deliveries are irregular, and a safety stock is needed to avoid shortages.

- Due to quality issues, all the supplier's products are required to go through incoming inspection or testing.

Suppliers with subpar performance in any area are of course on notice that they must improve or they are being phased out, and you would expect that, over time, there would be none left. In reality, however, there will always be a few. New products with new technology requiring some debugging will have components that suppliers have difficulty making and that will need to be watched until they mature. Stellar performers will also lapse as a result of management changes, mergers and acquisitions, bad outsourcing decisions, and many other reasons.

Grouping items by source or by destination

Figure 6-4 shows different strategies for grouping items in materials stores. As discussed above., direct delivery from Receiving to the line side as in Figure 6-4(C) is best when possible, but isn't always possible. When using intermediate stores, there are many ways to organize them, of which two are of particular interest.

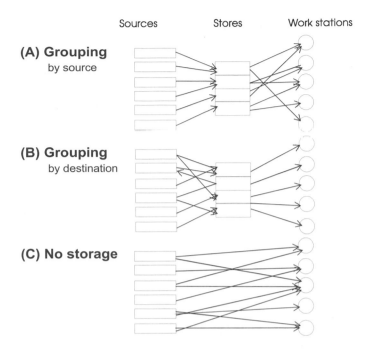

FIGURE 6-4. Item grouping strategies

In Figure 6-4 (A), the items are grouped by source, which is done in the central warehouse. The reasons for choosing this approach may vary. Car assembly plants typically have two materials services area, one on each side of the assembly line. One is used to receive parts from local suppliers; the other from remote or overseas suppliers, whose lead times are substantially longer, and whose products may require customs clearance. If a supplier is on a watch list, it will be easier to monitor its performance if all its items are collocated in the warehouse. Shortages, overages, wrong items, and defective items will be easier to trace and respond to.

If only one item is on a watch list, as opposed to all items from a given supplier, it can be stored with other items going to the same destination, but must be flagged appropriately. We have seen one company hang diapers above racks containing such items, as a sign that they need "baby sitting"—that is, a detour through Quality Assurance before release to Production.

In Figure 6-4 (B), the items are grouped by destination, usually in a local supermarket near that destination. Parts from one source may go into different locations, but retrieval for one station is now one-stop shopping. Grouping parts by destination is also what Toyota does in its Chicago consolidation center, where parts from multiple suppliers are sorted by destinations on the shop floors of NUMMI and the Georgetown plants and loaded onto intermodal containers that are sequenced and indexed by unloading dock at the plant, as discussed in Chapter 7.

Taking advantage of the vertical structure

The multiple levels in a pallet rack can be given different roles, as can be seen in warehouse clubs. This is shown in Figure 6-5 .

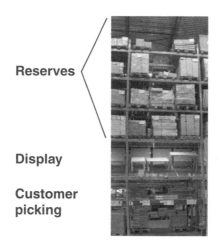

Reserves

Display

Customer
picking

FIGURE 6-5. Specializing shelf use (IKEA)

The bottom level is available for consumers to pick products, disassembled in cardboard boxes. The next shelf is used to display the assembled products, and all the shelves above hold reserves. Forklifts periodically come by to bring pallets down to the floor level and replenish the upper levels.

Figure 6-6 shows a similar approach for a warehouse where materials arrive in pallets of bins and leave in individual bins, mix-loaded on a train of tow carts.

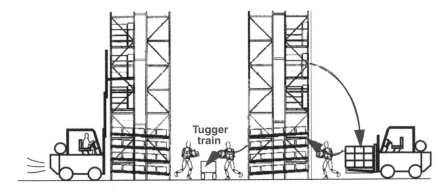

FIGURE 6-6. Beaver Materials' Pallet rack/flow rack combination

Stores for work in process and semi-finished goods

It is common in factories that do not practice lean manufacturing for work in process (WIP) to be stored in a warehouse between every two operations. After a batch of parts undergoes a turning operation, it checks into the warehouse, under the control of the materials group, and checks back out days or weeks later to go into drilling. This practice is unsound for the following reasons:

1. It generates unnecessary handling work, which not only wastes the time of materials handlers but also increases the risk of handling damage.

2. It reduces WIP visibility and, as a result, WIP quantities tend to grow out of control.

3. It extends lead times.

In a lean plant, there is no warehousing of work in process. It is held on the production floor by Production, on lineside shelves, in input and output buffers around production lines, or in supermarkets for water spiders to pick from. The role of Materials is limited to moving WIP between production lines, in response to pull signals. Figure 6-7 shows two ways of transferring parts from a fabrication machine or cell to assembly.

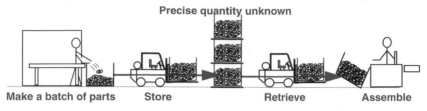

(A.) Handling in large bins with WIP warehousing

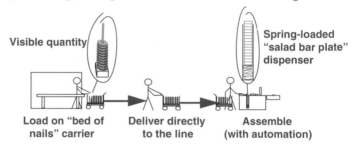

(B.) Direct delivery in custom carrier, with automation

FIGURE 6-7. **WIP warehousing versus direct delivery**

In Figure 6-7 (A), bagel-shaped parts are thrown into large bins, and put away in a warehouse prior to being delivered to manual assembly; in Figure 6-7 (B), they are neatly stacked on a custom cart that uses the parts' center hole to hold them on pins, and delivered directly to assembly. There, the operator transfers the parts one column at a time onto spring-loaded devices patterned after the plate dispensers used in salad bars, which presents the parts one at a time in a controlled orientation for automatic assembly.

On the drawing, it is tempting to collocate the fabrication machine with assembly and eliminate the transfer, and, if it can be done right away, it should be. In many situations, however, besides capacity mismatches, the current work environments of fabrication and assembly may be too different to be integrated. Collocating diecasting with assembly, for example, would make assemblers work in an environment that contains vats of molten aluminum, hot dies, and coolant mist. Or the environments may be compatible, but the engineers have not gotten around to integrating them yet and, until they do, the transportation step remains necessary.

There is a distinction, however, between WIP and semi-finished goods. It is common in many industries to make a small number of components or generic models, to be configured or customized just before shipping. Following are just a few examples:

1. Cosmetics are compounded in bulk, and then the same compound goes into a variety of bottles, tubes or jars that may further be aggregated into gift sets.

2. Materials in the form of plastic tubes or sheets are first made in rolls, and then cut to custom dimensions as needed.

3. Semiconductor wafers are fabricated into generic master slices, that are burned into 100 times more different application-specific integrated circuits at the last operation.

4. Commercial trucks are painted with the customer's colors and logos.

Where that pattern is present, it often makes sense to make the generic item to stock and customize it to order. One consequence of this policy is that items that are neither incoming materials nor finished goods are warehoused and managed during that time by Materials rather than by Production. These items are often called "semi-finished goods."

The difference between WIP and semi-finished goods is in the eye of the beholder. What makes an item one or the other is not its physical nature but management decision. Returning to the example of a part that undergoes turning and drilling, the holes drilled into it may serve to mount it on the customer's product. If this part is mounted differently on multiple products, then drilling can be treated either as one step performed in a flexible machining cell, or as a customization step, with the part between turning and drilling handled as semi-finished goods rather than WIP. While storing semi-finished goods can reduce the cost of mass customization by supporting delayed differentiation, unless management is vigilant, this strategy can easily degenerate into a return to the mass production practice of warehousing WIP.

Semi-finished goods are generic units made in much larger quantities than they are consumed in. Table 6-1 shows possible patterns for a few types of semi-finished goods.

TABLE 6-1. Storage and retrieval pattern for semi-finished goods

Type of semi-finished goods	Arrival quantities	Picking quantities
Discrete pieces	Pallets	Bins
Film, plate, fabric, tubes	Rolls	Cut pieces
Liquid or paste	Drum	Bucket
...	...	...

Semi-finished goods stores should exist only to support customization. The same item can be both *WIP* where used in its standard form in a high-volume product with a dedicated assembly line, and *semi-finished* when customized into multiple, low-volume products. In this case, the WIP fraction of its demand should be delivered directly to assembly, and only the rest should be stored in the semi-finished goods warehouse.

The semi-finished goods warehouse should also only hold items for which customization adds up to a steady demand for the generic item. If an item made in house is consumed so rarely that it would not justify a dedicated location as an incoming material, then it should be excluded from the semi-finished goods warehouse. If a generic lot would last six months, the finished product should be made to order from scratch using a residual job-shop set aside for such random requests. These concepts are shown in an example in Figure 6-8.

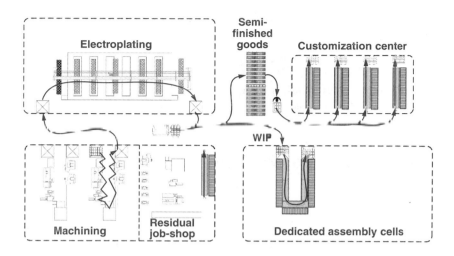

FIGURE 6-8. WIP and semi-finished goods

Finished goods stores

The need for finished goods stores

If all products are made based on pull signals from customers, then all units can be shipped immediately and there is no need for stores of finished goods. It is, however, a big "if." When factories get to this point, it is frequently because, in fact, their customer is the sales department. Sales issues orders to the factory that commingle actual customer orders with orders based on its own forecast and promotion plan, and owns the finished goods as soon as they leave the factory. In this case, the factory and the manufacturing organization as a whole don't have to worry about finished goods inventories, but the sales department and the company as a whole do.

Body-on-sequence suppliers to the automobile industry genuinely have no finished goods inventory. They do not start making a product unit until they receive a signal from the car assembly plant that the car it goes into has started on the first station of final assembly and ship it on the next milk run.

Injex Industries, of Hayward, CA, has been a body-on-sequence supplier of door panels to NUMMI in Fremont, CA, since 1993.[1] Finished goods inventories of door panels at Injex went from a 14 days' supply in 1985 to 2 days in 1990, 4 hours in 1992, and none as of 1993. While this obviously required a sustained effort, it also shows a transition period of *8 years*, during which the company had finished goods stores to look after.

What is a "finished good"?

In principle, finished goods are ready to ship, and all a manufacturer has to do is load them on a truck. In reality, what is usually referred to as "finished goods" in the plant still has hurdles to clear before getting out the door. The operations performed on finished goods at shipping typically include the following:

- **Boxing.** In most cases, packaging is done in production. In others, it is done as part of shipping. There are many different motivations for this:
    - Items are much bulkier after packaging
    - Packaging materials cannot be brought onto the production floor.
    - Customers have special packaging requirements.
- **Shrinkwrapping.** Pallets are often not shrinkwrapped until shipping, because otherwise it may have to be undone in order to ship half a pallet.
- **Recombining boxes.** Breaking down single-item pallets and recombining boxes into mix-loaded pallets.
- **Labeling.** Affixing custom labels on boxes and pallets.
- **Quality assurance.** Performing quality checks of varying scope demanded by customers.

The boxing station shown in Figure 6-9 looks like, and in fact is, an assembly station as found in production. It shows that the separation between

---

1. Hormoz Mogharei, personal communication (2004)

production and logistics is not as sharp as one might wish, and the trend towards more last minute customization *outside the plant* further blurs the line.

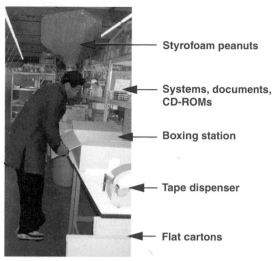

— Styrofoam peanuts

— Systems, documents, CD-ROMs

— Boxing station

— Tape dispenser

— Flat cartons

FIGURE 6-9. Boxing station within shipping

In the previous section, we called "semi-finished goods" items that are stored inside the plant in generic form, and retrieved for customization prior to shipping. But customization does not stop at the plant's shipping dock. More is done at multiple levels in the distribution network. Common examples include the following:

- Dealer-installed options in cars
- Paint color matching in the hardware store
- Matching makeup foundation to a customer's skin in a department store
- Cutting tubes or rolls of fabric to length

What gets into customers' hands has not entirely been made inside the factory. As a consequence, some level of *production* skill and product knowledge are needed in the distribution chain. Since, in the eyes of the customers, the manufacturer is responsible for quality regardless of where customization takes place, the manufacturer needs control over how the work is done.

Services requiring product knowledge are beyond the scope of 3rd party logistics or distributors. Customization must be done either by employees of the manufacturer located in service centers next to customers, or by employees of dealers who are trained and certified by the manufacturer. Even then, however, the level of control cannot match that achieved in the factory environment. It is simply more difficult to ensure that a spoiler is installed exactly the same way in 2,000 dealerships than at one assembly station. This constrains customization operations to be simpler and more mistake-proof than those carried out internally.

In some industries, products are *configured* by dealers rather than customized. For example, supplying an excavator with a particular bucket involves no modification of the machine, but requires having a range of buckets available, as shown in Figure 6-10.

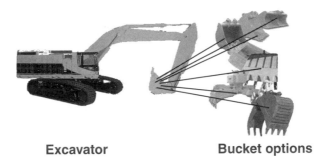

Excavator   **Bucket options**

FIGURE 6-10. **Excavator with bucket options**

There are usually too many options for all dealers to have available at all times. The manufacture's sales department then maintains a database of the inventory of buckets available at all dealerships, allowing dealers to locate where the nearest available bucket of a given type can be found, and the logistics of this activity include shipments between dealers.

Volume occupied by finished goods versus raw materials

Finished goods rarely occupy the same amount of space as the materials they came from. In activities like extraction, refinement, or smelting the finished goods are smaller than the raw materials; in most processes, however, it is the opposite, with finished goods containing more air than the materials, and protected by bulky packaging.

All the materials that come into a factory eventually leave it, either as part of finished goods or as scrap. In some activities, scrap is limited to disposable packaging materials and irreparably defective product; in others, a large proportion of the materials themselves are scrapped as part of normal operations. This includes not only extraction processes, but also machining. In aerospace machining, for example, coffin-shaped forgings are hollowed out to 10% of their original weight while the remaining 90% returns to the forging shop as chips to be recycled, as shown in Figure 6-11.

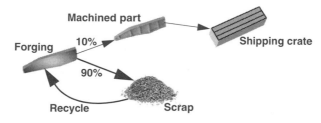

FIGURE 6-11. Aerospace machined part

The finished part, however, takes up as much space as the original forging, and more once crated. Meanwhile, the scrap metal in chip form also contains more air and takes up more space than it did when part of the incoming forging. In addition, the finished part is much more sensitive to handling damage than the original forging, on which a thin oxidized layer didn't matter since it was going to be machined away.

Figure 6-12 shows another product taking up more and more space as it moves from raw materials to finished goods. Not only does a finished, packaged frying pan take up 20 times more space than the aluminum disk, the coating, the handle, the rivets, and the carton, but then even the package must be protected from handling damage.

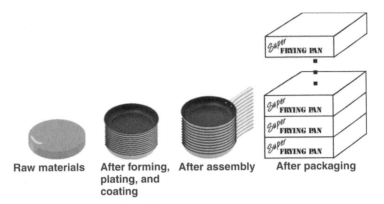

FIGURE 6-12. **Bulk of finished goods versus raw materials**

Where it occurs, this expansion in volume has the following consequences:

- Warehouse space that can hold a month of raw materials may hold only a day of finished goods. Forgetting this may lead to wrong conclusions about existing warehouse sizes, or to mistakes in warehouse design.

- Shipping from the factory may involve many more trucks than receiving. Docks used for shipping may be much busier than those used for receiving, or there may be more shipping docks than receiving docks. As shown in Figure 6-13, a flow-through building with equal dock capacity for receiving and shipping may not be as well suited as one where both activities are collocated on the same side.

- These considerations have an impact on plant location. If there are 20 trucks going to customers for each truck delivering materials, then you want to minimize the transportation of finished goods by locating plants near customers. If, on the other had, the plant refines a raw material and 90% of the output bulk is scrap, then the volume shipped to customers is small and it makes sense to locate the plant near the source of raw materials.

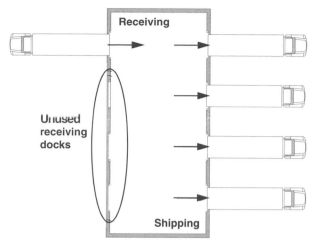

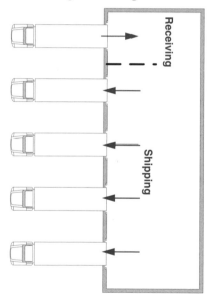

(A) Flow-through building with dock number imbalance

(B) U-shaped flow within building

FIGURE 6-13. **Balancing shipping and receiving dock capacity**

This chapter concludes the discussion of in-plant material flows. Starting with the next, the focus switches to inbound and outbound logistics.

PART III *Material flow in the supply chain*

Where the discussion extends outside the plant, to cover the movements of materials from suppliers to customers and the innovative business arrangements that have emerged as part of lean logistics.

CHAPTER 7

Supplier milk runs

Summary

A supplier milk run is a scheduled pickup of parts from multiple suppliers in matching quantities, and are a more sophisticated approach than a hub, reducing inventories of incoming materials, making lead times predictable even for items with variable consumption, smoothing the receiving workload, and providing an infrastructure for the transmission of pull signals.

Milk runs work primarily with local suppliers, but a local milk run can include a remote supplier who maintains a local warehouse. Clusters of remote suppliers can also be served by milk runs, with crossdocks or consolidation centers providing an interface to long-haul transportation by truck or intermodal railroad.

Milk runs should not involve more than four or five suppliers, who are usually chosen for geographical proximity. If many are close to one another, then destination within the plant can also be used as a grouping criterion. Milk run routes can be planned using on-line mapping services, but taking into consideration factors like border crossings, traffic and weather conditions, and road work in progress requires a more dynamic analysis that can be conducted with Access or Excel.

Once decided, the supplier sequence can be turned into a milk run schedule, with arrival and departure times at each site. The execution of the milk run is then tracked against the schedule to refine it and to prevent schedule drift from affecting the supply of materials to the plant.

In-plant milk runs were introduced in Chapter 3 as a tool to make movements of parts smoother and more predictable. Milk runs also work, on a different scale, to collect parts and distribute goods in the supply chain, and this chapter explains how.

The supplier milk run concept

A supplier milk run is a scheduled pickup of parts from multiple suppliers designed to support a given production level. Instead of using the plant as a hub with trucks each shuttling back and forth to a single supplier bringing the same items by the full truckload, you have trucks making the rounds of multiple suppliers, returning empty containers and picking up less-than-truckload matching quantities of many different items, adding up to a full truckload.

The differences between the two approaches can be seen from working out the implications of the patterns shown in Figure 7-1. Milk runs are a more sophisticated system than a hub, and require more work to implement. As we will see in the following sections, however, their advantages justify the extra effort.

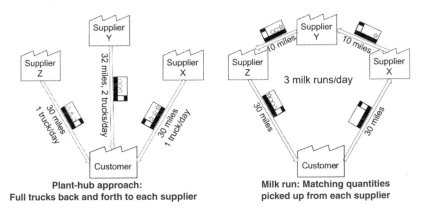

Plant-hub approach:
Full trucks back and forth to each supplier

Milk run: Matching quantities
picked up from each supplier

FIGURE 7-1. **Supplier milk run versus traditional approach**

Because it only requires coordination between the customer and each supplier individually, the hub model is easier to set up than the milk run, which involves all the participants in each trip. In addition, the milk run may require more truck mileage to deliver the same volume of parts. In Figure 7-1, the milk run diagram assumes that the truck is large enough to hold 1/3 of a day's worth of X, Y, and Z. If that is true, the total truck mileage is about the same for both approaches.

The hub model diagram shows *four* truckloads delivered each day, requiring $2 \times 30 + 4 \times 32 + 2 \times 30 = 248$ truck-miles/day. Unless the X, Y, and Z parts have exactly the same dimensions and one truckload covers exactly 1 day, half a day, and 1 day of production, respectively, then the trucks will not all be full. Mix-loading trucks in the milk run mode may afford an opportunity to supply all three items in only three truckloads and the milk run requires $3 \times (30+10+10+30) = 240$ truck-miles/day.

If the policy is to order only full trucks from each supplier, it is unlikely to result in exactly one truck/day or two trucks/day. The delivery frequency will then not be as shown in Figure 7-1 but instead will vary for each item, resulting in alternations of congestion and low activity at receiving. If the trucks are truly full, then there is no way their content will fit into the *three* truckloads on the milk run side, and the customer will either need more milk runs or a bigger truck.

The advantages of milk runs

This discussion is centered on the example of Figure 7-1, but, more information is needed to compare the performance of the two approaches depicted in Figure 7-1. The deliveries from the suppliers are done under the following conditions:

- Trucks going from the plant to the suppliers carry empty pallets and returnable containers.

- Suppliers X, Y, and Z each provides one item going into the same assembly, at the rate of one per unit for X and Z, and two per unit for Y.

- Assembly proceeds at a constant pace.

- The same truck is used for all three suppliers, so that, in the hub mode, the trips to the three suppliers are staggered throughout the day.

The following sections describe the advantages of milk runs.

Advantage 1: Milk runs reduce inventory

Figure 7-2 compares the impact of the two approaches on the inventory of the corresponding items inside the customer plant. The saw-tooth pattern, with a smooth linear decrease between deliveries, is generated by constant production at assembly. The safety stock serves to protect production against fluctuations in travel times.

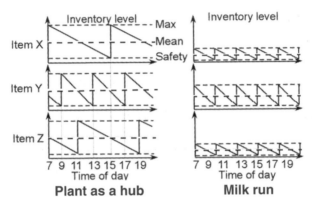

FIGURE 7-2. Inventory levels with hub versus milk run

For items X and Z, by multiplying the delivery frequency by 3, the milk run approach reduces the amount of inventory to 1/3 of the hub level; for item Y, to 2/3 of the hub level. Likewise, milk runs involving 5 or 6 suppliers stand to reduce inventories by 80% or more.

The number of pallet locations, pallets, and returnable containers required is proportionately reduced. The frequency of use of returnable containers is closely tied to their economic justification. Since they only become cheaper than disposable containers after about 20 uses, the faster they accumulate these 20 uses, the earlier they pay for themselves.

Advantage 2: Predictable replenishment lead times

The value of milk runs is not limited to items of constant consumption. A milk run is in fact a predictable transportation channel. A regularly scheduled truck arrives every two hours or every three hours; its content may vary but its arrival time doesn't. In practice, milk run trucks arrive at each site on their route within a 15-minute window.

Figure 7-2 shows *three* items with constant consumption. Real manufacturing situations, however, involve not three but 50, 500, or even 5,000 items with different delivery frequencies. Getting them delivered individually by the truckload then becomes a complex problem, regardless of whether the customer owns the truck or third parties are involved. Then milk runs *reduce* complexity and make it possible to order quantities that are less than truckloads without generating enormous transportation costs.

The advantages of milk runs are even more compelling when item consumption is variable, because, in a hub system, trucks cannot be counted on to be available whenever needed and can only be used economically for sufficiently large quantities. This adds a layer of unpredictability in lead times that the procurement process doesn't need.

The stocks of materials and components inside the plant are sized so to be just large enough to support consumption until the next delivery. Consumption rates are based on production plans that are internally developed to meet the demand. The replenishment lead times, on the other hand, depend on the supply network, and their variability is one of the most common complaints of production control managers.

Advantage 3: Better inventory visibility

With the staggered delivery pattern of a hub system, as shown on the left side of Figure 7-2, the amount of materials of any item on warehouse shelves provides little information. Racks can be full of X's and nearly empty of Z's without it signifying any abnormality. By contrast, milk runs deliver matched quantities of multiple items at the same time, so that, in normal operations, the racks of the different items are full, half-empty, or nearly empty all at the same time. As a result, any visible imbalance between available quantities among these items is an immediate cause for concern.

Advantage 4: Improved supplier communication

Using milk runs means visiting suppliers more often, which in turn provides numerous opportunities for communication with the supplier about delivery or quality. How well both sides are able to take advantage of these opportunities, however, depends on how the milk runs are set up. If the pickup operations are handled by a 3rd party, then the drivers will have no particular knowledge or concern about the customer's products. On the other hand, if the drivers are employees of the customer plant, their role can be enhanced to include verifying at least that they are given the right parts in the right quantities, and passing on replenishment orders together with empty containers.

Where milk runs don't work

As stated earlier, one of the key characteristics of lean logistics is that it is not a one-size-fits-all approach. While milk runs are a powerful tool, they are not applicable to the procurement of every part from every supplier. Milk runs are primarily used for items that are frequently used in moderate quantities and come from suppliers that are within tens of miles of the plant and of each other. We shall discuss some adaptations of the concept to clusters of remote suppliers—that is, groups of suppliers that are close to one another but remote from the customer plant.

Following are some circumstances where the milk run concept is not applicable:

- An item is needed in multiple truckloads every day. Then it makes sense to dedicate trucks to it, and possibly to have the vendor take charge of maintaining the supply in the plant.

- An item is required only sporadically, in small quantities, from a supplier who does not provide any regularly used items. Then common carriers can be a better solution.

- The supplier is geographically far from any other that could be combined with it in a milk run route. Then the cost of making a truck take a side trip through that supplier's location cannot be justified.

The determination of whether a group of suppliers is a milk run opportunity requires a quantitative analysis that is specific to the industry and the companies involved. Expressions like "tens of miles" or "every day" apply in the automotive industry. In aerospace, by contrast, milk runs can be justified for the procurement of items costing in the tens of thousands of dollars per unit, from a cluster of suppliers that is hundreds of miles away, and needed twice a week.

As of this writing, supplier milk runs are not commonplace in the United States Victor Fung,[1] from Hong Kong's apparel distributor Li & Fung, reported collecting assortments ordered by customers from up to ten manufacturers by milk runs. In this application the materials are needed only for shipping, and therefore the timing requirements are less stringent than for assembly.

Using milk runs and remote suppliers

The milk run concept, as described above, applies to suppliers that are within 25 to 40 miles of the customer plant. Many plants, however, have suppliers that are hundreds or thousands of miles away, or even overseas, and the following paragraphs describe four approaches that have been used to adapt the milk run concept to such circumstances.

Approach 1: Supplier warehouses near the customer plant

The most straightforward way to extend the use of milk runs is for remote suppliers to maintain warehouses near the customer plant, as shown in Figure 7-3. If the supplier customizes the items in any way for this customer, then the supplier can eventually grow the warehouse into a finished facility.

---

1. *Fast, global, and entrepreneurial*, Harvard Business Review, reprint 98507 (1998)

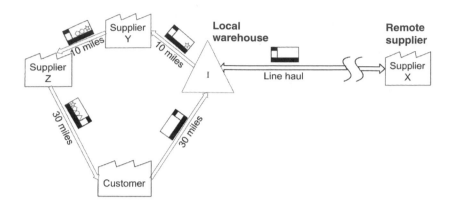

FIGURE 7-3. Remote supplier using a local warehouse

When remote suppliers are too small to afford a local warehouse, then a distributor may establish one instead. Such a facility, however, cannot turn into the kind of finishing shop that a warehouse operated by a single supplier can.

Some manufacturing companies have taken this idea further and established consolidation centers near their plants that receive parts from tens of even hundreds of remote suppliers. These consolidation centers take on such additional functions as transferring parts from disposable to returnable containers, and kitting and sequencing. This type of consolidation center is discussed in Chapter 8.

Approach 2: The "local-far" milk run

The milk run concept can be extended geographically when there is a cluster of suppliers that are close to one another even though they are collectively far from the customer plant. In the automotive industry, this works for supplier clusters up to 600 miles from the customer plant, with the same trucks doing a line haul between the customer plant and the cluster, and doing milk runs within the cluster, as shown in Figure 7-4.

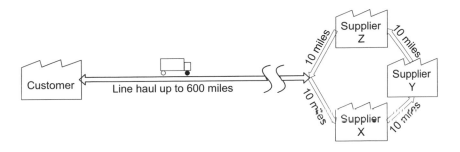

FIGURE 7-4. "Local-far" milk run

The main limitation of this approach when compared with the pure local milk run is that the turnaround time for a truck is on the order of two days rather than a few hours. If, in a local milk run, a truck carries replenishment orders in the form of cards—kanbans—these orders can be received and acted upon all within one shift. If, on the other hand, the truck needs to be driven for 8 to 10 hours to the supplier cluster before the orders can be in suppliers' hands, then there is a clear advantage to transmitting that information electronically instead.

The use of the line haul/milk run combination also has consequences in how drivers can be managed, because it is not possible for one driver to drive down the line, pick up the items along the milk run and drive back within one shift. Either the time has to be extended to include the driver's rest, or at least two drivers need to be involved.

The "slip-seat" system shown in Figure 7-5 is a workaround for this problem. It consists of having one designated meeting point half way along the line haul where drivers coming up and down meet and exchange trucks. This has the double advantages of allowing both drivers to go home every night and the company saves on travel expenses.

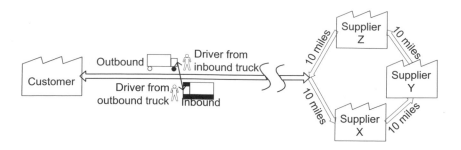

FIGURE 7-5. Local-far milk run with slip-seat system

Approach 3: Local-far milk runs with crossdock near suppliers

The next refinement is to consolidate the materials from multiple milk runs prior to trucking them to the plant, as shown in Figure 7-6. It is applicable when there are subclusters of suppliers whose output fits in larger trucks for the line-haul. A crossdock is a facility in which incoming materials are immediately sorted and shipped. The output of multiple local milk runs may, for example, be rearranged to collocate parts bound for thesame section of the customer plant inside the truck

Approach 4: Long-distance milk runs

The economics of transportation shift when the distance between a cluster of suppliers and the assembly plant exceeds a threshold. In the United States, when it exceeds 600 miles and the volume requirements are sufficiently high, it pays to set up a consolidation center at the "center of gravity" of the supplier cluster, and use that center to transfer the parts to intermodal containers, sequenced-based on the assembly factory's production schedule, and to transport these containers by train to a yard near the assembly plant. The final leg of the journey is done by truck again. This system is used by NUMMI and Toyota-Georgetown with their Michigan suppliers, and by Toyota's Kyushu plant with its suppliers in the Nagoya area.

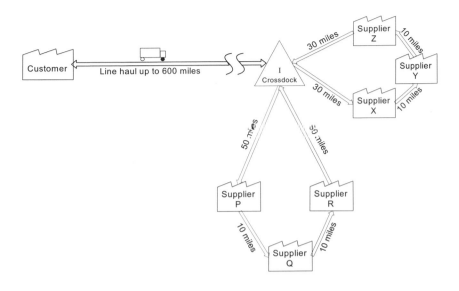

FIGURE 7-6. Local-far milk run with crossdock near suppliers

This system shows that it is possible to still use the milk run concept with remote suppliers, but the transportation time by rail is 5 to 7 days from Michigan to California, which constrains the assembly factory schedule. Clearly, this is not the best way to procure the parts that are most sensitive to model and option choices accepted by Toyota up to three days before a car rolls off the line. We do not know of this method being used outside the automobile industry.

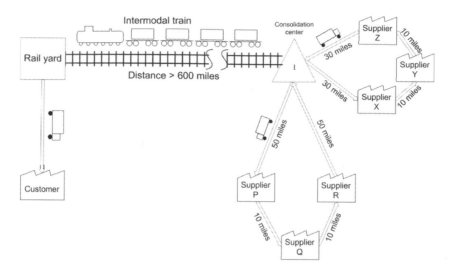

FIGURE 7-7. Remote milk runs with consolidation center

Details of supplier milk run operations

Reducing the concept of a supplier milk run to practice requires settling
many details that will vary too much based on company size, product mix,
and types of purchased materials and other characteristics to be tractable
by a single approach. The discussion below is based on the practices of the
automobile industry, and it is up to each reader to establish how the ideas
can be adapted to other, unique circumstances.

Control over the means of transportation

One would imagine that supplier milk runs could be executed by any
trucker, but in fact the routine contacts with many suppliers are opportunities to do more than just drop off empty containers and pallets and load
full ones. These additional functions include the following:

1. Verifying part numbers and quantities for the items received.

2. Performing some quick quality checks on the parts, within the limits of having no measurement instruments and limited time at each supplier.

3. Scanning barcodes or using other auto-ID devices to perform the receiving transaction on the spot.

4. Reporting any problems to the customer plant immediately.

5. Delivering orders to the supplier in the form of kanbans, as explained in Chapter 11.

Most companies would not entrust these functions to 3rd party truckers, who would take responsibility for delivering freight but not for what is in it. They take pallets from suppliers and deliver them to the customer, but any validation of the content is up to the customer's receiving organization. If anything is wrong with a shipment, it is obviously far better to discover it before it leaves the supplier's plant than after it has been delivered, but the practical consequence of putting the necessary process in place is that the truck drivers can only be employees of the customer company, which must also own or lease the trucks.

What kind of truck for a milk run?

The use of trailers or semitrailers provides some flexibility. If need be, a cab can be unhitched from a trailer at a receiving dock or even in the parking lot, and immediately hitched onto another trailer pre-loaded with empty pallets, returnable containers, and kanbans for another milk run.

Most trucks are loaded and unloaded from the back, through docks that, in the United States, are 9 to 12 feet wide, and raised 42 to 60 inches above the ground. These trucks can only be unloaded in last-in–first-out (LIFO) mode. If they contain materials from five suppliers, then the contribution from the first supplier on the run is at the front of the truck and only available after the materials from the following four are unloaded. The unloading speed is also limited by the width of the truck. The much less common side-loading trucks provide much better access to their loads. In particular, materials handlers can unload at the same time as materials from different suppliers bound for the same destination inside the plant. The differences between the two approaches are shown in Figure 7-8.

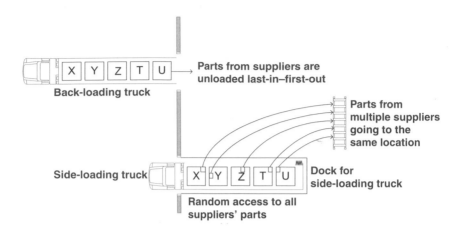

FIGURE 7-8. Back-loading versus side-loading trucks

The unloading time can also be reduced by applying more handlers concurrently. Side-loading trucks, however, remain a minority for two reasons:

1. They require docks that can be up to 50 feet long and practically have to be inside the building. This is not a common configuration and would have to be present at all plants along the milk run.

2. The load/unload side of the truck is usually closed by some form of curtain, which does not provide the mechanical, thermal, or humidity protection to the freight that the solid walls of back-loading trucks do, as shown in Figure 7-9.

FIGURE 7-9. Side-loading truck with curtain closure

Key disciplines for suppliers on milk runs

While it has many advantages, the milk run system is also vulnerable. Suppliers must have good parts ready on time, in the right quantities, and staged at a loading dock. The trucks have a 15-minute window within which to arrive at each supplier, in the face of changing weather and traffic conditions.

When customers order by the truckload, it is usually not at regular intervals; when suppliers make product by the truckload, it is usually with equipment setups that are both long and variable, involving trial runs. To deal with variability both on the demand side and on the production side, the supplier maintains at least one truckload of finished goods as safety stock.

Milk runs first affect this pattern in two ways:

1. They make the demand more regular.
2. They reduce the size of the safety stock needed to ship the next order when production fails to deliver on time.

Initially, the supplier is most likely not able to cut production runs, and will still make product by the truckload while shipping it by the 1/4 truckload. Thus breaking down the production run will create additional handling work.

Reducing the size of production runs to avoid this inconvenience and this expense, however, is not a simple matter. In fact, it requires the supplier to reduce setup times, reorganize production into cells where applicable, and change the approach used for production planning and scheduling. In short, the supplier needs to convert operations to lean manufacturing, and this is one of the reasons customers who are already lean create "supplier support" groups of engineers within their purchasing organizations.

Three-quarters of it needs to be put away in storage and retrieved in increments of one-quarter for every milk run. Figure 7-10 shows the finished goods inventory pattern for a product going through the phases described above.

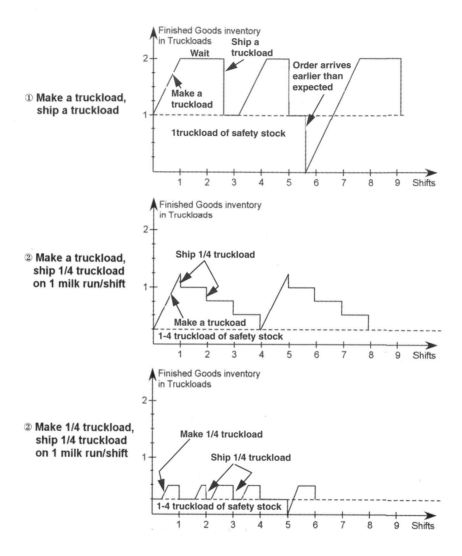

FIGURE 7-10. Milk run quantities, production runs, and finished goods

Key disciplines for the customer plant operating milk runs

Likewise, the customer plant must be ready to receive the milk run truck. Either semitrailers in the parking lot serve as incoming materials stores or the receiving docks must be scheduled for unloading. If the trailers carry intermodal containers filled in a consolidation center, then their content is sorted by destination in the customer plant and sequenced. In this case, it makes sense to use the parking lot as a staging area, bring the trailer to the dock serving the destination area, and deliver the content straight to the production or to a supermarket near by.

But if the trucks, whether with trailers or not, return directly from a milk run, then parts used in the same production operation may be in different trucks, and parts in different trucks may go to the same operation. In this case, the trucks need to be unloaded to sort the parts prior to delivering them to production, and the docks need to be scheduled for this purpose. The logistics organization has full control over the docks, but not over truck arrival times, which vary with weather and traffic conditions. As a result, the docks will be scheduled differently depending on the following:

- *Truck priority.* If the policy is to unload trucks as soon as they arrive, then some slack time needs to be planned into the use of the docks.

- *Dock priority.* If the objective is instead to keep receiving docks busy unloading at all times, then trucks have to wait for their turn, and there is value in separating cabs from trailers as described above.

How many suppliers should there be in one milk run?

When first starting with milk runs, a customer is lucky to find two or three suppliers willing and able to play along, and designing milk runs is not a problem. Once the first milk runs are working, however, new challenges arise when the customer plant wants to apply the concept more broadly.

The following considerations practically limit the number of suppliers on a run to four or five:

- Supplier milk runs are intended to recur every few hours. A given run can be daily, twice a day, or four times a day, but not twenty times in a day.

- A trailer can host contributions from four or five different suppliers but not twenty.

- As the number of suppliers on a given run rises, so does the ratio of the time spent driving between suppliers to the time spent driving to and from the customer plant.

If a customer plant has, say, 20 suppliers in a geographical area who can participate in milk runs, then it usually makes sense to split them into four or five groups.

Physical proximity is usually the primary clustering criterion. Factories are not evenly spread through the landscape but instead are concentrated in industrial parks, and having several suppliers in the same park is a strong incentive to put them in the same milk run. If there are enough suppliers in the area, it may also make sense to partition them based on where their products are used in the *customer* plant.

Route planning

Milk runs are on tight schedules, but traffic conditions are not controllable by any of the participants, which gives a special importance to the planning of the truck routes. Following are several methods to do it, all of which use inexpensive and readily available software.

Method 1: Use on-line services on the internet. Assume the plant is located on Remington Dr. in Sunnyvale, CA, and needs to pick up parts from the following suppliers:

- Chin Widgets, Inc., 961 Maude Ave., Mountain View, CA
- Thorvald West, 265 Ellis St., Mountain View, CA
- Crusher Technologies, 1000 San Antonio Rd., Palo Alto, CA
- Alphacom, Inc., 551 N Shoreline Blvd., Mountain View, CA
- Tupac International, Inc., 765 Fremont Ave., Los Altos, CA

Using a web browser, log in to http://www.mapsonus.com, select "Plan New Route," look up the suppliers by name, enter them as intermediate destinations, and click "Plan Best Tour," which automatically generates the shortest path through all these suppliers. This results in the map shown in Figure 7-11, followed by turn-by-turn directions.

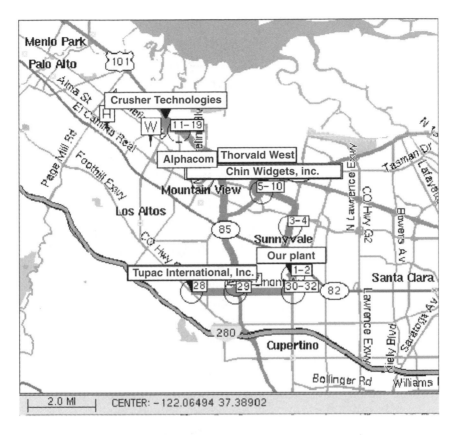

FIGURE 7-11. Minimum distance path through five suppliers

According to MapsOnUs, the best milk run from "Our plant" through all five suppliers totals 21.1 miles and requires 41 minutes with 32 turns, in the following sequence:

1. Chin Widgets, Inc.
2. Thorvald West
3. Crusher Technologies
4. Alphacom
5. Tupac International, Inc.

This is a convenient starting point, particularly considering that this service is free. It does, however, have the following limitations:

- *Minimizing total mileage or total time?* Minimizing the total mileage on a milk run is not always the primary objective. The time it takes to go through the run may be a more relevant metric, and a shortcut that takes the truck on a narrow, congested road with stoplights may not save any time.

- *Accuracy.* MapsOnUs's maps are not 100% accurate, and occasionally prompt the driver to take non-existent freeway exits. Also, the method used to sequence the destinations is not revealed, and, as we shall see, not perfect.

- *Border crossings.* The maps are limited to the United States, and therefore cannot serve, for example, U.S. plants with suppliers across the border in Mexico. Border crossings also add substantial time to a trip for almost no mileage, and this time is also asymmetric, since crossing from the United States to Mexico can be five or ten times faster than crossing in the opposite direction.

- *Variability of travel time.* The travel time between two plants is also not the same at 8:00 AM, 2:00 PM, or 1:00 AM. It also depends on the weather, or roadwork in progress, none of which are considered in the MapsOnUs system. The software just assumes an average speed of $21.1 \times 60 / 41 = 31$ m.p.h.

With these numbers, the total time needed for one milk run works out as follows:

Total travel	41 min.
Unload and load parts from 5 suppliers at 15 min./supplier	75 min.
Unload and load full truck at customer plant	<u>60 min.</u>
Total milk run time	176 min.

It should therefore be possible for one truck to make two milk runs per shift.

Method 2: Use Access or Excel to plant the route. The fastest route from one plant through five destinations can be found be enumerating all 120 possible itineraries, calculating how long they should take, and selecting the shortest one. This brute force method is not practical with pencil and paper, but is straightforward and fast with the software available on every engineer's desktop. Let us first examine the results of doing this with Access in Figure 7-12, and then explain how these results were obtained.

Site 1	Site 2	Site 3	Site 4	Site 5	Total travel minutes
Tupac International, Inc.	Crusher Technologies	Alphacom	Thorvald West	Chin Widgets, Inc.	3
Chin Widgets, Inc.	Thorvald West	Alphacom	Crusher Technologies	Tupac International, Inc.	3
Tupac International, Inc.	Chin Widgets, Inc.	Thorvald West	Alphacom	Crusher Technologies	3
Chin Widgets, Inc.	Thorvald West	Crusher Technologies	Alphacom	Tupac International, Inc.	3
Tupac International, Inc.	Alphacom	Crusher Technologies	Thorvald West	Chin Widgets, Inc.	3
Crusher Technologies	Alphacom	Thorvald West	Chin Widgets, Inc.	Tupac International, Inc.	3
...	...	...	...	...	..
Crusher Technologies	Chin Widgets, Inc.	Thorvald West	Tupac International, Inc.	Alphacom	5
Alphacom	Chin Widgets, Inc.	Crusher Technologies	Tupac International, Inc.	Thorvald West	5
Thorvald West	Tupac International, Inc.	Alphacom	Chin Widgets, Inc.	Crusher Technologies	5

Record: 119 of 120

FIGURE 7-12.   Enumeration of all possible itineraries

Figure 7-12 shows the top and bottom of a table of all the possible itineraries sorted by increasing total travel time in minutes. The shortest time itinerary is as follows:

1. Tupac International, Inc.
2. Crusher Technologies
3. Alphacom
4. Thorvald West
5. Chin Widgets, Inc.

The most remarkable result is that this itinerary is different from the one suggested by MapOnUs and, at 37 minutes, is 10% better. This is confirmed by forcing MapsOnUs to calculate the Access itinerary.

The Access database used to generate Figure 7-12 has two tables and one query. The first table is a list of site names; the second, a list of travel times between pairs of sites.

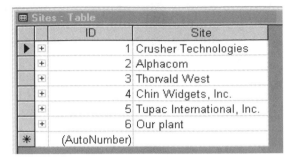

FIGURE 7-13. Table of sites

The table of travel times in minutes is shown in Figure 7-14. Site names are entered through pull-down lists from the table of sites. The travel times can be changed and do not have to be symmetric. As indicated above, it may take longer to go from A to B than from B to A if, for example, A is in Mexico and B is in Texas.

This information can also be visualized as a matrix of travel times as shown in Figure 7-15, generated as a pivot table report in Excel from a copy of the table in Figure 7-14. The matrix is easier to read, but the table is needed for the calculations. The query that generates Figure 7-12 is based on multiple joins of the list of sites with the list of travel times as shown in Figure 7-16. The first and the last site are constrained to be "Our plant," and the selection on each copy of the Sites table excludes the sites already chosen, so as to exclude itineraries with loops.

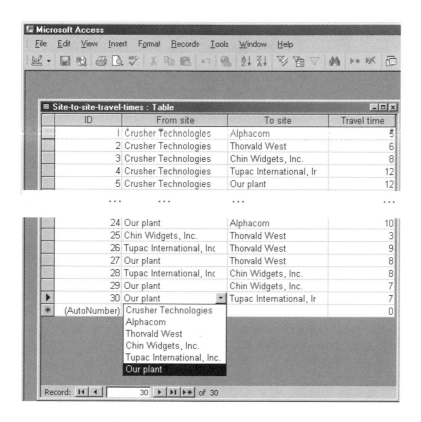

FIGURE 7-14. Table of travel times

Travel times in minutes

From site	Alphacom	Chin Widgets, Inc.	Crusher Technologies	Our plant	Thorvald West	Tupac International, Inc.
Alphacom		5	5	10	3	10
Chin Widgets, Inc.	5		8	7	3	8
Crusher Technologies	5	8		12	6	12
Our plant	10	7	12		8	7
Thorvald West	3	3	6	8		9
Tupac International, Inc.	10	8	12	7	9	

FIGURE 7-15. Matrix of travel times in minutes between sites

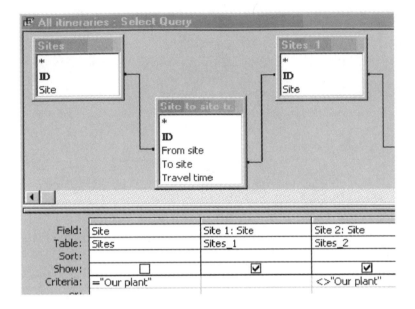

FIGURE 7-16. Design of the itinerary query

Method 3: Using an Excel add-on program. If programming Access as described above is too difficult, another option is to use an Excel add-in called Premium Solver. Ordinary Solver is supplied with Excel, but is not a good fit for this problem. Premium Solver is a separate commercial product, of which an "education version," sufficient for milk runs, is supplied on CD-ROM with some management textbooks (See http://www.solver.com/academic2.htm).

The matrix representation of travel times shown in Figure 7-15 is used directly in the calculation. The sites are identified by index numbers pointing to their row and column numbers in Figure 7-15 and used to retrieve the travel times to the next site. We ask Premium Solver to shuffle the site indexes in the black frame so as to minimize the total travel time in the red frame. This is specified in the Premium Solver problem setup form by the constraint that the variables indexed in the black frame must be "alldifferent."

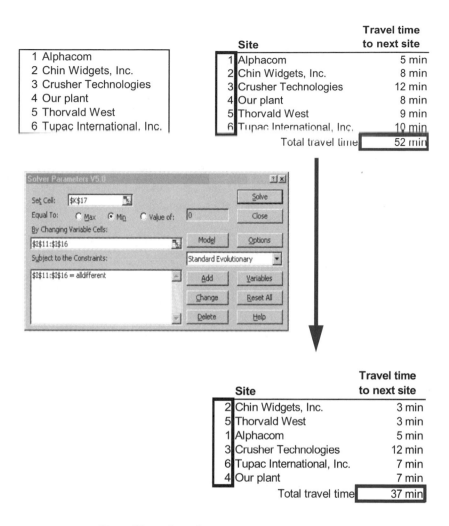

FIGURE 7-17. Use of Premium Solver

This is easily set up and produces the same result as the full enumeration in Access. When comparing the two approaches, the following points stand out:

- Premium Solver scales up much better than full enumeration, which for as few as 10 sites would involve a table of more than 3.5 million rows, but this advantage is moot for supplier milk runs, because they don't involve that many sites.

- Full enumeration is understandable to everybody, whereas the algorithms used in Premium Solver are not. As we have seen above, a software supplier's secret algorithm cannot always be trusted.

- Full enumeration boils down to an elaborate query against a relational database. It can be automatically formulated in the SQL language and run against a relational database based on a system other than Access and containing the customer company's supplier data. Not having to copy this data into Excel also means not having to worry about it being up to date and consistent with other information about the same suppliers.

Generating a milk run schedule

Having established the sequence of suppliers to visit, the next step is for the customer plant's logistics group to generate an actual milk run schedule for the driver to follow, and to monitor its execution—first to validate it, and then to detect changes or anomalies. An example is shown in Table 1.

If roadwork on the freeway changes the milk run sequence, then all the affected suppliers need to be notified and the truck does not arrive to find the parts still in production. The easiest way to verify the effectiveness of the schedule is to share it with every supplier and analyze feedback.

TABLE 1. Example of a milk run schedule

Time	Action
8:10AM	Load empty returnables and pallets
8:30AM	Leave Our plant
8:37AM	Arrive at Tupac International, Inc.
8:52AM	Leave
9:04AM	Arrive at Crusher Technologies
9:19AM	Leave

TABLE 1. Example of a milk run schedule

Time	Action
9:24AM	Arrive at Alphacom
9:39AM	Leave
9:42AM	Arrive at Thorvald West
9:57AM	Leave
10:00AM	Arrive at Chin Widgets
10:15AM	Leave
10:22AM	Arrive at Our plant
11:02AM	Unload complete

As we have seen, supplier milk runs are more complicated to set up than in-plant milk runs, but their benefits are ample reward for the effort. In the next chapter, we describe another structure that is commonly set up by customer companies that is an extension of the idea of a local warehouse maintained by a remote supplier: a consolidation center receiving parts from multiple remote suppliers and acting like a local supplier to the plant.

CHAPTER 8   *Consolidation centers near the plant*

Summary

A consolidation center located near a manufacturing plant receives components and parts from many suppliers and delivers them to the plant. Manufacturers use such centers to insulate the factory from overseas suppliers with long lead times and from domestic suppliers who cannot or will not work with kanbans, returnable containers, and truck milk runs. In addition, in the automobile industry, consolidation centers allow materials handling work to be paid at its market rate rather than the high rate of car assembly.

The design of a consolidation center should be driven by an analysis of the in-and-out flows of parts, pallets, packing materials, returnable containers, and kanbans. The objectives should be to avoid multiple handling and make the handling work productive and error-free. Possible methods include storing parts in trailers until needed, and using lift-and-rotate tables to present parts to operators.

A consolidation center inside the plant sounds ideal, but keeping it too close to production may entangle the plant management in its operations, while creating tension among operators who are paid different wages for similar work. Location within the same industrial park as the plant is common. Location a few miles away from the plant is usually the result of hiring a preexisting distribution company into the role of consolidation center.

Consolidation centers also provide a handling service for parts that are bought directly by the manufacturing company. The insulation of the plant, however, is more complete when the consolidation center acts as a trading company.

This chapter defines what a consolidation center is and examines the reasons for practitioners of lean production to resort to this structure rather than deal directly with their suppliers. It then describes the work that can be profitably off-loaded to the consolidation center, the physical organization of how this work is or should be done, where the consolidation center should be located, and the type of work that is best *not* entrusted to the consolidation center but kept in house. Moving up from brick, mortar, and equipment, the discussion moves to possible business structures for the consolidation center and its relationship with the manufacturing plant.

Definition of a consolidation center and motivation for using one

A consolidation center is a facility located near a manufacturing plant that receives components and parts from many suppliers and delivers them to the plant (See Figure 8-1). It is usually operated by a separate company, in which the manufacturer may or may not own equity.

In general, adding a middleman between suppliers and users does not enhance a supply chain, and it is therefore surprising to find leading, lean car makers doing it. They have many different motivations. A consolidation center can shield the factory from dealing with overseas suppliers with lead times in months. The consolidation center is then a domestic supplier, working with the plant as if it made its own parts on a day-to-day basis.

The complexities and risks of working with remote suppliers and four-month lead times do not disappear, but, rather than dealing with them, the customer plant prefers to pay the consolidation center to do so. The plant staff has its hands full keeping assembly lines and machines running, and can do without the additional work load.

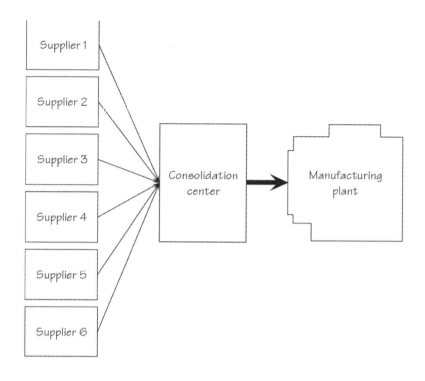

FIGURE 8-1. Definition of a consolidation center

A second, similar motivation is to insulate the plant from domestic suppliers who won't work with kanbans or returnable containers. These suppliers should convert or be weeded out, but this process takes time, and, meanwhile, their products still need to be delivered to the plant. Again, the consolidation center relieves the plant from having to accept large, sporadic deliveries of inappropriately packaged parts.

While the first two reasons for using a consolidation center apply to other industries as well, labor cost reduction is a strong third one that is special to the automobile industry. In every country where it exists, the automobile industry is and has been paying high wages to its operators, whether they work on the assembly line or in the warehouse. Outside of it, a consolidation center can recruit warehouse personnel for half or even one third of a car assembler's wages. It cannot do all the materials handling for the manufacturing plant, but what it does, it can make a profit on while saving money for the plant.

How a consolidation center works

The flows of materials into a plant that uses a consolidation center are as shown in Figure 8-2, and discussed in the following paragraphs.

Not every item needs to go through the consolidation center. Let us assume that its purpose is to insulate the plant from overseas suppliers and from domestic suppliers who do not deliver at the frequencies, in the quantities, and in the containers that the plant wants. Then the suppliers of all other items should deliver them directly to the plant.

In particular, the following types of items should *not* go through the consolidation center:

- *Body-on-sequence items.* The supplier is notified electronically when each unit starts final assembly and starts making it at that time in order to deliver it to the appropriate assembly station just when the unit reaches it. This is used in the car business for such model, and option-dependent items as seats and body upholstery.

- *Pay-per-build items.* The supplier is responsible for maintaining stocks at or near the line side, and is paid based on the bill of materials for finished products leaving the assembly line. In car assembly, this is used for nuts, bolts, washers, and similar standard items. The suppliers of these items may in fact consolidate inputs from second-tier suppliers, but that is not the same thing as going through *the* consolidation center of the plant.

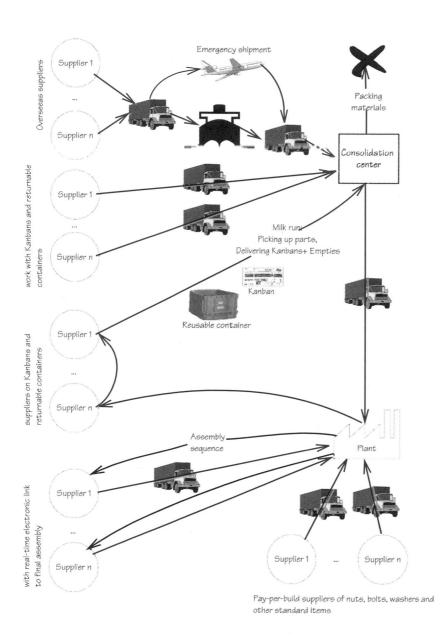

FIGURE 8-2. Material flows to an assembly plant

Over time, the plant will most certainly attempt to localize sourcing for all items, and the populations of both overseas suppliers and uncooperative domestic suppliers will wither. The consolidation center should therefore be needed most when the plant is new, and less and less as the plant matures. No matter how far we look, however, not every supplier will have a factory within 10 miles of the plant, and those who don't will be under pressure to open at least a warehouse there. The consolidation center can find a long-term mission in serving as a common warehouse for a group of these suppliers.

Physical organization of the work

The consolidation center receives large shipments; breaks them down into the smaller quantities that the plant needs; disposes of the supplier's transportation crates, boxes, and bags; places the parts in the plant's reusable containers, and delivers them either to Plant Receiving or directly to the line side. Because it breaks large quantities into small ones, the consolidation center holds substantial inventory and needs a warehouse.

A concept for a consolidation center is shown in Figure 8-3. It is radical in the sense that it uses trailers for storage and is free of forklifts, and there are many more alternative ways of doing this, for example, using side-loading trailers and flowracks that hold entire pallets.

Before considering the details of the concept in Figure 8-3, however, you should recognize its *limitations*:

- It is intended for parts like automotive pumps, compressors, or head-lights that fit in the type of containers shown in Figure 8-3. It wouldn't apply to 2-dimensional parts like sheet metal or 1-dimensional parts like bars or wire harnesses.
- It is intended for parts that have been packed so that they will not be damaged by exposure to humidity and temperature changes that may occur during storage—parts shipped by sea certainly meet this condition. Parts from remote domestic suppliers may or may not.

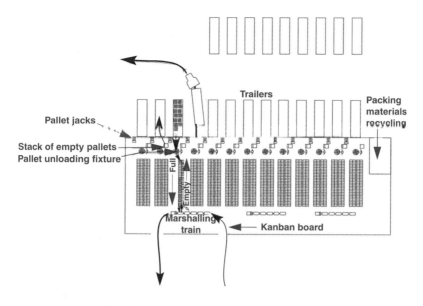

FIGURE 8-3. A consolidation center concept

- It requires the same item to always be delivered to the same loading dock. If the dock is occupied, there is no opportunity to unload at another.

- Items are grouped by destination on the assembly line, to support contiguous if not one-stop shopping for tugger trains. With reliable suppliers, this is appropriate, but, for questionable suppliers, you may prefer to organize stores by source, for easier performance monitoring.

To avoid multiple handling of pallets, all stocks are kept in *trailers*. As long as the orders placed four months ago match today's demand, for each item, there is one trailer being unloaded and some trailers on the road in various phases of fetching the next load. If too many orders were placed for today's consumption, then full trailers accumulate on the parking lot. The economics of this option depend heavily on the relative costs of real estate and construction in the area, since a classical warehouse will have a much smaller footprint for the same amount of storage space. The trailers used must be roadworks, and can be rented. As a storage system, they have the advantage that their number can easily be adjusted up or down.

Each loading bay has a pallet jack the operators use to move pallets from trailers one at a time, onto a lift-and-turn table to present the boxes in a consistent, ergonomically adequate position. If the flow rack for full item-specific returnable containers is not full, the operator then places the parts into the next container picked from the empties' flow rack.

For pallet unloading, tables that rise and rotate or tilt are available from several vendors as shown in Figure 8-4. Tables that both rotate and tilt, on the other hand, do not appear readily available. If only one of the functions is available, then rotation is more important than tilting. These devices may also need to be recessed into the ground for loading by pallet jacks.

FIGURE 8-4. **Lift & Tilt versus Lift & Rotate tables.**

The operator stacks empty pallets for reuse, along with any skids or item-specific, blow-molded separators used in transportation. Disposable packing materials are conveyed to recycling by an underground or an overhead conveyor not shown in Figure 8-3.

On the opposite side of the flow racks, Figure 8-3 shows tugger trains delivering empty containers and picking up full ones. If the consolidation center is in the same industrial park as the plant, the tugger trains can go directly to the lines to deliver the parts. Otherwise, the full tugger trains can roll onto trucks and roll straight off the trucks onto the shop floor at the plant.

The kanban board is useful if not all the kanbans picked up at the plant are for immediate delivery. For example, they may specify that delivery should take place in the milk run after next, which may be done by a different train. The driver therefore places the cards on the board in the corresponding column, and picks up the cards that are due on the current run.

To increase the number of items available for picking at a single train stop, you can do the following:

- Use the narrowest possible flow racks.
- Place the return rack for empties above the rack for full containers rather than side-by-side.
- Stack more than one level of flow racks.
- Use mirror-image flow racks with docks on both sides of the building and trains going down a central aisle.

Locating a consolidation center

From a strict logistics point of view, the best location for the consolidation center would be inside the plant building. Transportation from the consolidation center to the line side could then rely on the same tugger trains or carts used for other items, and the weather would not matter.

If, however, the purpose of the consolidation center is to insulate the plant from certain supply problems, collocating the two in the same building may not be the best way to achieve it. At the management level, proximity and the sharing of food service facilities may make it difficult for plant materials managers to refrain from intervening in the management of the consolidation center. In addition, close daily contact between operators who make different wages for similar jobs is bound to create tension.

Consolidation centers are often located in a separate building within the same industrial park as the plant. If the climate permits it, it is still possible to directly load vehicles that go to the line side at the consolidation center. Otherwise an additional transfer is needed when the parts reach the plant. The consolidation center staff still comes from the same labor pool as the plant staff, but corporate identities are more clearly separated, and daily contacts are few.

Manufacturing companies usually do not set up from scratch a consolidation center that is several miles from their plant, because transportation would then require road trucks. This sort of situation arises mostly when an *existing* trading company is drafted into the role of consolidation center. If it has a facility that is less than a 15- to 20-minute drive from the plant, then it isn't worth building a new one nearer. This facility then taps into a *different* labor pool from the plant, and can recruit employees for whom the wages it offers are an improvement.

Three functions a consolidation center should *not* perform

There are limits to what can be reasonably asked of a consolidation center. Following are three examples of work that, for different reasons, must be kept in house.

Example 1: Kitting

The consolidation center should not be asked to pick kits for production, for several reasons:

- To pick kits, you need pick lists based on the product's bill of materials, and sharing a bill of materials with the consolidation center means not only letting out key proprietary information but keeping it up to date. Whenever engineering changes are implemented in the plant, they must also be at the consolidation center. The corresponding exchanges of data are much more complex than if the consolidation center only deals with individual items.

- The best time and place to pick a kit is next to the assembly line and just before it is assembled. The pickers can be experienced assemblers who will do a more careful and thorough job as a result of knowing what each part is for. Missing or defective components can be easily replaced, and there is no need to manage and transport a stock of kits.

Example 2: Incoming quality assurance

Again, the issue here is the information that consolidation center employees need to have. They would have to be trained both on the plant's Quality Assurance (QA) methods but also on the characteristics of the parts. This is better done inside the plant—without sharing technical information with outsiders—and where engineers are present who can analyze problems as they are detected.

Example 3: Sorting empty boxes and dunnage

The temptation is great on the production shop floor to throw all the empty boxes and dunnage together at random and count on the consolidation center to sort it out. After all, consolidation center labor is cheaper than assembly plant labor, and therefore why not do it?

The reason it is a bad idea is that it is not a transfer of work to the consolidation center but the creation of work that otherwise wouldn't need to be done. The empties on the shop floor are found where the parts have been consumed. They come out automatically organized by item, operation, and product line. By scrambling the boxes, production is actually destroying a structure it already had and that the consolidation center must later reconstruct. In this case, it is more economical to organize the pickup of empties by item.

CHAPTER 9

Packaging and returnable containers

Summary

While returnable containers are the most common form for shipment between suppliers and industrial customers in Japan, they are only now being adopted in the United States, concurrently with milk runs. Returnable containers protect parts better than disposables, are cheaper if used enough times and often enough, and are friendlier to the environment. When used exclusively for an item, they also cap the inventory of this item in circulation.

Stackable containers are preferred in local supplier milk runs. Empty nestable containers take up less space, but cannot hold dunnage, their slanted walls do not securely hold multiple identical layers, and they are slightly unstable in stacks. Collapsible containers are used over long distances where there are opportunities for return freight. Dunnage options range from none to part-specific molded inserts.

Returnable container ownership can either be on the customer side or the supplier side, or shared between the two in an arrangement that motivates both sides to make them work. Container maintenance and replacement is usually a supplier duty. Customers, on the other hand, are responsible for ensuring that the same containers are used for delivery of the same item to multiple sites. Container tracking involves both visible management and computer-based information systems.

Containers designed for transportation are not always fit for part presentation on the line side. Finally, disposable containers remain the norm for shipping finished goods to consumers, and can therefore never be completely eliminated.

In Japan, the use of returnable packages in shipments between suppliers and industrial customers has been the norm for 30 years, and is not even a topic of discussion in Japanese books and periodicals. U.S. publications have not paid it much more attention either, but many suppliers today, under pressure from customers, struggle through the conversion from disposable to returnable containers. The challenge is to manage the flow of containers both within plants and between plants to provide the best logistics service at a lower cost than with disposable containers. This chapter covers the main issues that have been encountered in practice.

Assessing packaging needs

Except for ships, large airplanes, and semi trucks that are themselves means of transportation, few products travel unpacked. As seen in Table 9-1, the packaging used for different products ranges from nothing to multiple layers that occupy a much greater volume than the product itself and, in the case of consumer goods like toiletries, may actually cost more and be more difficult to procure than the contents.

Since packaging does not change a manufactured product in any way, it is tempting to dismiss it as a "non value-added" activity, but the importance of packaging should not be easily dismissed. Following is a partial list of the reasons why:

- Protecting the product against:
  - *Mechanical damage.* This is the most obvious. During loading, transportation, unloading, storage, retrieval, etc. the product is at risk of being dropped, hit, or shaken.
  - *Electrostatic discharge (ESD).* This mostly affects integrated circuits and printed circuit boards handled inside a plant and is prevented by using metallized bags or conductive totes that enclose the part in a Faraday cage. Although one might expect electronic components to also require protection against magnetic fields, it is much less of a concern than ESD.

TABLE 9-1. Packaging for a variety of industrial products

Cars travel "naked" on trucks custom-designed for this purpose. This is due to their size, their ability to move under their own power, the fact that they are intended to be exposed to the elements, and the volume of transportation they generate.

Motorcycles travel in crates that can go inside any standard truck, but the crates require labor to assemble, load, unload, and recirculate. Motorcyles are sold in a much lower volume than cars and therefore do not justify custom trucks.

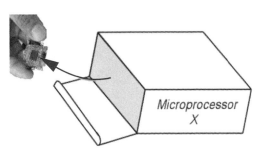

Microprocessors, with documentation, travel in individual boxes that are many times their size, in multiple layers of protection against electrical as well as mechanical shocks. Not only does packing and unpacking require labor, but the boxes are disposable.

- *Corrosion.* Automotive parts with exposed metallic surfaces are often packed in grease for protection against corrosion, particularly when exposed to sea air during maritime transportation.

- *Contamination.* Ingredients going into pharmaceutical or cosmetics products require sterile packaging that seals them off from biological contamination.

- *Dust.* Parts and products have varying levels of cleanliness requirements, the most stringent being those of semiconductor wafers, which must not only be fabricated in clean rooms, but also moved in containers that keep dust out.

- *Heat and light.* Products that are sensitive to heat and light include not only the obvious foodstuffs and photographic materials, but also painted surfaces that can crack or be discolored.

- *Theft.* Products that are both expensive and small are often protected from theft by outsize packages that make them more difficult to conceal.

- Protecting the environment against hazardous materials, particularly in the form of chemical leaks and radiation from nuclear materials.

- Protecting handlers against sharp edges the product may have. Knives have sharp edges, but so do many other products.

- For consumer goods, assuring consumers that products are new and untampered, and enhancing the products' appeal on store shelves.

- Presenting industrial goods for convenient picking.

- Communicating information about the product through labels, kanbans, color-codes, or by making the content visible by transparency as in bottles or wire-mesh baskets.

- Placing a cap on inventory. If there is a fixed number of packages in circulation, then the amount of inventory of the item in those packages is limited to their content.

Choosing between disposable and returnable containers

The cons of disposable containers

While disposable containers will continue to be the norm for consumer goods, their use in manufacturing logistics is being challenged by returnable containers. If we consider the case of cartons used in shipping parts from a component supplier to an assembly customer, it involves the following activities that would not be needed with returnable containers:

1. The supplier carries out a commercial transaction for each purchase of cartons.

2. The cartons themselves come in palletized bundles that need to be unpacked prior to being brought to their point of use.

3. Operators in the supplier plant need to erect the cartons and insert dunnage, as shown in Figure 9-1.

4. In the customer plant, used empty cartons need to be collapsed and bundled, sometimes requiring the kind of heavy equipment shown in Figure 9-2.

5. The bundles of empty cartons need to be shipped either to landfills or to recycling plants, to be turned into building insulation, animal bedding, magazine paper, or newsprint.

FIGURE 9-1. Erecting cartons

FIGURE 9-2. Processing of empty cartons

In addition, disposable containers place no limit on the amount of inventory in circulation between the supplier and the customer. From a production control standpoint, cartons can be treated as a resource in unlimited supply.

Pros and cons of returnable containers

Returnable containers must also be bought, but purchases of returnable containers are two orders of magnitude less frequent than purchases of disposables. Contrary to disposables, their supply is perceptibly finite: management decides how many containers are in circulation, and, in principle, the quantity of any given item in circulation between supplier and customer cannot exceed what fits in these containers. When daily volumes fluctuate within a narrow band around a stable average, this is a means of preventing overproduction. It is, however, not an advantage when demand suddenly doubles or is cut in half, or when customers require suppliers to ship in disposable containers when returnables are short.

The process of returning empties to where they can be refilled involves the following:

1. *Sorting.* The customer organization needs to sort the empty containers by item and ship-to container Management Center (CMC) to route them accurately back to suppliers. Suppliers also need to keep track of containers by customer. Empty containers on the shop floor are per-

ceived as a nuisance to be disposed of as quickly as possible, and many assembly organizations respond by just throwing them together, relying on the logistics organization, perhaps in a CMC, to separate them by supplier and item.

The logic behind this policy is that, if 3rd-party materials handlers off site are paid 1/3 the wages of the customer's employee doing similar work, then it makes sense to offload this task. The reality, however, is that this sorting would not be necessary if the customer organization didn't scramble the containers in the first place.

2. *Storing.* Storage space is needed by both customers and suppliers for empty containers before shipping and after receiving. Figure 9-3 shows a storage shed used for this purpose. Since it is not fully closed, the containers are exposed to changes in temperature and humidity, and to dust, but they are protected against rain and snow.

FIGURE 9-3. Storage shed for returnable containers

In some cases, such as in urban areas, sheds are either not secure enough or not allowed by local zoning ordinances, in which case warehouse space inside the plant needs to be set aside for empty returnable containers.

As discussed in Chapter 4, supplier milk runs reduce the storage requirements for empty returnables by one order of magnitude over the single-item full truckload approach.

3. *Transportation between plants.* Empty returnables must be trucked from the customer plant back to the supplier. Here again, supplier milk runs

are key, because they allow the containers to hitch a ride in trucks that would otherwise travel the same route empty.

4. *Transportation within the plant.* Empty returnables must be delivered to the filling point, and in-plant milk runs also provide the opportunity for empty containers to ride on vehicles that would otherwise travel empty.

Economics of returnable and disposable containers

In their promotion of the concept, the suppliers of returnable containers emphasize the following:

1. *Packaging quality.* Plastic containers, particularly stackables with part-specific dunnage, are simply better protection against handling damage than disposable, corrugated cardboard boxes. The best way to quantify this is to measure the results on a pilot implementation and extrapolating to the entire product mix.

2. *Costs.* While a switch to returnable containers eliminates some activities, it requires others, and we have no basis to say that the cost of handling returnables is *always* lower than that of disposables. These operational costs, however, are small compared to the costs of the containers themselves, and this is where the differences appear, as discussed in detail below.

3. *Environmental responsibility.* Disposable containers generate waste that returnable containers don't. Some managements view the switch to returnable containers as a way of "greening" the company. The public relations benefits of this may be substantial but are difficult to quantify.

If a disposable package costs \$2/unit and a returnable costs \$40/unit, then the returnables become cheaper once they have been used more than 20 times. The number of times a returnable container can be used is clearly key to its economic value, but its frequency of use is equally important. The payback period on our \$40 returnable container is 20 years if used once a year, but 4 weeks if used daily. Household coffee makers are sold to consumers in disposable packages because they don't buy one every day. A car assembly line, on the other hand, uses 1,000 sets of rear view mirrors every day, or 50 returnable containers with 20 sets each.

Customers do not like the idea of paying to ship empty containers back to suppliers. As we have seen above, this problem is solved with supplier milk runs. The conditions for making returnable containers pay are therefore as follows.

1. Handle them with care to maximize the number of uses.

2. Use them only for items with steady demand.

3. Keep their numbers low enough for them to rotate frequently between customer and supplier.

4. Take advantage of available transportation.

Types of returnable containers

Stackable containers

Stackable containers, as shown in Figure 9-4, are the most commonly used in local supplier milk runs. They take up as much space empty as full, but that is not a problem in the absence of return freight opportunities from the customer back to the supplier. The container's vertical walls enable them to hold multiple identical layers of parts, and the corresponding dunnage can remain in the empty returning container. In addition, stackable containers have lips intended to hold the containers above securely and do not need lids.

FIGURE 9-4. Stackable containers (Courtesy of Orbis-Menasha)

Nestable containers

By contrast, the empty nestable containers shown in Figure 9-5 occupy only a fraction of the volume they take up when full, but they cannot hold multiple identical layers of parts and the dunnage must either be disposed of or transported back to the supplier separately, which can nullify the space savings. Their stacking stability is also inferior to that of stackables and they require lids. The main limitation of nestables listed in Kulwiec's *Materials Handling Handbook* is their tendency to "ride up" when bumping into each other on a conveyor. From our perspective, however, dunnage and stability are more important issues.

FIGURE 9-5. Nestable containers (Courtesy of Orbis-Menasha)

Collapsible containers

Pallet-size wire baskets are collapsible containers and used in many machine shops, but are generally too large for the size of parts they contain. Smaller, collapsible containers, such as are shown in Figure 9-6, are used for transporting automobiles parts across oceans.

FIGURE 9-6. Collapsible totes (Courtesy of Orbis-Menasha)

By collapsing to 1/3 of their erected size, these totes allow their users to fill ocean-going containers with return freight, and they commonly establish trading companies for the purpose of finding such freight.

Collapsible containers are sometimes also used domestically, but they have two drawbacks:

1. They obviously do not allow dunnage to recirculate with them.
2. Operators describe them as "finger pinchers." Erecting and collapsing these containers quickly and safely requires special skills and dexterity.

Types of dunnage

Figure 9-7 shows several dunnage options in increasing order of cost and function. None of these options is excluded by lean manufacturing. The key point is that this level of operational detail should be designed based on an analysis of the needs.

a. No dunnage   b. Disposable dividers   c. Reusable dividers   d. Part-specific dunnage

FIGURE 9-7. A few dunnage options

Provided they are not subject to damage as a result, parts can simply be heaped in a returnable container without any dunnage, as shown in Figure 9-7.a. This has the following drawbacks:

- *No mistake-proofing.* Wrong parts can easily contaminate the bin.

- *Counting by weight only.* Weighing the bin is the only practical way of knowing how many parts are in it. It requires a scale and may not be sufficiently precise.

- *Random orientation of parts.* Randomly oriented parts take longer to pick by hand, and are a challenge for pick-and-place robots.

Disposable cardboard dividers, such as shown in Figure 9-7(b) provide more structure, by, for example, separating the parts into sets that each go into one unit of finished goods. They also make parts easier to count, but they do not provide mistake-proofing or orientation control.

The reusable dividers in Figure 9-7(c) go one step further. They do provide limited orientation control, but it is still possible to insert a part upside down and to insert a wrong part. Only the part-specific dunnage in Figure 9-7(d) provides easy counting, mistake-proofing and orientation control.

Factors affecting customer–supplier collaboration on returnables

Ownership of containers

However container ownership is settled, it is eventually reflected in the price paid by the customer. If customers buy the containers, they pay correspondingly less for the goods than if they ask the suppliers to make that investment. The issue is not which side profits the most but what incentives each side has to be diligent and effective in managing the flow of containers.

When returnable containers were used to deliver milk or beer to consumers, they were owned by the suppliers, who had to motivate the consumers to return them, for example by giving them a few cents back for each empty bottle. By contrast, returnable containers used between manufacturing companies are often owned by the *customer* side. Some customers ask suppliers to design and buy the containers, and then buy them back from the supplier over time.

Among the reasons for this, the most fundamental is that it ensures that the containers do recirculate and are handled with care. Customers are neither careful nor prompt in returning containers owned by their suppliers. Suppliers, on the other hand, are keen to "take care of their customers" by handling containers as the customers wish and are in a hurry to return them full of their own products. In addition, customers often specify protection requirements for the parts they buy, and these requirements are easiest to meet if the customer owns the containers and the dunnage.

On the other hand, if any one side owns all the containers used for a given product, then the other side has no strong incentive to reduce the number in circulation. According to Naotake Yanai,[1] a common pattern in Japan is for ownership to be split. Assume, as shown in Figure 9-8, that there are 30 containers in circulation, with an average of 10 in the customer plant, 10 in transit, and 10 in the supplier plant. Then the customer may own 20

---

1. Personal communication, 9/2003

of the containers and the supplier the remaining 10, which ensures that *both sides* are motivated to make do with as few containers as possible.

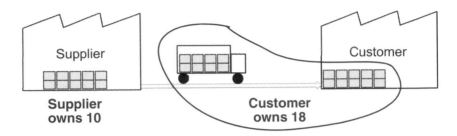

FIGURE 9-8. Ownership split for returnable containers

Cleaning, maintenance, repair, and replacement of containers

The supplier cleans, maintains, repairs, and replaces the containers as needed. Supporting suppliers is not an American tradition, and this is reflected in the condition of empty containers arriving at supplier plants. It is not uncommon for them to be smeared with oil, broken, or commingled with other suppliers' containers, as in the examples shown in Figure 9-9. Customers also tend to use the suppliers' yards as free storage of extra containers.

Most of the costs incurred by suppliers for these reasons would be avoided if the customers paid more attention to the flow of returning containers. They don't because they are busy attending to their own customers and feel that their suppliers should do the same. This attitude towards suppliers, however, can only have one of two consequences:

1. The supplier decides that cleaning up after the customer, while being browbeaten into lowering prices by Purchasing, is not worth the hassle and gets out of the business.

2. The cost of these operations is built into the price of the products and eventually are borne by the customer.

FIGURE 9-9. Supplier yard used as overflow storage of empty containers

Compared with this approach, working together with the supplier to avoid generating extra work is the way for the customer to get lower prices while allowing the supplier to make a profit.

Container standardization

Different customers require different types of containers even if they buy the same product, forcing suppliers to sort empty containers by customer. That different companies should use different containers may be regrettable but is not surprising.

What is more shocking is that different *factories* of the same company should demand different containers for the same item. Ford is bucking this trend and has issued a "one part–one pack" policy to allow a common part to be shipped in the same container to all receiving facilities. As of this writing, however, many other major manufacturing companies have no such policy.

Countermeasures against container shortages

As discussed earlier in this chapter, having a fixed number of containers in circulation places a cap on the inventory of the corresponding item. There cannot be more material in the loop than can fit in the containers available, and, if container circulation is properly managed, there should be no case where the supplier needs to ship parts but has no container with which to do it.

In the Toyota supply chain, this is indeed a rare event. When it does occur, the supplier's response is to notify the customer plant and request an emergency shipment of empty containers. The supplier is neither expected nor allowed to revert to disposable containers. American car manufacturers do not have this policy. Ford,[1] for example, *requires* suppliers to maintain a stock of disposable packages to use when returnables are not available, which suggests a less than wholehearted commitment to the concept. Figure 9-10 shows a finished goods flow rack with several rows of disposable containers behind the returnable containers that are standard for this product.

Disposable containers   **Returnable containers**

FIGURE 9-10. **Disposable containers used in conjunction with returnables**

If the elimination of handling damage is a stated goal of the move to returnable containers, then how can the customer allow some of the goods to be knowingly shipped in containers that offer inferior protection? Concurrently using both types of containers for the same item also complicates the task of measuring the reduction in handling damage, and requiring suppliers to maintain stocks of disposable containers drives costs up.

---

1. Production Part Returnable Packaging Guidelines for North America, 3/2001

Container tracking

When hundreds or thousands of items are handled in returnable containers, keeping track of the number and location of each type of container is not a minor task. There are two complementary approaches:

- Visible management through color codes, labels, and signage.
- Computer based information systems.

Color coding is a time-honored way of enhancing the distinctiveness of otherwise similar looking objects, thereby making them less likely for handlers to confuse. It is easier to use with returnable containers, that come standard in multiple colors, than with cartons, that are brown unless custom-printed. There are, however, limitations to keep in mind:

1. Boxes come in a limited number of colors. In addition, the human eye can tell apart only so many colors reliably over time, as they fade and boxes get dirty. As a result, colors have to be assigned to categories of parts rather than individual items.

2. There are cultural constraints on color choices. Red, for example, is commonly used for defectives, and should therefore not be used for anything else.

3. Color-coding limits flexibility in the use of containers. Regardless of changes in volume, green containers cannot be reconfigured to hold the same parts as blue containers.

These limitations are sufficiently severe for some manufacturers to decide that color-coding is not worth the trouble.

Labeling requirements are issued by customers. Ford, for example, requires hot stamps on two sides of each container, bearing the following:

- The supplier company's name, city, and state.
- A Ford container code.
- A "ship from" location code.

The information actually carried on container labels, however, varies wildly. Figure 9-11 shows empty nestable containers delivered to a supplier that belong to other suppliers and are labeled inconsistently.

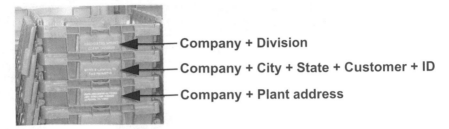

Company + Division

Company + City + State + Customer + ID

Company + Plant address

FIGURE 9-11. Returnable containers from multiple suppliers

In addition to this permanent identification, containers also bear stick-on labels designating the parts they carry, and, if the kanban system is used, a plastic pocket or other device to hold a kanban.

Figure 9-12 shows an example of an in-house production kanban held in a container's card pocket in an injection molding shop. In this example, the card pocket is used to hold other data as well. The backflush card goes to Accounting and the traveler to Quality Assurance.

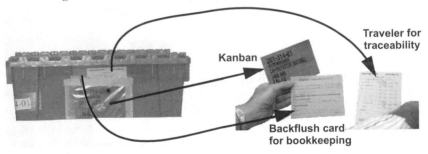

Traveler for traceability

Kanban

Backflush card for bookkeeping

FIGURE 9-12. Returnable container with kanban in card pocket

It is easy to attach such a card pocket to plastic totes as in Figure 9-12, but other types of containers, such as wire baskets, are more of a challenge. Finding a way to attach kanbans to containers that is both convenient and sturdy is often a challenge when implementing the kanban system. Alternatives to card pockets include velcro, magnets, and the kind of clips that are used to attach badges to clothing.

Signs on the walls and markings of storage locations assist in moving containers appropriately. As everywhere else, the actual visibility of the signage and the maintenance of its accuracy require sustained attention. If just a few the signs on the shop floor are inaccurate, the credibility of all signs is destroyed in the minds of materials handlers and operators.

Visibility tools, however, are insufficient and must be supplemented by an information system. For some purposes, the level of detail in Figure 9-13 is sufficient. We need to know the types and quantities of containers in different states, but we don't need to track each container individually.

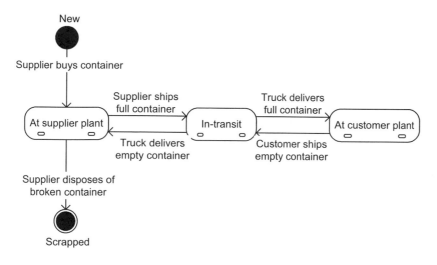

FIGURE 9-13. Container states, high-level view

The number of containers in each state can be gleaned from data already collected through basic production control transactions. In routine operations the numbers of containers at the customer's location, in transit, or at the supplier's location should vary within bounds around an average, and large deviations can be used as early warnings of shortages.

Also, the average number of times containers are reused before being scrapped can be inferred from this data. In steady state, we have:

$$\text{Container life expectancy} = \frac{\text{Number of containers in circulation}}{\text{Scrap rate}}$$

If the supplier scraps five containers every month out of 50 in circulation, then, on average, a container lasts 10 months. If the supplier ships 500 boxes per month, then each box makes 10 round trips per month, or 100 round trips in ten months. We know then that a box is reused 100 times on average.

Tracking individual containers is not worth the trouble if it requires manual data entry, and labeling requirements generally do not include a serial number for each container. The container itself becomes an easily tracked unit if it is fitted with an RFID (Radio-Frequency ID) tag, but that is not a common practice as of this writing.

The software industry does not, at this date, provide "Returnable container management systems." Large car makers have internally developed systems and let suppliers access them. Suppliers either use paper-based systems or define the containers as items in their ERP/MRP systems. Using database records for purposes other than those intended by the system's developers is often tempting but rarely a good idea, because the system's outputs are based on the assumption that these records are used as intended and may become difficult or impossible to interpret.

Scope of use of returnable containers

The containers used to transport parts between facilities exist for the purpose of handling and protecting parts in transit, not to present parts appropriately to production operators at the customer site. On occasion they may be usable for this purpose but that is not common. There usually is either a size mismatch with the need of the line or a part presentation issue; both problems are discussed in the following sections.

Problem 1: Containers size mismatch

The most common issue is that transportation containers are too large for lineside use. One full pallet-size bin, as unloaded from the truck, may contain two weeks' worth of a part that goes into one out of ten products assembled on a given line. While other products are being assembled, their parts need the line side space taken up by the bin, which must therefore be removed, returned to stores as a "partial," to be retrieved when needed later. Since parts are often just heaped into these bins, knowing how many are in a partial bin is practically impossible. Therefore, in addition to creating extra handling work, the manipulations of partial bins make inventory accuracy unmaintainable.

When there is no alternative to receiving parts in large bins, in-plant logistics needs to break them down for lineside delivery into bins that are small enough to be allowed to stay in place until empty, so that the parts' trip from the warehouse to the line is strictly one-way. The content of the warehouse is decremented by a whole number of small bins and never has to be adjusted back up for partials afterwards. As shown in an example in Figure 9-14, this also results in saving 60% of the floor space around the cell, using narrower aisles, and eliminating forklift traffic from the production area.

The situation shown in Figure 9-14 (A) commonly emerges in the early stages of lean conversion, as a result of cell implementation. Logistics improvements then allow the plant to migrate to Figure 9-14 (B).

(A) Bringing pallet-size bins to an assembly cell

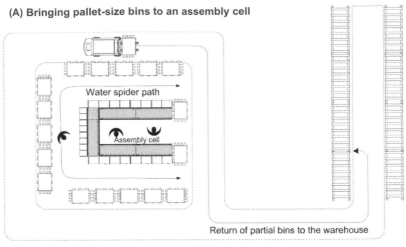

(B) Bringing small bins on mix-loaded carts to an assembly cell

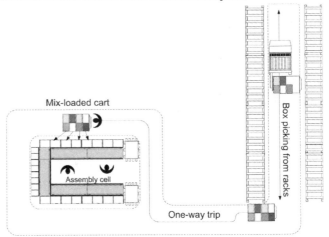

FIGURE 9-14. Impact of bin size on delivery to an assembly cell

While breaking down large bins adds handling labor *up front*, it is justified by the following benefits:

- Reduction in the amount of labor required later to handle partial bins.

- Simplification in information system requirements, by the elimination of return transactions for partials.

- Enhanced shop floor visibility. The flows of materials are easier to follow when they go in only one direction.

- Improved inventory accuracy. The actual number of parts in partial bins is often inaccurately recorded.

Problem 2: Part presentation

Chapter 11 of *Lean Assembly* discusses the need to present parts to assemblers unpacked, within arm's reach, with their smallest dimensions facing out, and oriented for easy installation, with single-piece presentation and kitting as needed. Transportation containers are designed to meet other needs, and, as a consequence, are frequently inadequate by the line side.

Some plants transfer parts to lineside bins right at receiving and the transportation containers never make it to the inside. This is mostly done with disposable, cardboard containers, and where the dust associated with cardboard on the shop floor would hurt the products. This strategy is used, for example, by semiconductor equipment maker Applied Materials.

Other plants deliver the transportation containers to supermarkets near the production lines, where the assembly operators called "water spiders" unpack parts and kit them for delivery to the line.

Sizing the containers

Converting all handling from large to small bins increases the packaging cost per unit, but it only results in a cost increase if the small bins are used to handle the *same quantities* of parts. If, as shown in Figure 9-14, the small bins are used to reduce the amount of parts handled, their use does not result in an increase in overall packaging cost. The point of reducing bin size is not to replace one large bin with 27 small ones but with 1 small one. It is impossible to reduce the quantities handled while using large bins. Small bins are necessary to make that possible.

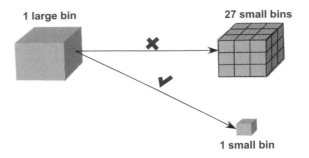

FIGURE 9-15. Large versus small bins

Preparation of shipping containers

A manufacturer cannot control the type of containers customers want parts shipped in, and even plants that make every effort to use returnable containers both internally and with suppliers often must package their finished goods in disposable containers.

The flow of disposable containers was discussed earlier in this chapter. On the shop floor, it needs to be organized as a production process and synchronized with the production of the goods. Strictly speaking, packaging goods is part of the production process and not logistics, but in most plants at least part of the responsibility for it is in the Logistics organization. Sometimes the work is divided between Production and Logistics. For example, packing detergent powder into boxes and grouping the boxes into display cases are Production tasks, but Logistics palletizes the cases and shrinkwraps the pallets. There may be a variety of reasons for this:

1. The pallet configuration for shipment is not known at the time of production.

2. There is last-minute customization. For example, individually boxed items sent to department stores may require customer-specific price tags.

3. Production's outgoing quality may not be trusted, and Quality Assurance demands a final inspection prior to shipment.

The automatic packaging machines used with mass market consumer goods like detergents or personal products pick, erect, and fill packages one at a time. Manual packaging, on the other hand, is often not designed with the same care as other production operations and involves operators building a stock of erected boxes ahead of need. This practice is unsound for the following reasons:

1. It adds storage and retrieval work between erecting and filling a box. Even though it is done in the name of "efficiency," it in fact adds labor to the process.

2. Boxes take up about 20 times more space erect than flat. Empty erect boxes not only take up valuable line side space but also clutter the work space and reduce visibility.

3. The risk of closing and shipping an empty or partially filled box is higher when there are many empty erect boxes around than when the only erect box around is the one currently being filled.

As should be clear from the above discussions, returnable containers require more attention than disposables, but protect parts better, and cost less over time (as long as the parts are used on a regular basis). Starting with the next chapter, we begin our discussion of the information flows that trigger, accompany, and document the movements of materials.

PART IV *Logistics information systems*

Which describes the information superstructure that is built on top and enabled by the material flow infrastructure outlined in Parts I through III.

CHAPTER 10

Pull systems

Summary

Pull systems drive the materials through signals triggered by downstream consumption. Pull systems are a counterintuitive way to deliver products faster, but the push alternative increases WIP, multiplies handling steps, and needs more handling equipment. In the old reorder point system, one single pull signal is issued for an item when the stock crosses a threshold, and it is still used where sufficient.

More often, multiple pull signals provide a richer information flow. In a dedicated line, a pull system needs a stable demand. In a mixed-flow line, production runs and deliveries are synchronized by leveled sequencing combined with parameters on pull signals that specify delivery on the nth milk run after issue. Pull loop sizing formulas are based on Little's law, but they provide only lower bounds.

The effect on inventory of using a given number of signals can be simulated. The replenishment logic assumes the immediate future to be like the present, which works for auto parts. Other industries like toys, or electronics, are subject to explosive growth—during which replenishment can't keep up—followed by catastrophic declines—during which it accumulates inventory. In such cases, "dynamic pull" with sophisticated short-term forecasting may be an improvement.

"Pull" is not make-to-order, and even Toyota builds cars it hasn't sold. Buying involves decisions, but responding to pull signals doesn't. Production operators or materials handlers should do it, not schedulers or expediters. A pull system directs activity without central coordination, which does not work for final assembly and fabrication with complex setups, which require explicit scheduling. Pull signals can be physical tokens or electronic messages.

This chapter discusses the concept of a pull system independently of any devices through which it may be implemented. Bins, fixtures, marked spaces, cards, golf balls, and various forms of electronic messages can all be used as pull signals. Before going into the details of how they work and where they apply, however, this chapter discusses what they have in common that sets them apart. We feel that understanding these issues at this level is a prerequisite for success in implementing a pull system, whatever form it may assume.

How pull systems differ from push systems

In materials handling, a pull system moves parts between locations when and only when the destination location signals that it is ready for them; in production, likewise, it feeds parts to the first station of a line when and only when the end of the line signals that it is ready. Sometimes, but not always, the same signal triggers both the production of parts and their move after completion.

In a pull system parts, or lots, don't move until the downstream operation is ready, as shown in a machine shop example in . In a push system, parts move as soon as *they* are ready; in a pull system, as soon as the *next operation* is ready, as evidenced by a pull signal. In Figure 2-3, the upstream machine does not wait for the signal to make the *next* part. Instead, it has the previously made part in its output buffer waiting for the signal to move.

A complete picture requires an understanding of what "ready" means and the response lead time. The pull signals are not based on anyone's subjective assessment of readiness; instead, they are triggered by part movements or consumption, and are intended to replenish stores at the issuing location up to a specified level. The action taken in response to the signal is not expected to be instantaneous. In lean plants, delivery through milk runs and production with leveled sequencing has predictable lead times, which the pull system relies upon.

Taiichi Ohno[1] describes the pull system as being one in which "the downstream operation comes to take away the materials," as opposed to having the upstream operation bringing them unsolicited. This conjures up the image of the output buffer of the upstream operation being like a retail store where the downstream operation comes to help itself. While this is a powerful image, it should not be taken to mean that an *operator* from the downstream line leaves it to go fetch parts. Between two lines, the issuance of a pull signal causes a *materials handler* to move the parts in a process that is more akin to mail order than to walking to the nearest convenience store.

Pull systems: A counterintuitive approach

Pulling is simple but counterintuitive, and many plant managers have a difficult time understanding its implications. Lean manufacturing aims to move product units through the production process as fast as possible, and in particular, with the least amount of waiting time between operations.

Holding parts in the output buffer of the operation they just completed hardly seems like the way to get them out the door faster. On the contrary, moving them as soon as they are done to the next operation appears to be the way to expedite their completion. "You can't get anything to move" is the most common complaint of production managers about the materials organization.

But if the next operation is not ready for the parts, the only effects of moving them are as follows:

1. Shift work in process downstream without reducing the production lead time.

2. Deprive the operators of the upstream operation of information on the downstream operation's ability to absorb their output. The output is

---

1. *Toyota Production System,* Taiichi Ohno, Productivity Press, (1988)

out of sight, and they can see neither how much of it there is nor how quickly it is being consumed.

3. Deprive the downstream operators of control over their environment, as materials handlers deliver pallet after pallet of unsolicited materials, overflowing shelves, encroaching on transportation aisles, and reducing visibility by stacking pallets in open areas.

Figure 10-1 shows an example of the push approach in action. As soon as a pallet is full of parts, the upstream operator brings it with a pallet jack to a staging area. A materials handler driving a forklift then transfers the pallets to a pallet rack. The pallet is then transferred from the rack to the downstream operation.

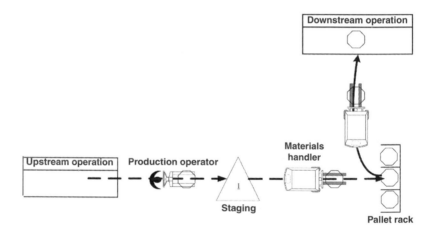

FIGURE 10-1. Push system example

In this mode, the parts are transported three times and stored twice on their way between the two operations. While this clearly appears wasteful, eliminating it requires asking "why?" several times, as follows:

• Why is there a staging area?

  Management does not want forklifts in the production area, and therefore production operators need to bring the full pallets to a location where forklifts are allowed.

In addition, the output area of the upstream operation is used to stage empty containers and pallets.

- Why do we need forklifts?

  Pallet jacks cannot store and retrieve pallets in the upper levels of a pallet rack.

- Why do we need a pallet rack?

  The upstream operation has longer setup times than the downstream operation, and therefore longer production runs. The production run is, say, six bins upstream and one bin downstream. The pallet rack is needed to hold at least one upstream production run of every item.

- Why stage empty containers near the machine?

  The materials handler has the time to do it and the space is available.

Figure 10-2 shows the same operations connected in a pull system.

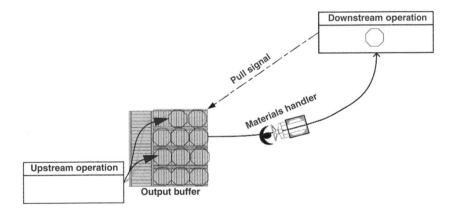

FIGURE 10-2. Conversion to a pull system

The space next to the upstream operation is no longer used to store empty containers. In fact, the operation needs, at most, one empty container in addition to the one currently being filled. The output buffer shown in Figure 10-2 has parallel flow racks, each of which can hold one production run of one item, and the end of the rack is sufficiently low for a pallet to be picked up with a pallet jack. Setup time reduction (SMED) efforts at the upstream operation have made it possible to cut the size of the production runs in half to three bins.

The content of the output buffer is an order of magnitude lower than the content of the staging area and the pallet rack of Figure 10-1, and, as a result, the throughput time of the material is reduced from days to hours. It is possible because the pull signals synchronize production between the upstream and downstream operations.

In Figure 10-2, we can see why the output of the upstream operation must be held next to it until pulled: it provides visibility for the operator. When the output is held in a separate staging area, as in Figure 10-1, the operator of the upstream operation loses sight of the downstream operation's consumption rate. If, for any reason, the downstream operation falls behind, the upstream operation is likely to overproduce until the staging area and the pallet rack overflow.

Because the amount of WIP between the two operations is limited to the output buffer of the upstream operation, it does not require a multilevel pallet rack, and therefore it needs neither a forklift nor a driver. Note also that, by contrast with Figure 10-1, in Figure 10-2, the pallet jack is pushed by a materials handler instead of the production operator, which allows the production operator to focus on production, as he or she should.

The answers to the "Why?" questions above highlight the implementation challenges. Pulling is faster and cheaper than pushing, but requires more effort in designing the logistics between operations, as well as more discipline in execution, as we shall see in the following chapters.

Issuing pull signals

The downstream operation can communicate its needs upstream in many ways. An approach that predates lean manufacturing is the reorder point system, in which a replenishment request is issued when the inventory on hand crosses a lower limit. In the reorder point system, the quantity requested is intended to bring the inventory level back up to a maximum quantity.

In terms of consumption of the item, the result is shown in Figure 10-3. The cumulative consumption of the item is flat when the line is stopped or making a product that doesn't need it, and rises linearly when it is being consumed per the line's production rate.

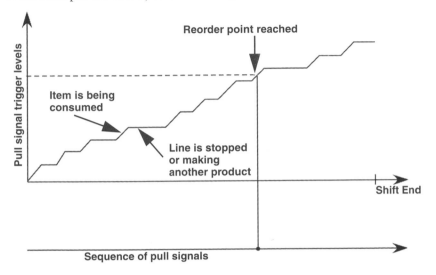

FIGURE 10-3. **Operation of the reorder point system**

The reorder point is set at such a level that the remaining inventory is sufficient to cover the demand during the replenishment lead time. Until the reorder point is crossed, no information is communicated back to the upstream operation, and there is at most one signal for the item being acted on at any time.

Where these limitations are not a problem, variants of the reorder point system are used in lean manufacturing, but the more common process of issuing pull signals over one shift is as shown in Figure 10-4. Each pull signal is for a fixed quantity, and is issued whenever the cumulative consumption crosses the corresponding levels.

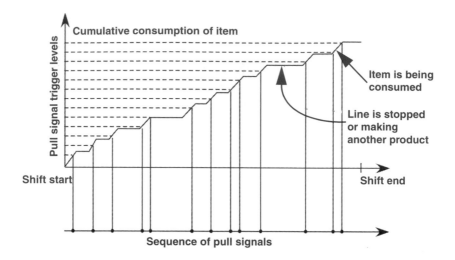

FIGURE 10-4. Pull signal issuing process

The flow of signals provides the upstream operation with visibility into the status of the downstream operation. As we shall see in the coming chapters, the generation and timely delivery of these signals is the most difficult challenge in making a pull system work.

The times between pull signals get shorter or longer in response to variations in the consumption rate. These variations are not an enemy of the pull system: in fact, they are the reason it exists. If there were no variability, and one bin were consumed like clockwork every 60 minutes, then no pull signal would be needed. The kinds of variability the pull system is designed to absorb, however, are as follows:

- Daily fluctuations around a fixed rate, such as are due to trucking times affected by traffic conditions, tool breakage on machines, or operators having the flu.
- Small changes in the demand.

Pull signals in dedicated versus mixed-flow lines

In a dedicated line, the applicability of the pull system depends on the stability of the demand; in a mixed-flow line, also on the relative length of production runs and the replenishment lead time.

The demand for automobile parts to go into new cars is stable for months at a time, and subject to local, short-term fluctuations due to disruptions in the supply chain. In this case, we can expect a naive forecast looking ahead a few hours to be quite accurate. On the other hand, the demand for a fashion item sold to teenagers is too erratic, and so is the demand for rarely needed spare parts.

For mixed-flow lines, Figure 10-5 shows the simple example of two products, with pull signals that are issued continuously during each run. If the production runs are longer than the replenishment lead times, then the naive forecast at the end of the run for product P1 is wrong, and parts for P1 are delivered during the beginning of the run for product P2. This effect is minimal when the replenishment lead time is very short compared to the production run, and worst when they are equal. On the other hand, the shorter production runs are compared to the delivery lead times, the better the forecast and the smoother the delivery pattern.

This can of course be accomplished by reducing and level-sequencing production runs, but it can also be done by postponing deliveries. Pull signals can carry parameters indicating that they are for delivery not on the next milk run but on the 2nd, 3rd, or *n*th milk run afterwards.

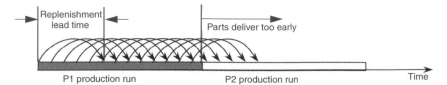

a. Production runs longer than the replenishment lead time

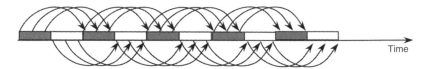

b. Production runs at half the replenishment lead time

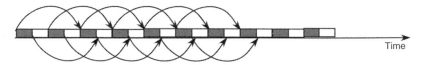

c. Production runs at 1/4 the replenishment lead time

FIGURE 10-5. **Production runs and replenishment lead times**

Sizing and simulating pull loops

As shown in Figure 10-5, the pull system determines how pull signals are issued and their fulfillment lead time. There are formulas for calculating the number of signals to put into circulation. The idea behind these formulas is to calculate the number of signals that would be needed if production and logistics worked perfectly, and apply a safety factor to compensate for their failure to do so.

The major weakness of these formulas is their dependence on an arbitrary safety factor. Its intent is to mitigate the risk of shortage without driving up the amount of downstream inventory any more than necessary. But this risk and the safety requirements can only be assessed based on the consumption pattern, which is not considered in the formulas.

The formulas are based on a very general principle called Little's law, illustrated in Figure 10-6. Little's law is obvious when the pace of work is constant. Blanks arrive at the plant at a constant rate, stay in for one lead time, and ship out. The difference between the cumulative numbers in and out is the number of blanks that have come in but not yet gotten out. In other words, it is the total inventory inside the plant. Since the slope of either of the cumulative lines is the throughput, then

$$\text{Throughput} = \frac{\text{Inventory}}{\text{Lead time}}$$

and

$$\text{Inventory} = \text{Throughput} \times \text{Lead time}$$

The point of Little's Law is that the formula remains valid about averages of throughput, inventory, and lead times, when both rates of arrivals of and departures are allowed to fluctuate randomly around a stable value. This simple law is to production as Ohm's law is to electricity.

In a general manufacturing supply chain, whether inside a plant or from supplier to customer, lead times vary, and finding the right lead time number to use in Little's law is not simple. As discussed in Chapters 3 and 7, however, lean logistics relies on milk runs, which, among other advantages, makes lead times *predictable*. Inside the plant, a train of carts may deliver an item every 20 minutes, while a truck may bring parts from 5 suppliers every three hours. This takes an unknown out of the calculations.

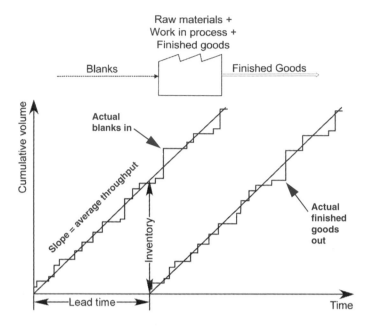

FIGURE 10-6. Little's law

Some lean manufacturers go as far as breaking down the work day into "pitches" corresponding to the minimum time between consecutive milk runs, as shown in Figure 10-7. Clocks on the shop floor display the current pitch number instead of the regular time, replenishment lead times are expressed in pitches, milk run periods are 1 pitch, 2 pitches, 3 pitches, etc., with corresponding delivery quantities.

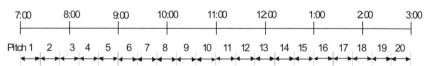

FIGURE 10-7. Clock time and pitches

While this approach does further simplify calculations, it is not without drawbacks, as it requires training the work force to reckon time in pitches instead of the familiar hours and minutes, and the organization of breaks is also a challenge. For example, if you want pitches to represent only worked time, then you could stop the pitch clock during breaks, but then it requires the entire plant to take breaks at the same time or else different lines could be at different pitch numbers at the same time.

Using pitches, Little's law, and a safety factor, we can calculate the number of pull signals as follows:

$$\text{Demand in pull signals per pitch} = \frac{\text{Demand in bins per pitch}}{\text{Number of bins per pull signal}}$$

$$\text{Min. number of pull signals} = \text{Demand in pull signals per pitch} \times \text{Lead time in pitches}$$

$$\text{Number of pull signals} = \text{Min. number of pull signals} \times \text{Safety factor}$$

As indicated earlier, the use of a safety factor is a severe limitation of the formula. In fact, its main use is to provide a lower bound to the number of signals in circulation. The most successful implementation strategy is to start out with enough signals to support the usually excessive quantity of WIP initially present in the loop, and then to whittle it down by removing signals one by one until reaching a limit below which shortages begin to occur.

Another approach that is gaining popularity is to simulate the loop's response to a variety of consumption patterns. Table 10-1 shows an example of simulation parameters, with which the above formulas stipulate the use of 26 pull signals.

TABLE 10-1. Simulation parameters

Average demand per pitch	5 bins
Replenishment lead time	5 pitches
Safety factor	1.01
Number of bins per pull signal	1

Figure 10-8 shows the results of a simulation made with Excel, in which the pitch demand is allowed to vary randomly by adding the 10-pitch moving average of a white noise to the average for every pitch. The demand is rounded up to the nearest whole number of bins and the replenishment lead time is fixed, so that the end-on-hand of every pitch is the quantity that was present at the beginning, decremented by what was shipped, and incremented by what had been shipped 5 pitches ago

.

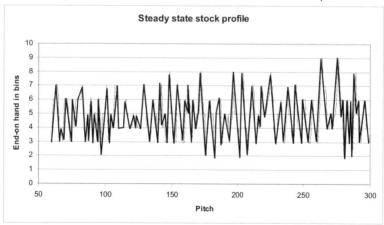

Pitch	Pitch demand (bins)	Bins shipped	End-on-hand (bins)	*Emergencies*
			26	
1	5.31	6	20	
2	5.63	6	14	
3	5.13	6	8	
4	5.91	6	2	
5	4.59	2	0	Stockout
6	3.49	0	6	
7	3.77	4	8	
8	5.73	6	8	
291	4.72	4	4	
292	7.42	4	4	
293	4.19	4	6	
294	6.16	6	5	
295	5.65	5	3	
296	3.97	3	4	
297	5.27	4	4	
298	5.13	4	4	
299	5.91	4	6	
300	5.18	6	5	

FIGURE 10-8. Sample simulation results

The simulation starts with all signals attached to bins and 26 bins on hand, and "warms up" through the first few pitches until it reaches a steady state, which is what we are interested in. It shows the end-on-hand quantity ranging from 2 to 9 bins, with an average of 5.

Such a simulation can be played with in a variety of ways, primarily to check out the effect of different demand patterns. Instead of the simulated random demand of Figure 10-8, for example, the actual pitch-by-pitch demand of the past two weeks could be used if it is available. Other patterns to be tried include the following:

- A fixed demand.

- A linearly rising or falling demand.

- A demand with a step increase or decrease.

One caveat about this approach is that simulation is addictive and can become a distraction.

Relationship between pull systems and market mechanisms

Do pull systems affect the customer experience?

"Pull," write James Womack[1] and Dan Jones, "[...] means that no one upstream should produce a good or service until the customer downstream asks for it." This definition adds the concepts of *service* and *customer* which were not present in Ohno's formulation. In the context of manufacturing logistics, we can take "service" to refer to the movement of parts, as opposed to their production.

---

1. *Lean Thinking*, James Womak and Dan Jones, Simon & Schuster, (1996), p. 67

On the other hand, "customer" can be easily misunderstood. In the car supply chain, for example, it could be taken to mean any of the following:

- *The end-user.* The ultimate customer is the consumer who buys a car. The new Toyotas in Figure 10-9 are waiting for buyers at a dealership and have not been made because any consumer specifically asked for them. The definition could mislead the reader to think that "pull" is synonymous with make-to-order. Most Toyotas sold in North America are not made to order. Even in the Japanese market, about 70% are made to order, but 30% are not.

FIGURE 10-9. New Toyotas at Jim Pattison's dealership in Vancouver, BC

- *The dealer.* Car makers sell to dealers, not to consumers, and therefore "customer" can be interpreted to mean the dealers. The dealers maintain an inventory of new cars and the pull system to them means ordering a new Corolla when they sell a Corolla and a new Camry when they sell a Camry. There are, however, exceptions to this mode of operation, for example during promotions or new product launches. Also, the three Toyota dealerships in North Dakota are isolated from each other and because they are hundreds of miles from the nearest production site, cannot have sufficiently frequent deliveries to operate in this manner.

- *The car maker's sales department.* The factories do not sell directly to dealers but to the car maker's sales department, which does not simply pass on dealer orders but also supplements them with orders based on forecasts, plans for promotions, and product launches. Another common misunderstanding at this point is the assumption that manufacturing then acts on the unfiltered flow of orders from Sales on a First-In–First-Out basis (FIFO). In fact, the lean approach consists of sequencing final assembly with the goal of smoothing the work flow of upstream feeder processes as well as supplier deliveries, which, as discussed in Chapter 2, is not directly related to customers.

- *The downstream production line.* In a pull system, the next process behaves like a customer in a supermarket, but with two notable differences:

  - There is no payment involved.

  - The next process does not have the option to get the parts from another supplier.

"The next process is the customer." is a metaphor from Total Quality Control. The point of it was to say the next process, or production line, should be *treated* as if it were a customer. In the decades since, this metaphor has become popular to the point of being taken literally, and a term that normally designates independent economic agents who decide whether to buy is being applied to internal departments with no such freedom.

In fact the flow between stores, cells, feeder lines, and final assembly inside the plant, where the term "customer" only applies metaphorically, is the primary application area of the pull system. Only when pull signals are used with outside suppliers does the term apply literally, and it imposes constraints on the types of signals used that are not present within the walls of the plant.

How commercial transactions differ from pull system operations

In general, the money a customer pays for goods is a form of pull signal, albeit an excessively generic one: it tells the seller that *something* has moved, but it doesn't say *what.* Before its sales system was entirely computerized in the mid 1980s, the campus bookstore at Stanford University kept an identification card inside each of the half-million books it had available. Sales were processed at supermarket-style check stands, where the clerks removed the cards from the books and placed them in a collection box.

These cards provided item-specific signals that were used to trigger replenishment.

The sale of the book involved a purchasing decision; the processing of the cards, by contrast, involved only the application of rules in a prescribed manner. What an operator does in response to a pull signal, including the issuance of other pull signals, is the execution of a protocol. The operator does not need to make a judgment as to what to work on next, and the supervisor does not need to arbitrate between conflicting requirements, because the protocol provides unambiguous direction.

Many factories using push have an information system that provides dispatch lists of production tasks sorted by priority. Usually, these lists are not directly actionable. They are for lots that need to be aggregated into production runs, which then need to be sequenced based on the equipment's setup structure. Execution is contingent on the retrieval and preparation of needed materials, fixtures, tools, process programs, and instructions. All these tasks are done by specialists called "planners," "schedulers" or "expediters."

When you switch to a pull system, who should be receiving the signals? Most organizations that make the transition to pull systems want to keep the schedulers/expediters in charge. They receive the signals, process them, issue the same work orders to operator, and expedite as before. This approach is contrary to the spirit of the pull system. It is intended to be self-sustaining. The cell leaders who release work into a cell and the handlers who move the parts act directly on the signals and issue new signals to others, simply by executing the protocol.

There is no intermediary in routine operations. It is a desirable outcome, but it has preconditions:

1. Following the rules must tell the operator exactly and unambiguously what needs to be done.

2. The participants must be trained to the point where following the rules becomes second nature.

3. The flow of materials must be organized so that, whatever the pull signal says, the needed parts are readily available.

4. The production line must be flexible enough. It does not need one-touch setups, but it does need setups to be short and of predictable durations.

Pull systems use distributed control

The similarity that remains between a pull system and a market is that both direct activity without a central coordinating authority. As production operators and materials handlers—or buyers and sellers—go about their tasks, they issue signals which trigger other tasks. The move to a pull system on the shop floor is a partial reversal of the trend observed from the 1840s to the 1970s, away from market mechanisms and towards what Alfred Chandler[1] called "the visible hand" of management to allocate resources and work within companies and industries. The attempt to use MRP to plan and schedule the shop floor can be seen as the extreme of the visible hand reaching into operational details and prescribing from a central location which parts should be run when through each machine.

There are cases where central sequencing or scheduling cannot be dispensed with. Barges on canals and trucks on roads do not need it, because traffic laws provide a protocol that drivers can follow. Railroads, on the other hand, need central scheduling: there is no protocol that can possibly manage the sharing of a track by two trains going in opposite directions. Figure 10-10 shows the traditional technique of the Ybry chart used to solve this problem.[2] Each slanted line on the chart represent a train's progress over time. Where these lines cross, there must be sidings allowing one train to wait while the other goes by, and the configuration of sidings is shown on the left.

---

1. *The Visible Hand*, Alfred Chandler, Harvard University Press, (1977)
2. *Envisioning Information*, E. Tufte, Graphics Press, (1990)

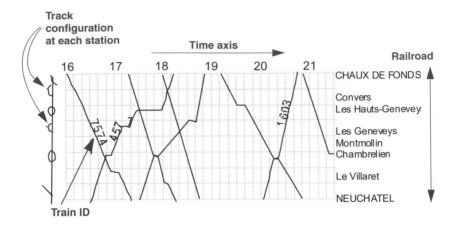

FIGURE 10-10. Railroad scheduling on a shared track in the Swiss Alps

Likewise, on the shop floor, many activities lend themselves to self-regulation through pull signals, but others do not. Final assembly has already been mentioned, but fabrication through machines with complex setup structures is another example.

Where applicable, pull systems are effective, because local decisions are controlled locally, using a logic that makes these decisions naturally consistent with global business needs. The concept is simple; making it work on the ground, with actual products, processes, people, and equipment is not.

How pull systems work within production control

In a lean manufacturing environment, pull signals are the main (but not the only) devices used to trigger production in lines or cells and to regulate the flows of materials between lines or cells in the same process, between storage areas and production lines, and between supplier and customer plants.

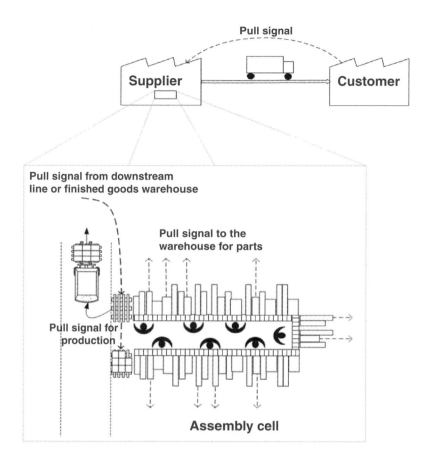

FIGURE 10-11. Push versus pull in a machine shop

The concept of a pull system is not relevant between two operations inside a production line, where no decision is required. Once a part is released to the first station of an assembly line or to the first machine in a cell, it moves through like a train on rails all the way to the end. Pull signals, on the other hand, can be used to decide which parts to release to the first station.

Pull signals are usually not used alone, but in conjunction with other systems that forecast activity and generate explicit sequences and schedules for pacemaker lines, most commonly final assembly, from which pull signals are issued that drive the rest of the plant. Explicit sequencing and scheduling is required in the following circumstances:

1. The line stops for setups and following the raw sequence of pull signals would require so many setups that the line would not have the capacity to keep up.

2. The raw sequence of pull signals contains random variations in product mix that are better smoothed out before passing the flow of signals on to upstream feeder lines and suppliers.

At the opposite end of the spectrum is production to a stable demand using an equally stable process. Electricity meters last 20 years, and, in a 20-million meter market, are needed at a constant rate of 1 million/year. They are mature products, made with well-established processes in dedicated lines. In such circumstances, production needs are so predictable that pull signals are no more than an administrative burden.

Pull signals need simple protocols

The signals and the protocols for using them must do the job of implementing a pull system, and be as simple to execute on the shop floor as we can make them. Setting them up may require hard thinking on the part of managers and engineers in production, production control, and materials management/logistics, but executing them shouldn't. Protocols executed by people are constrained to be simple, as can be seen in the example of a crossroad with 4-way stops on U.S. roads, as shown in Figure 10-12. The rule is that the car that has been waiting the longest from any direction gets to cross next. This is as complex a protocol as human beings in large numbers can use, and the only reason it works is that the stakes are high, since violating it could result in fender benders or injuries. Even as simple as it is, there are many countries that find it too dangerous to use.

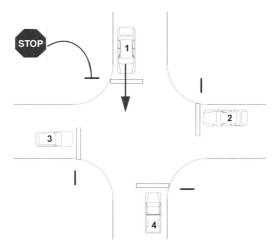

FIGURE 10-12. **The 4-way stop protocol**

Imagine what would happen if it were made more complex, for example as follows:

1. A Mercedes has first priority.

2. If there is more than one Mercedes waiting, then the one that has been waiting the longest goes first.

3. If there are no Mercedes, then the first car in the direction with most cars waiting goes first.

It is not difficult to imagine how any attempt to use this protocol would fail, simply because the people involved would get confused or balk at its unfairness. Another sure way to generate chaos would be to have different rules apply at different crossroads.

Computer operating systems and communication networks use much more complicated protocols, but these protocols do not require human intervention, and this is why they can work. Manufacturing logistics is complex, but it is the job of the professionals in the field to reduce it to rules that are easy to follow for operators, materials handlers, or truck drivers, and applied consistently. The signals must be easy to see and understand, and they must also have the same meaning wherever used inside the plant or with suppliers. Consistency in the signals from customers is also desirable, but a supplier is rarely in a position to demand it.

There are pull signals for every occasion. In increasing order of complexity, first comes the use of devices that are already on the shop floor and are pressed into service as pull signals through minor modifications. Then comes the use of physical tokens that circulate along the loop, bearing various amounts of data. Finally, comes the use of computer, communications, and video technology. Each category is examined in detail in Chapter 11, which covers manual pull signals, and Chapter 12, which covers hybrid and electronic pull signals.

CHAPTER 11

Manual pull signals

Summary

Marked locations, lights, and drop-down plates can be used as pull signals provided the respondent has the required materials on hand when the device is visible. By contrast, fixtures, pallets, or bins can travel, and therefore, when used as a pull signal, have a range that is not limited by the line of sight from the destination point, but their bulk and weight limit information handling.

This restriction is lifted by using kanbans—*that is, cards, tags, or other small and mobile physical tokens used as pull signals and carrying only information. Kanbans can be sequenced and posted on boards and can carry bar codes as well as human-readable data.*

They exist in many variations, and are used both in-house and with suppliers. Move kanbans authorize transfers of parts; production kanbans, the processing of parts; common kanbans, both processing and transfer; and tunnel kanbans, processing through a sequence of operations.

The reorder point system is still used for bulk supplies, and two cards in combination are used for lines with substantial setups, with the first card, a signal to get ready, and the second, to start production. Other card-based approaches include Spearman & Hopp's CONWIP and Rajan Suri's POLCA.

Manual pull signals are easiest to set up, in experiments or pilot projects, but in many cases for full implementation in production as well. This is why they are the subject of this first of three chapters on pull signals.

Using fixed devices

Empty marked locations, lights on semaphores, or drop-down plates, as discussed below, are all devices that can be used to signal a need. Their common limitation is range: they cannot be perceived and acted upon beyond the line of sight of the devices. In addition, the agent who sees the signal must be equipped to act on it. If, for example, a materials handler who notices that a tote of item X is needed at cell A does not have such a tote at hand, he or she cannot act on the signal. Writing down the item requirement in a shopping list for bringing a tote from the warehouse is not acting on the signal but creating a new one.

As a consequence, the use of this type of signal is restricted to items consumed at a sufficiently steady rate to make it feasible for the handler to always carry a spare tote or bin on milk runs.

Marked locations

With cells that are in close proximity, an empty space on the floor with proper markings can be an effective pull signal. This is the way actual supermarkets work: employees keep shelves full, and replenish any empty space they see. For this to work as an alternative to kanbans, operators at the upstream operation must be able to see the input buffer of the downstream operation.

Between operations that both practice one-piece flow, this space can be just a painted shape on the floor. It does, however, need more structure when the upstream and downstream operations have different batch structures.

In the example in Figure 11-1, the upstream operation tries to keep the flow racks full with parts in lots, and the downstream operators kit the parts across the face of the row of racks.

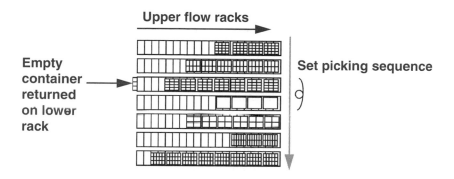

Upper flow racks

Empty container returned on lower rack

Set picking sequence

FIGURE 11-1. **Empty spaces on flow racks used as pull signals**

Figure 11-2 shows the same approach applied to parts that don't readily fit on flow racks. What it shows is a "piano-key buffer," between a machining operation that produces long and narrow parts two at a time, using two spindles and another operation that takes these parts one at a time, sequenced as sets for assembly into the same product unit.

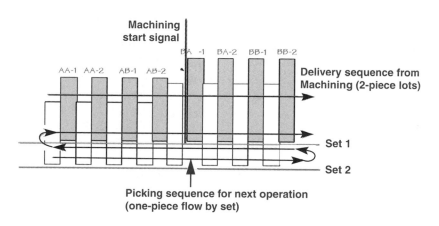

Machining start signal

AA-1 AA-2 AB-1 AB-2   BA-1 BA-2 BB-1 BB-2

Delivery sequence from Machining (2-piece lots)

Set 1

Set 2

Picking sequence for next operation
(one-piece flow by set)

FIGURE 11-2. **The piano key buffer concept**

The upstream machining operation makes two sets' worth of a piece at a time, which are placed in staggered locations in the piano-key buffer. The delivery sequence is left to right. The picking sequence, on the other hand, is left to right on the front set first—the white piano keys—and then left to right again on the back set—the black keys.

The upstream machines also make other products and therefore can make the required sets faster than the downstream operation can consume them. The red line in the buffer marks when the upstream operation must get started on the next two sets if it is to avoid causing a shortage.

The piano key buffer is an elaborate visible management tool, and its success hinges on support by the operators and handlers who make it work on a daily basis. In practice, they support only if they feel they have invented it, and they will invent it if they have been exposed to similar tools that they can adapt.

Because it is a visible management tool, the piano key buffer must be located on the shop floor between the upstream and the downstream machine where the operators can see it.

Drop-down plates

The mechanism shown in Figure 11-3 has a hinged plate requesting replenishment that falls into place on the back of the flow rack for the materials handlers to see as they make their rounds. This is best for small items that they routinely carry around on a cart. If they don't have the item available when they see the plate, then they need to write it down to bring it next time, and a normal kanban would be simpler.

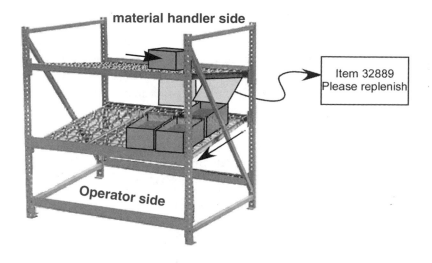

material handler side

Item 32889
Please replenish

Operator side

FIGURE 11-3. **Drop-down plate replenishment signal**

Using mobile devices you already have

Mobile devices, like fixtures, pallets, or bins can travel, and therefore, when used as a pull signal, have a range that is not limited by the line of sight from the destination point. Also, since the devices used are required to move the parts, these signals cannot be bypassed.

On the other hand, their size and weight limits what can be done with them in the following ways:

- The number of fixtures or bins in circulation cannot be easily adjusted.
- The signal cannot be issued until the device is empty. If a bin is a signal, then it obviously cannot be sent to replenishment as long as there is at least one part in it.
- They cannot be shuffled or placed on boards.

However, these restrictions can be lifted and the signals subjected to more sophisticated handling by separating the pull signals from physical devices.

Empty fixtures or pallets

The flow of materials between operations can sometimes be regulated by controlling the number of a particular type of device in circulation. Figure 11-4 shows a machining process that involves roughing and finishing on two different machines that are not collocated. The obvious solution of bringing the machines together into a cell is not feasible because the present situation is not expected to endure long enough to pay back the cost of moving the equipment. A new machine is scheduled to arrive within six months that will do all cuts from raw casting to finished part.

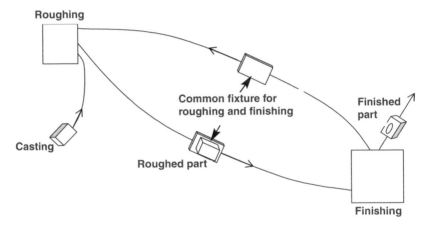

FIGURE 11-4. Using fixtures as pull signals

If both the roughing and the finishing operations can be engineered to use the same fixture, it not only saves the cost of taking parts on and off between operations, but it turns an empty fixture into a pull signal that cannot be ignored. It is physically impossible for the roughing operators to start a part unless they have a fixture to hold it.

Bins

The two-bin system is the grandfather of all pull systems, but still appropriate in the right circumstances. Two containers are used for the item, and an empty container is a replenishment request, as shown in Figure 11-5. The system works as long as a full container is delivered before the other one is empty. They must therefore be dimensioned so that one bin covers the production needs during the replenishment lead time.

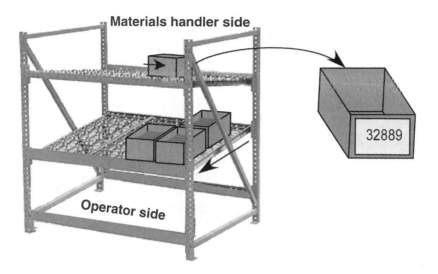

FIGURE 11-5. The two-bin system implemented with flow racks

The containers must be marked with all the item and shelf location information required for proper routing. The container is dedicated to the item, but this is true anyway for all the items for which there are slots and dunnage in reusable containers.

The two-bin system constrains the handling of empty containers. If the containers serve as pull signals, then any empty bin must directly return to where it can be filled. If empty containers are just empty containers, they can wait, be stacked, and picked up by a separate service at a much lower frequency than pull signals.

Also, with this method, the pull signal cannot be issued until the container is empty, whereas a kanban is pulled as soon as the first part is taken from the container.

Using physical tokens

The approaches we have seen so far either provide signals with a range limited to the line of sight from the destination or with severely limited information handling capabilities. The key to freeing ourselves from these restrictions, where needed, is to separate the information from devices used to handle the materials.

Information today is thought of primarily in electronic form and traveling across computer networks. Fifty years ago, when Taiichi Ohno and Kiichiro Toyoda were developing the Toyota Production System, it meant hardcopy carried by vehicles and people. Today, the need for hardcopy has vanished for some functions, but it is easy to forget that it still has not for others. In particular, as long as people are involved in production or logistics, they will need human-readable documents attached to parts or containers.

While Toyota no longer uses the pure hardcopy system, it still applies the same logic. We will first explain this logic originally developed as "the kanban system," and then discuss how it changes as a result of applying modern information technology.

"Kanban" is a common everyday Japanese word meaning: sign, doorplate, or shingle, as shown in Figure 11-6. As we shall see, in production control, the meaning is quite different. Everyday life kanbans don't usually move; shop floor and supplier kanbans do.

In a lean manufacturing and logistics environment, a kanban is a physical token used as a pull signal. What separates a kanban from the signals discussed above is that it is small, mobile, and carries only information. As in the example of Figure 11-7, kanbans are most commonly cards of varying sizes, but, on occasion, metal plates or golf balls have also been used.

FIGURE 11-6. Kanbans in everyday life

FIGURE 11-7. Supplier kanban from the Toyota website

A kanban carries all the information needed to act. As in Figure 11-7, it is often in both human- and machine-readable form. It specifies what should be made, moved, or shipped, from and to which locations, when, and in what quantities. This information not only tells operators, materials handlers, or shipping & receiving clerks what to do but also provides guidance in the execution of these actions, replacing previously existing paperwork, such as dispatch lists, travelers, routing slips, or order slips.

That kanbans carry information that is indispensable in daily operations is key to the success of the system. Many plants initially put kanbans in circulation *in addition to* the existing paperwork rather than as a replacement for it. This is a mistake for two reasons:

1. It creates more work and adds complexity. To be successful, the kanbans system must make the work simpler, not harder, for all those who have to handle the cards.

2. It allows operations to continue with missing kanbans. The kanbans are not indispensable, and can therefore be ignored without penalty.

In the plant, kanbans move according to rules described below, as a result of operational activity, and these moves, in turn, cause more work to be sequenced. As a result, a kanban loop is self sustaining, and in particular eliminates expediting. Making the kanban system work requires effort on the part of the supervisors, but at the level of making sure that each loop makes sense and that operators follow the rules. He or she does not have to look for parts.

In addition to its immediate operational role, the kanban system is also a tool for driving process improvement. By quietly removing one or two cards from a given loop, supervisors test the practical limits of WIP reduction. When they "succeed" in causing shortages, it points out areas of potential improvement.

Kanbans versus other types of pull signals

While many have taken to calling any kind of pull signal, or even a shelf, a "kanban," we feel that the discussion of these matters is better served if we reserve the term for its original meaning of a physical token, usually a card, used as a pull signal.

Saying that there is no difference between kanbans and the types of pull signals described above is like saying that credit cards and coins are the same, or that personally waiting in line is the same as holding a ticket. The differences are not primarily in the sequencing logic, but instead in the practical, operational impact of applying it. Credit cards and coins are both money, but one is heavier than the other and leaves you no recourse if robbed. Likewise, a kanban and an empty bin are both pull signals, but one is lighter and smaller than the other, can be moved more easily, and can be mounted not only on containers but on boards as well as part of visual management.

Common kanbans

A *common* kanban authorizes both production and movement. It is discussed first, because it is often the first choice of initial implementers. It is an appropriate choice in many cases, but not always, and the implementers need to know that there are alternatives.

Figure 11-8 shows its application in a plant where a fabrication shop makes components that are each assembled with purchased components into many different finished goods. The fabrication process may be injection molding, plastics extrusion, diecasting, or a variety of other processes that are performing on a set of parallel and interchangeable machines or lines.

Management's policy is to make the components to stock and assemble them to order. It has decided to use just one type of kanban and have assembly's pull of a pallet from the semi-finished goods store to trigger both the fabrication of a replenishment pallet for the same component and its transportation to the semi-finished goods store.

The way retrieval from the semi-finished goods store is organized is not our topic here, and we just assume that it is in place. The only feature of it that is relevant to our discussion is the obligation placed on the materials handler serving assembly is to detach the kanban attached to a pallet on its way to the assembly cell and deposit it in the collection box.

The materials handler in charge of replenishing the store "picks up the mail" from the collection box and delivers it to fabrication. The common kanban may look as the example in Figure 11-9. It shows both the production line that is to make the part and the store address to which it is to be delivered. The "delivery cycle" number tells the production operator when the materials handler will need to pick up the full pallet.

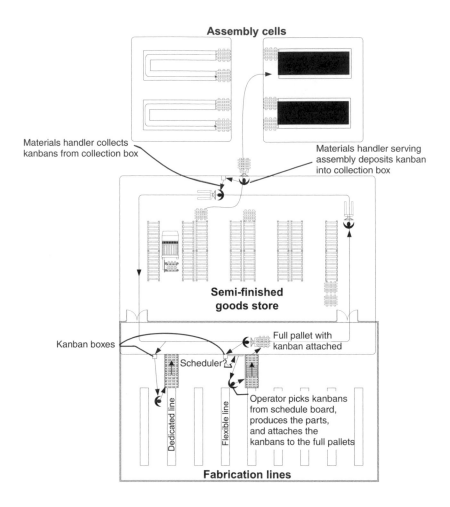

FIGURE 11-8. Use of a common kanban

Some but not all kanbans are serialized as the one in Figure 11-9. It is marked as number 6 of 10 issued. From a strict production control point of view, this number should not matter: as long as we have one card authorizing an action on a given quantity of parts, it shouldn't matter which one. If the cards, however, are acted on in order of their serial numbers, then, once attached to bins, they represent the order in which the bins were made. The full bins arrive at the destination point with kanbans numbers 1 though 10, and then back to 1. As long as not all the bins are at the destination point, as shown in Figure 11-10, the kanban serial numbers provide unambiguous information about the process sequence, which is useful for traceability and quality control.

Bar codes for traceability

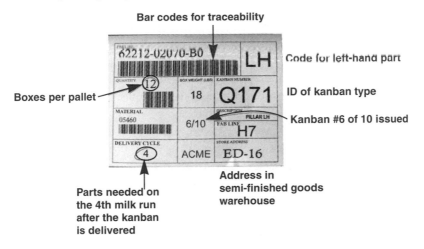

Boxes per pallet

Parts needed on
the 4th milk run
after the kanban
is delivered

Code for left-hand part

ID of kanban type

Kanban #6 of 10 issued

Address in
semi-finished goods
warehouse

FIGURE 11-9. **Example of a common kanban.**

Bin process sequence

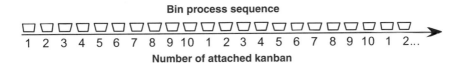

Number of attached kanban

FIGURE 11-10. **Bins with serialized kanbans**

For fabrication lines that are dedicated to one item, the kanbans may simply be dropped into a box, to be acted upon in sequence by the production operator. The line is fully occupied making just this item—or it wouldn't be dedicated to it—and has no opportunity to produce a pallet earlier than needed. The role of the kanban flow to this line is to slow it down or stop it if consumption drops.

The processing of the kanbans is more complex at lines that make more than one item, because fabrication lines have setups that constrain the size of production runs. Setup time reduction eliminates this problem, but not instantly. Projects in this area may have reduced setups from two hours to 45 minutes on all the machines, but it will take another two years to get them under 10 minutes, and another five years to make them instantaneous. In the meantime, it is common for a line that is assigned, say, five different items, to have insufficient capacity to make one-pallet runs in the order the kanbans are received.

A scheduling board is then used to organize the flow of incoming kanbans into a sequence of multi-pallet production runs. If it is simple enough, the materials handler can place kanbans directly on the board. The complexity of the scheduling board, however, often requires the intervention of a specialized scheduler. Then it is time to consider some of the different approaches discussed below.

At this point, the same kanban is moved by a materials handler, sequenced by a scheduler, and produced to by an operator. It would less likely to be damaged or misplaced if it triggered only one action by one person, instead of three actions by three agents with different bosses. This is one reason to want to separate *production* kanbans, which authorize only making the parts, from *move* kanbans, which authorize only their movement between two locations.

Because of the time taken up by setups, production runs may be constrained to include more than one pallet, and since there is one kanban per pallet, for more than one kanban. If production runs are designed to cover the demand for different items over the same period of time, then the production run for a heavily used item may be five pallets, with five kanbans, while that for a less frequently used item may be only one pallet, with one kanban.

Figure 11-11 shows devices used to post common kanbans on scheduling boards. The board on the left side holds kanbans for more products than the one on the right, but does not provide visibility into production run sizes. In fact, the kanbans do not arrive individually, but in production run bundles held together by rubber bands. On the right, the kanbans arrive one by one, and gradually fill up color-coded columns that, in aggregate, represent the total amount of storage allocated to each item in the semi-finished goods stores. As long as the top kanban in the column is still in the green zone at the bottom, there is not enough demand for a full production run, and the item won't be made unless there is nothing else to do. At the opposite end, if there are enough kanbans on the board to reach the red zone at the top, it means that the semi-finished goods store is at risk of shortage for this item. Scheduling boards are discussed in details in Chapter 15.

Common kanbans in slots

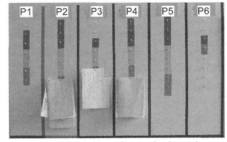

Common kanbans in vertical stacks

FIGURE 11-11. Posting common kanbans on scheduling boards

So far, the focus of discussion has been the communication of the pull signal back to fabrication. There is also the other part of the loop to consider, in which the materials handler picks up full pallets of fabricated materials and delivers them to the semi-finished goods store. As discussed in the previous chapter, in a pull system, the handler should not pick up pallets from fabrication without a signal from stores authorizing it. But the common kanbans authorize *production* instead, and the reason full pallets are picked up is that they are ready. In other words, we have a *push* system for transfer of materials from fabrication to the semi-finished goods store, and if, anywhere else in the plant, kanbans authorize movement, the system is as inconsistent as a road network with different priority rules at different crossroads with 4-way stops.

The dual-card system with production and move kanbans

The dual-card system, with different kanbans to authorize production and movements is less popular, because it appears to be more complicated, requiring two types of cards instead of one. The complexity that it adds, however, is in management. In execution on the shop floor, it actually makes the system *simpler* when dealing with flexible lines and production runs that are multiples of the quantities moved and vary by product.

The differences with the common kanban system are shown in Figure 11-12. What happens between the semi-finished goods store and the assembly cells is unchanged from Figure 11-8, and therefore omitted. What happens at the end of the fabrication line, on the other hand, is quite different, as shown in the enlargement.

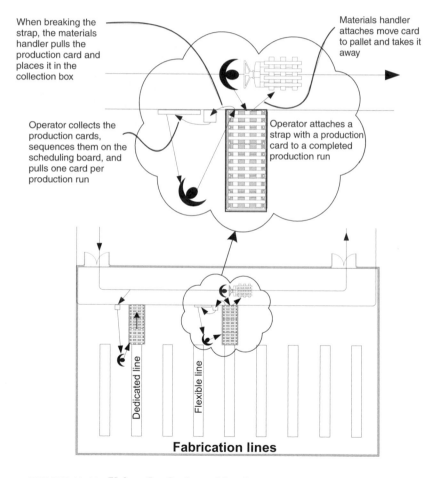

FIGURE 11-12. **Using the dual-card kanban system**

The production operator only touches the production kanbans, and there is exactly one for each production run, and, for each item, the number of pallets in the production run is written on the kanban. When completing a production run, the operator puts a strap around the pallets comprising the run and hangs the production card on this strap.

The materials handler may pull a pallet from a partial production run by attaching a *move* kanban to it and taking it away. To break a new production run, the materials handler has to remove the strap and dispose of the attached *production* kanban, by placing it into the collection box. Then, he or she attaches a move kanban to the first pallet in the run and takes it away. The scheduling board is designed so that the next production run is finished shortly before the last pallet of the previous one is taken away.

At the cost of having two types of kanbans instead of one, this approach addresses the issues raised in the previous section:

- *Responsibility.* The materials handler is responsible for the move kanbans; the production operator, for the production kanban. Each kanban has a simple loop, and the two loops intersect where the handler detaches the production kanban to place it into a collection box.
- *Posting on a scheduling board.* Since there is exactly one production kanban for one production run, the issues of mapping a stack of kanbans to a production run go away. As a result, a simpler scheduling board can accommodate more items, and the need for a specialized scheduler to organize the kanbans on the board goes away.
- *Consistency.* The handler only takes away a pallet with a corresponding move kanban in hand. The operation is therefore completely consistent with a pull system.

Another advantage of using both production and move kanbans is that it decouples improvement efforts on both sides, since the number of move kanbans in circulation or the size of the production runs can be reduced independently. While the common kanban only allows you to control the total amount of material in fabrication and the semi-finished goods warehouse, it does not enable you to control each one separately.

Figure 11-13 shows how the information on the common kanban is split among the move and production kanbans. Since each production kanban is for multiple pallets, there are fewer in circulation than move kanbans.

Move kanban for 1 pallet   Production kanban for a run of 4 pallets

FIGURE 11-13. **Move and production kanbans**

Supplier kanbans

The most commonly told story about the origin of the kanban system is that Taiichi Ohno was inspired by seeing the replenishment system of American supermarkets in 1950. While supermarket clerks strive to keep the shelves full, however, they don't use kanbans. An alternative story is that, about the same time, Kiichiro Toyoda first used kanbans when the nearly bankrupt Toyota could only afford to pay suppliers for the parts it had actually consumed.

This plausible story makes the supplier kanban the first type to have been used. Today, while the logic of the supplier kanban system is used in lean supply chain, the stack of recirculating hardcopy kanbans delivered to suppliers by milk runs is a thing of the past. This chapter describes below several schemes involving both electronic communication and hardcopy that are used to emulate it.

The differences between an in-house move kanban and a supplier kanban are due to the need for it to be used by two different companies, between which it serves as a commercially binding order. Incidentally, in 1950, the Japanese tax authorities required documentation on commercial transactions that the circulation of kanbans did not provide. Today, supplier kanbans—or their electronic images—are triggers within the framework of a blanket purchase order specifying terms and conditions. Kanbans, in the form of one-time use hardcopy, travel with parts, and the shipping and receiving transactions are recorded by scanning barcodes. Figure 11-14 shows an example of an elaborate supplier kanban.

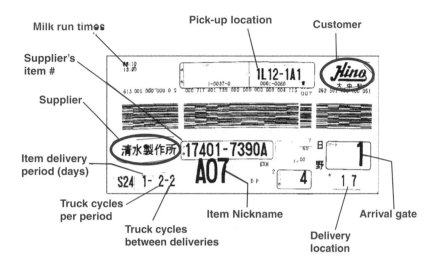

FIGURE 11-14. **Supplier kanban between Shimizu and Hino**

The customer's and the supplier's item numbers may or may not match. If they don't, then both item numbers are needed on the card. The item nickname, also called "item back number," is the short name that operators use to refer to the part among themselves instead of the tongue-twisting, confusing full item number.

The "1-2-2" on the bottom left describe the delivery cycle as follows:

- The "1" means that the parts are delivered within one day of the kanban being issued.
- The first "2" means that a truck delivers parts from this supplier to the customer plant twice a day.
- The second "2" means that a kanban leaving on one truck comes back with parts not on the next truck but on the one after it.

The reorder point system

The reorder point system is often confused with the kanban system. In a Best Manufacturing Practices[1] survey, for example, United Electric Controls of Watertown, MA, reports that it "notifies the supplier whenever the stock in the central stores reaches a one-week supply" and describes this as a "supplier kanban" system. There is a place for reorder point among the methods that can be used to trigger replenishment, but the discussion is clearer if we call it just that. This is appropriate for easy-to-procure commodities where the value of having your finger on the pulse of the consumption is not worth the trouble. Figure 11-15 shows more examples from Korry Electronics, where the reorder point is one bag for the item on the left and the red line for the item on the right. Note that the reorder card is attached to the shelf and not to the item, and that pulling it uncovers a sign saying "on order" as on the left side. Separators on the shelf between the items ensure that they remain aligned with the proper signs.

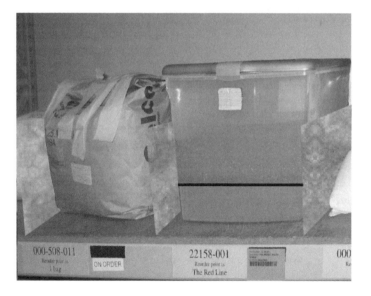

FIGURE 11-15. Reorder points at Korry Electronics

---

1. www.bmpcoe.org/bestpractices/internal/uec/uec_11.html (04/22/2003)

Signal and material kanbans

This variation on the reorder point system was originally developed for automotive stamping plants. As a result of setup time reduction efforts, most of the work needed to change dies in stamping presses was externalized, meaning that it could be done while the press was still stamping the previous product. But how do the stamping plant operators know when to do the external setup? An explicit production schedule will provide that information, but it will not be tied to consumption as in a pull loop.

The combination of material and signal kanbans shown in Figure 11-16 addresses this issue. "Material and signal kanban" is the established term for this system, but it would more aptly be described as a "ready-set-go" system. As welders work their way through a stack of roof stampings, they encounter and pull the rectangular "material kanban," which tells the stamping plant to get ready to stamp more roofs.

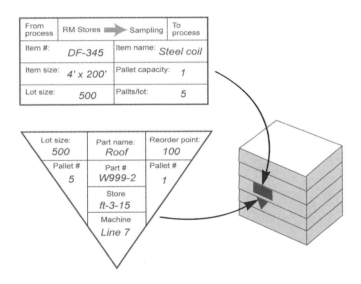

FIGURE 11-16. Material and signal kanbans

In response, the stamping plant operators retrieve the specified coils of steel from the warehouse, position the dies next to the line of stamping presses and make them ready to be swapped into the presses. Meanwhile, the welders keep eating through the stack of stampings and reach the triangular "signal kanban," which tells the stamping operators that it is time to change the dies and start producing and delivering the roofs.

Beyond stamping, this approach is applicable in diecasting, injection molding, machining, and other processes with the common characteristic of having substantial setups that have been externalized through setup time reduction projects.

Tunnel kanbans and CONWIPs

There are circumstances, however, where it is practical to control the total amount of materials within a segment of a process without controlling the flow between every pair of operations or lines. Imagine, for example, that you machine parts in house, send them to an outside contractor for electroplating, and bring them back in house for painting. Then you may want to use kanbans between Painting and Machining without having any action taken on the kanbans while inside the electroplating "tunnel." Kanbans travel and stay with machined parts throughout their journey to the contractor and back, to be pulled at Painting and returned to Machining. The tunnel kanbans cap the total number of parts in the plating loop as a whole, but do not affect where in that loop they may be. This concept is illustrated in Figure 11-17.

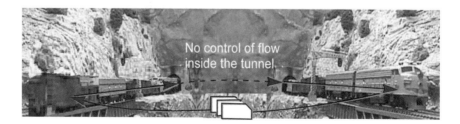
No control of flow inside the tunnel

FIGURE 11-17. The tunnel kanban concept

This concept of capping WIP without controlling where it is on the floor can also be used to manage the residual job shops that remain after a plant has been converted to lean manufacturing. These job-shops typically perform the following functions:

- *Production of C-items*—that is, the large number of products that are made sporadically and in small volumes, accounting in aggregate for possibly 5% of the production volume but 80% of the product catalog.
- *Production of fixtures or refurbishment of tools or dies.* A standard process exists only at a high level, and the detailed routing of parts through machines vary with each unit.
- *R&D and pilot production.* Since the work performed is all experimentation, by definition the work cannot be standardized and is non-repetitive.

In these circumstances, restricting the aggregate amount of work in process in the shop avoids congestions and lets jobs proceed quickly through whatever ad-hoc route they may follow. Inside the shop, the work can be sequenced visually as in the example of Figure 11-18, for a machine shop that makes custom jobs with parts small enough to fit, together with their paperwork, tools, fixtures and NC programs on a cafeteria tray.

The policy is that, say, no more than 50 jobs are allowed in the shop at any one time. If 50 jobs are in process, then the next one waits until one job completes. The high level common process is that, for example, milling is done before heat treat, and grinding afterwards, and this high-level process is used to map the progress of all 50 jobs in process on an Ybry chart.

All the job shuffling and priority games are played by the gate keeper before a job is released. Once released, it proceeds first-in–first-out (FIFO) in every center specified on its traveller through gravity flow racks. Since the WIP is capped at a low level, all jobs complete quickly once they are released. In Figure 11-18, the milling center is laid out as a pseudo cell. Since it is comprised of equivalent machines working in parallel, it is not a cell, but the layout borrows as much from cells as possible.

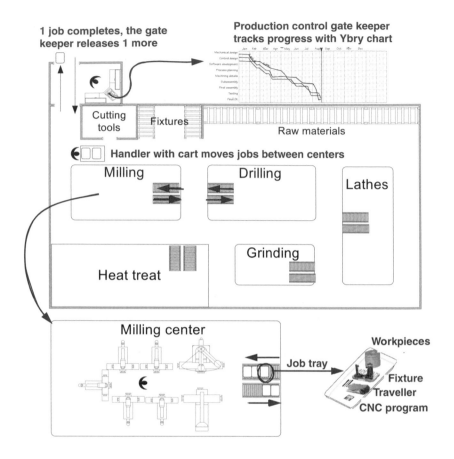

FIGURE 11-18. Visual FIFO sequencing inside a machining job-shop

Hopp and Spearman[1] describe a concept they call "CONWIP," for "constant WIP," which, as first sight, looks identical to tunnel kanbans and appear to implement the same logic as described in Figure 11-18. There is, however, a difference. In the job-shop system of Figure 11-18, priorities serve to sequence jobs prior to release but not once they are on the floor.

---

1. *Factory Physics*, Spearman & Hopp, Irwin, (1996)

With CONWIPs, sequencing in every center is done through dispatch lists based on priorities.

While FIFO is not particularly desirable from a strictly scheduling point of view, it helps control quality by making the process easier to trace, and it can be implemented by simple devices like gravity flow racks. Dispatch lists, by contrast, require a system to produce them and require random-access storage for WIP. While capping the WIP can produce improvements in the shop's performance, using dispatch list might possibly provide a few more percentage points, and it is not clear that it is worth the cost, in particular the loss of process traceability.

Other approaches that have been proposed for low-volume–high-mix environments include Rajan Suri's[1] "Paired-cell Overlapping Loops of Cards with Authorization" (POLCA).

Each of the manual methods described in this chapter works well in its domain of applicability, but, as the number of pull loops in a plant rises, so does the administrative burden of managing the flow of physical signals, as well as the risks of misrouting. As a consequence the full or partial automation of these tasks using information technology becomes ever more tempting. The next chapter describes several solutions adopted by Toyota and other manufacturers.

---

1. *Quick Response Manufacturing*, R. Suri, Productivity Press, (1999)

CHAPTER 12

Hybrid and electronic pull signals

Summary

The kanban system is from the 1950s, and the two-bin system predates it. Computer networks practically usable as a pull system infrastructure, however, became available in the 1990s, prompting efforts to replace hardcopy with electronic messages that have met with varying degrees of success.

In the automotive supply chain, most orders are placed through Electronic Data Interchange (EDI) rather than kanbans, but human-readable documents will need to accompany materials in transit or on the shop floor as long as people are involved. Toyota's e-kanban system is a hybrid, automating the error-prone and labor-intensive part of a supplier kanban's cycle, when it returns unattached to the supplier, and turning it into hardcopy when attached to materials on the way to the customer. Other companies use supplier kanbans internally, to trigger the issuance of orders by EDI or FAX to suppliers who are not aware of the kanban system.

"Electronic kanbans," however, automate a logic designed for hardcopy. Other approaches that take full advantage of the power of computer networks include body-on-sequence and variations of vendor-managed inventory (VMI). The kanban system is based on the assumption that the next few hours will be like the last few, which is true in the automotive industry but not of manufacturing in general. While more sophisticated forecasting schemes are not possible with hardcopy, they are with computer systems.

There have been many attempts to replace kanbans with electronic equivalents. This has taken multiple forms, including the following:

- Products offered as "flow manufacturing software" by several companies.

- "Kanban modules" included in major ERP products.

- Custom systems built by system integrators based on specs from a manufacturing company.

- In-house efforts in manufacturing companies that have development capabilities in their IT groups.

Kanbans and information technology

While moving cards around seems like an antiquated way of working, attempts to modernize it through computer systems have not been as successful as expected, for two primary reasons:

- *Shop floor interface issues.* Materials moving in a supply network need IDs and information attached about where they come from and where they are going. No matter what logic it implements, the computer system must generate the IDs, they must be attached to the materials and read as needed by machines or people.

  Printing human-readable paperwork is not difficult, but the manipulation of this paperwork from the printer to the materials, and the communication of updates back to the computer system can generate so much work, take so long, and include enough errors to negate the value of the computer system.

  Machine-readable documents have until recently been limited to barcodes that are limited in content and require a human operator to properly position the label in front of a scanner. While successful at accelerating data entry and eliminating input errors, barcode systems have not completely eliminated manual data entry work.

  RFID is the first technology to make work in process automatically self-identifying in many industries, but its use is not widespread yet.

Once it is, the passage of a bin in front of a reader will be able to trigger the issuance of a pull signal without any human intervention.

- *Computerized kanbans as a horseless carriage.* The kanban system was designed for cards and embodies a logic that can be implemented with cards. A computer-based kanban system is therefore more like a horseless carriage than like a car. Computers are not limited to automating manual procedures. Their power can be used instead to implement more sophisticated approaches that require it.

  Examples include the body-on-sequence method, some vendor-managed inventory (VMI) schemes, and in what might be called "dynamic replenishment," in which more information is used to set replenishment quantities than just the immediate quantity consumed.

For use inside the plant, kanbans are still competitive today with electronic signals, but the development of various forms of electronic ordering has displaced them through all or part of the pull loops in the inbound and outbound supply chain. While electronic ordering is a small but growing fraction of retail trade, it is dominant at least in the automobile supply chain. An auto parts manufacturer today typically receives most of its orders through electronic data interchange (EDI), most of the remainder by email, and a small fraction by FAX.

EDI is the exchange of such commercial documents as orders, invoices, and shipping notices in electronic form between a customer and a supplier, directly from a computer application in one organization to an application in another over a communication network. EDI protocols such as X.12 in the United States or the international EDIFACT predate the Internet, and, until the 1990s participation in EDI required an investment of thousands of dollars in dedicated hardware and software. The spread of EDI since then is largely due to a reduction in this cost through the use of the Internet, and in particular through the following technologies:

- *Web-based EDI.* Once web-based EDI is set up by a customer, all a supplier needs to participate is a computer, an internet connection, and a web browser.
- *XML.* XML stands for "extensible markup language" and provides a way for trading partners to exchange EDI messages in the form of

tagged text files that can be correctly interpreted by different software applications on both sides.

Unlike orders received through EDI, orders in plain emails or FAXes have no fixed structure and need to be interpreted by customer service clerks.

There is an abundant literature on the technology supporting electronic commerce. This technology, however, is only an enabler. In this chapter, rather than its technical details, we discuss how it can be put to work implementing a pull system.

Toyota's e-kanban system

Toyota's e-kanban system is partial automation of the kanban system, focused on the part of the kanban cycle that is most subject to human error. The supplier kanban stays with a box of parts until a production operator pulls the first part from the box. What happens afterwards with a classical hardcopy kanban is as follow:

1. The *operator* deposits the kanban into a mailbox.
2. Several times a day, the *team leader* picks up the kanbans from the mailboxes and places them in a collection box.
3. The *kanban postman* collects the contents of the collection box and takes it to a kanban sorting room to sort them by supplier.
4. The *truck drivers* who deliver parts pick up the kanbans from the sorting room for the suppliers on their routes.

This procedure involves four different players manipulating a detached kanban before it makes it out the door and is rife with opportunities for mistakes. To make it work requires intensive training and a level of discipline that few organizations are able to sustain. From the instant the kanban is detached from the parts, however, its handling is of the type that on-line transaction processing (OLTP) systems do better, faster ,and cheaper than humans.

Recognizing this, Toyota has replaced the manual procedure on its website with a computer-based system called "e-kanban," which works as shown in Figure 12-1.

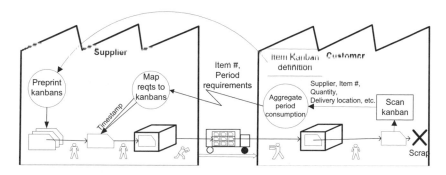

FIGURE 12-1. E-kanban flow between customer and supplier

Forward movement, associated with parts, is shown on the bottom as involving hardcopy and manual handling. Instead of returning to the supplier, however, the kanban pulled from the box is scanned and destroyed. The item and quantity information retrieved from the kanban is aggregated by period, which may be a shift or a day, or a fraction of a shift, and communicated electronically back to the supplier.

The supplier has kanbans preprinted by a local shop and matches them against the requirements received from the customer. Because the kanbans are used only once, they can be timestamped with an easy-to-read explicit date instead of bearing cryptic delivery cycle data. The handling of the kanban through shipping and receiving is then identical to what it was with the reusable kanbans.

Using kanbans with suppliers who don't

A car company with $150B/year in sales can tell a $50M/year supplier how to take orders, but a $50M/year company is rarely in a position to do the same to *its* suppliers. In particular, training them to use kanbans may not be an option. Companies in this situation sometimes find a way to use supplier kanbans without their suppliers even realizing it, by circulating kanbans in-house and cutting orders to suppliers that match exactly the conditions specified on the kanbans, using EDI, or whatever order entry system the supplier has in place, as shown in Figure 12-2.

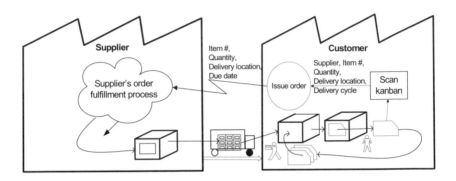

FIGURE 12-2. Making suppliers respond to kanbans without knowing it

As previously, the information on the kanban is scanned after pulling, but the kanban is not destroyed. Instead, it returns to Receiving to be attached to the next incoming box. The information on the kanban is used to generate an order, in whatever form the supplier may accept, be it EDI, email, or FAX. This order then enters the supplier's usual order fulfillment process. The supplier does not have to know that these orders are triggered by kanbans. The main difference the supplier may see is a steady flow of small orders replacing an erratic flow of large ones.

Figure 12-3 shows how Korry Electronics posts supplier kanbans at Receiving. The due date and number of the order issued by email for this order are marked on the kanban by hand, in erasable ink.

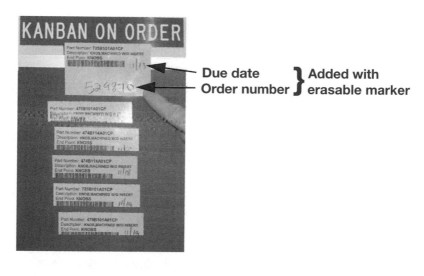

FIGURE 12-3. Supplier kanban board at Korry Electronics

The body-on-sequence system

The body-on-sequence system is used by many car makers under a variety of names, a few of which are listed in Table 12-1, but this system does not seem to be used outside the automobile industry.

TABLE 12-1. Sequencing systems of different car makers

Car maker	Sequencing system
Toyota	Just-in-time sequencing
Ford	In-line vehicle sequencing (ILVS)
GM	Just In Sequence
Chrysler	Sequence Parts Delivery (SPD)

The idea is to communicate the final assembly sequence to suppliers and require them to deliver parts in the same sequence, to the exact location, and at the time they are needed. This is a much tighter coupling of supplier and customer than is provided by the kanban system, and, at least in the version used by Toyota and GM, could not be implemented without computer networks.

Ford's ILVS system uses EDI to send sequences of vehicles to suppliers 6 days in advance. This means that either the system is used only for components whose sequence is not subject to change 6 days in advance or that last-minute alterations are made in the assembly plant, within the constraints of parts availability. Toyota also sequences parts from remote consolidation centers days in advance, but some model- and option-specific components made by local suppliers, like seats and upholstery components, are not ordered for each car until it starts at the first station of final assembly. Toyota and GM use a system called "broadcast pulse" to send the requirements for one car at a time to the suppliers.

The reason this happens at the start of final assembly is specific to the car industry: the preceding operation is *painting*, which is the least reliable of the entire car assembly process. Just because the sequence from Production Control says that the next unit should be a white Corolla does not guarantee that there is a corresponding painted body available. On the other hand, once a car starts through final assembly, it can be counted on to make it all the way through, and to be, for example, at the seat installation station at a predictable time.

Suppliers who are new to this system initially respond by building finished goods stocks and only picking to the customer's sequence. Within a few years, however, they develop the capability to actually build in sequence, and the *supplier's* assembly process is triggered by the broadcast pulse. At Injex in Hayward, CA, for example, the order fulfillment lead time is 220 minutes, from receipt of the broadcast pulse to delivery of the corresponding set of door panels to the proper dock at NUMMI, 14 miles down the road in Fremont. Injex holds no finished goods stocks and its trucks make 10 round trips per day.

For this system to work, the supplier must not see large swings in its own part requirements within a shift. In other words, the body-on-sequence system cannot operate on the receiving end of the bullwhip effect, and a prerequisite is for the customer needs to sequence its products with the goal of smoothing the flow of components from suppliers, using the techniques described in Chapter 16.

The broadcast pulses from the body-on-sequence system *are* pull signals, and are in fact the only type to eliminate any stocks between the supplier and the customer. In the supplier plant, there is work in process being assembled and a truck being loaded but nothing else. The logic of the body-on-sequence system is different from that of the kanban system, and it could not work without a computer network.

Vendor managed inventory (VMI)

Where the use of body-on-sequence implies a tight coupling between customer and supplier, VMI is at the opposite extreme and applies to items the customer does not feel a need to monitor closely. As the name suggests, VMI is an approach in which the management of the stock of an item at a customer site is left entirely to the supplier, and it is not a zero-inventory system. It can be used in outbound logistics, where a manufacturer or wholesaler assumes responsibility for keeping the shelves of a retailer stocked, and in inbound logistics, where a supplier of components or materials keeps them in stock in the customer's factory.

The extent to which the vendor manages the inventory varies.

* The customer makes the data about the supplier's products in the inventory database accessible. The supplier monitors the quantities on hand and makes deliveries as needed to keep it within agreed upon bounds. The materials from this supplier are received like other materials by the customer, and the supplier issues invoices together with advanced shipping notices (ASN).

* In addition to deciding when to replenish, the supplier takes charge of physically maintaining stores of the parts or materials on the customer's shop floor. Like the vendors replenishment food vending machines, supplier reps are allowed onto the shop floor. The supplier retains ownership of the materials until they are used, and is paid for the quantities specified in the bill of materials when finished product units leave

the production line. This is known as a consignment or pay-per-build arrangement.

By definition, VMI schemes apply to items that the customer does not feel are worth managing. In a retail situation, the supplier's items may not be given great importance by a distributor carrying thousands from multiple suppliers. VMI then enables the vendor to give these items more attention and in particular to receive better feedback on which ones move or don't move.

In inbound logistics, the approach is used in priority for commodities like nuts, bolts, and washers that may be used in large quantities but are inexpensive and easy to obtain. Chrysler reports using it for paint. The most unusual application reported[1] is the use of consignment by Ford for truck brakes, which is the kind of high-value, product-specific, safety part one would expect a customer to monitor closely.

Depending on the form it takes, VMI may or may not require extensive use of information technology. In the approach where the supplier remotely monitors quantities on hand, the supplier has to maintain an accurate inventory status database, make it accessible over the Internet, and make it secure, granting authorized suppliers access to data about their items.

On the other hand, if the supplier simply keeps bins full of bolts on the customer shop floor and gets paid on a consignment/pay-per-build basis, then the *customer*'s information system does not need to monitor quantities on hand or issue orders in any form. All it needs is an accurate bill of materials to credit the supplier for parts in finished goods.

We have seen cases where the adoption of consignment/pay-per-build for standard items reduced a customer's information systems costs by 10%, or about $1M/year.

---

1. *Reengineering the Corporation*, M. Hammer & J. Champy, Harper Business, New York, N.Y., (1996) p. 43

Dynamic replenishment

Pull systems are about replenishment, not order fulfillment. The signal to produce or deliver the amount of an item that has just been consumed is issued based on the assumption that the same amount will shortly be needed again, which is a naive, short-term forecast.

A "naive" forecast simply assumes that the future will be identical to the present, and, under the right circumstances, cannot be substantially improved upon by more sophisticated methods. If the sun shines in a cloudless sky now, the naive forecast that it will still do so in half an hour is about as accurate as a weather forecast can be. The accuracy of the naive weather forecast, however, drops dramatically if the sky is not cloudless or the horizon lengthens to a day or a week.

In a pull system, the term of the implicit forecast is the replenishment lead time, which may range from 15 minutes to one week. This raises the following questions:

1. What are the constraints on the downstream process for the naive forecast to be accurate?

2. Can more sophisticated forecasting methods improve the results?

In medium or long range production planning, naive forecasting is clearly insufficient, but pull system operations are not concerned with weeks and months but minutes and hours. In the automotive supply chain, where lean manufacturing originated, dramatic changes in *market demand* do not occur within this timeframe, but component suppliers and in-house subassembly lines on the receiving end of the bullwhip effect can be affected by changes in their customers' *production schedules*, that may be present even in the absence of any change in market demand. This is why pull systems go hand-in-hand with *leveled sequencing*.

A given number of pull signals can accommodate a range of activity levels simply by variations in their speed of rotation. In the automotive industry, the numbers of signals in a loop is reviewed periodically, every month or every other month, but is not changed by production control between reviews. During that time, production supervisors may withdraw signals from circulation to test the loop's ability to function with fewer signals, but this is not a response to a change in demand.

Other industries have different demand patterns. When a toy is a hit or an electronic device has pent-up demand, it is subject to explosive growth for a period of time. Figure 12-4 shows pent-up demand: a population of buyers discovers that it needs a product as a result of its introduction. Until the product existed, they didn't know they needed it, but, as soon as it is introduced, it becomes a must-have item. This pattern has been repeated over decades for products ranging from pocket calculators to PDA's. Demand explodes initially, but then trails off as the market saturates. The curve in Figure 12-4 can only be drawn after the fact. As the product life unfolds, neither the height nor the timing of the peak are known.

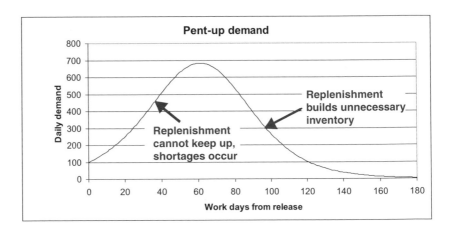

FIGURE 12-4. Pent-up demand pattern

This kind of demand is challenging in many respects, including the use of a pull system. A situation where demand doubles every month for three months is outside the domain of validity of Little's law, and the above formula is not applicable. This type of variability is intrinsic to the market and not a side-effect of a dysfunctional production scheduler.

In this context, a possible improvement over issuing signals to replenish exactly what has been consumed, is to adjust dynamically either the number of signals issued or the quantities associated with each signal based on the trend in the demand. This means putting to use not only the immediate information on consumption but its recent history. Depending on how the pull system is implemented, this may or may not be possible, based on the following:

- If the signals are in the form of cards, bins, or other hardware devices, then their numbers cannot practically be adjusted every shift or every day, and neither can associated part quantities.

- If electronic signals are used, in forms discussed in Chapter 12, then dynamic adjustments can be made without creating more manual work.

Time-series analysis techniques to forecast demand in the near future based on the recent past are now available in inexpensive software for PCs, but possessing such software is not sufficient. A substantial effort is also needed to understand how to use it.

Most lean manufacturing experts from the automotive industry view the development of what might be termed "dynamic pull" systems as a mistake, reflecting only a lack of understanding of pull systems. We view it instead as a legitimate effort to extend the concept of pull systems to domains where the demand does not have the same characteristics as that for cars and auto parts.

Other technology-based methods

Other technology-based approaches have been used over the years.

FAXbans

FAXbans are kanbans sent by FAX. With a long-distance pull loop, a FAXban can be in the supplier's hands two days earlier than a kanban carried by a truck driver. Since FAXes travel over the telephone network and almost every business has a FAX machine, FAXbans require little investment.

On the other hand, they require human intervention at least on the receiving end, and usually on the sending end as well. A customer using EDI with other suppliers may accommodate a technically lagging supplier by having the computer system automatically send FAXes through a modem, but the more common pattern for using FAXbans is to have a clerk feed hardcopy kanbans through a FAX machine. While we have seen FAXbans used successfully in industries ranging from medical devices to gas turbines, several characteristics and limitations have to be kept in mind.

FAXing replicates the FAXban on the other end rather than sending, as would happen with hardcopy kanbans in trucks. One difficulty is making sure that each FAXban is transmitted successfully to the right destination once and only once.

With EDI, the information in an order itself determines where it goes. With FAXbans, this is dependent on the operator selecting the right FAX number, and operator error is possible.

FAX transmission is not always successful on the first attempt. The line may be busy or the transmission fail. If the recipient uses a FAX modem and FAX management software, failed transmissions will be flagged. But an old FAX machine may generate a partial print, which the supplier may mistakenly use as an order, so that the later, successful transmission will create a duplicate order.

To avoid this, an effective practice is to number the FAXes, so that a recipient who has FAXes number 635 and 637 knows that 636 is missing and that, if there are two labeled 636, one is a duplicate that should be discarded.

Besides reliability, the less than perfect quality of FAX transmission is also an issue, and more for machine than for human readability. Operators have no problem reading FAXbans, but a barcode can easily be garbled beyond recognition.

Email

With email, the quality of transmission is not at issue, but its reliability still is. While it does not happen as often as failed FAX transmissions, emails do occasionally get lost, and it is a good idea to systematically request read receipts.

The second major issue with email is the lack of security. It is not a secure medium and its use can compromise confidential business information. "Secure email" software is available to encrypt messages and authenticate recipients and can be applied. Even with secure emails, however, an operator on the supplier side still needs to read the order and key it into the supplier's order entry system. This raises the question of whether the parties would not be better off just using EDI systems specifically designed to support business transactions and the automatic entry of orders into the supplier's computer system.

Live videos

For use inside the plant, we have seen a number of approaches in Chapter 11 that require the input buffer of the downstream operation to be *visible*, and this requirement limited their applicability. Video technology, however, can be used to extend the "line of sight."

Mounting one small black and white camera over a flow rack, running a cable to the materials services area, and showing the picture on a monitor is inexpensive and straightforward. Doing it for tens or even hundreds of locations, however, is neither cheap nor simple and is not necessarily the best method.

This chapter has shown how the information technology of the early 21st century can not only help meet the administrative challenges of a large-scale, manual pull system but also enable manufacturers to use logic that they couldn't with only a manual system. Whether manual or electronic, however, the success of the pull system hinges on the way *people* respond to its signals, which is the topic of the next chapter.

CHAPTER 13

Kanban operating policies

Summary

How kanbans are used is what makes them instruments of production control as opposed to simply pieces of paper. For this reason, the rules Toyota developed for the use of kanbans should be studied and not tampered with lightly. They are the protocol operators and materials handlers must follow in routine operations.

They specify that the kanban is pulled from a bin when the first unit is withdrawn, that replenishment is for the quantity marked on the kanban, that kanbans for the same items are processed first-in–first-out, that kanbans for multiple items may be sequenced on boards, as explained in Chapter 15, and that kanbans should never be knowingly attached to defectives.

In addition managers must convey to the work force the company's commitment to making the kanban system work, use it to identify improvement opportunities, prevent it from being abandoned at the first sign of trouble, and involve the workforce in designing implementation details. Beyond the pilot stage, Production Control must also set up a "kanban central bank" in charge of issuing kanbans and controlling the number in circulation.

This chapter first addresses the practically troublesome issue of when a kanban should be pulled from a bin or a part. Since this is how a signal is issued, it is critical to the operation of the pull system. Then it presents the complete set of rules for kanban handling, separating for clarity's sake those that apply to shop floor personnel from those that apply to management.

When should a kanban be pulled?

Toyota's rule is that a kanban is detached from a box when the first unit is pulled, and this rule is particularly difficult to get accepted on the shop floor. It seems that everybody wants to "improve" on it, by detaching the kanban when the box is two-thirds empty or even when pulling the last part.

The concern that is usually voiced about detaching the kanban when pulling the first part is that it causes the next box to arrive too early, resulting in having unnecessary stock on hand at the line side. In the ideal situation, the replenishment lead time is such that the next box arrives just when the operator is about to pick the last part from the current box. In reality, move kanbans in particular can return with a full box on the next milk run. If there is a milk run every 30 minutes and one box lasts 2 hours and 15 minutes, then the replenishment will be 1 hour and 45 minutes early.

Detaching the kanban part of the way through the box has the following problems:

- It makes sense only if there is only one box, in which case it is a return to the reorder point system, which provides less visibility into the item's consumption rate than the kanban system.
- It requires the operator to pay attention to the different reorder points set for each item, as opposed to having one simple and consistent rule for all items.

Detaching the kanban when the last part is pulled does not work either. If there is only one box by the line side, then the item is short until the next box arrives. If there is more than one box, then detaching the card when pulling the last part in box *n* rather than the first part of box *n+1*, differs only by one takt interval and will not affect the delivery time of the next box.

The proper way to solve this dilemma is to detach the kanban when the first part is pulled but specify the delivery cycle on the kanban itself. In our example, the kanban could say that it needs to return with a full box on the third milk run after it was collected. With a milk run every 30 minutes, it means that the full box will be delivered between 90 and 120 minutes after the kanban is detached, which works out to between 15 and 45 minutes before the box is needed.

This way, the requirements placed on the production operator are simple and consistent, and the responsibility for dealing with varying replenishment lead times rests where it belongs, with production control or materials management.

Kanban rules for operators and materials handlers

The way we handle kanbans—like the way we handle bank notes—is what makes them different from ordinary pieces of paper. The rules for using kanbans constitute the protocol executed on the shop floor, in the warehouse, and in the supply chain. They specify how the game is played, and must be second-nature to the participants to ensure success. This takes years to accomplish, and even experienced companies need to give periodic reminders and "booster shots" of training to prevent slippage.

There are many different kinds of kanbans used to authorize a variety of actions: production, in-house movements, the preparation of a machine for setup, or deliveries from suppliers. Since we are formulating rules here that apply to *all* kanbans, we refer only to *actions*. Likewise, the people who handle the kanbans may be operators, materials handlers, or shipping/receiving clerks, and, for the sake of generality, we refer to them as *agents*. We will fill in below the details that vary with each type of kanban.

It should be noted that the agents who act upon kanbans are *directly* involved in making, moving, shipping, or receiving parts. They are not specialized schedulers or planners. Schedulers have a role in setting up and monitoring the system but not in every transaction involving parts, which would be a continuation of—or return to—expediting.

The common rules governing the use of all types of kanbans are as follows:

Rule 1. An agent from a *downstream* operation detaches the kanban from materials when pulling them.

Rule 2. Each detached kanban authorizes a specific action at an *upstream* operation.

Rule 3. The kanban bears the following information:

- The nature of the action.
- The item number of the affected materials.
- The quantity of materials affected.
- The location from which the materials are to be picked.
- The location to which the materials are to be delivered.
- The timing of the action, if not immediate.

Rule 4. Kanbans for the same item are processed first-in–first-out.

Rule 5. Kanbans for different items at the same operation are sequenced using visible management tools with the goal of smoothing the flows of materials triggered by action on the kanbans.

Rule 6. The agent acting upon a kanban attaches it to the materials in a visible location, and it remains attached until the downstream agent pulls the materials.

Rule 7. Agents never knowingly attach kanbans to defective materials.

Rules for production and materials/logistics managers.

While the above rules describe what operators and materials handlers must do, managers also have key roles to play.

Rule 1. The first line managers must convey to the work force the company's determination. This includes oral and written communication, and sanctions for breaking the rules, losing, destroying, or tampering with kanbans.

Rule 2. The first line managers are also responsible for using the system to identify improvement opportunities, by gradually taking kanbans out of circulation.

Rule 3. Management must not allow abandonment of the system at the first sign of trouble. Otherwise the work force will mistakenly perceive the kanban system as brittle and unable to cope with machine breakdowns or exceptional orders.

Rule 4. The managers must involve the work force in the design of the system in a controlled manner, separating what is open for debate from what is not. The rules are not, but the shape of the kanbans and the means of attaching them to containers are.

Rule 5. As soon as the pilot implementation stage is past, production control must set up a "kanban central bank" with control over the number and types of kanbans in circulation, as if they were currency.

Other lists of kanban rules

Many other authors have published lists of kanban rules that differ somewhat from the above. But some of these rules are ambiguous or do not describe actions taken in daily operations. Hirano's six rules, for example, have the following problems:

- Rule 3 is that defective parts should never be passed on to the next process. If, however, a defect is buried inside the part where the agent cannot know of it, he or she cannot be blamed for passing it on. The only realistic requirement is not to *knowingly* pass on defective materials, which requires vigilance. That defects should be an exceptional event is a prerequisite for the system to work and the process must be engineered to this level prior to implementing the kanban system.

- Rule 4 says that leveled sequencing, or "heijunka," should be used, which is ambiguous, because, leveled sequencing of final assembly is implemented by production control, as described in Chapter 17, but kanban shuffling as described in rule 5 above also is a form of leveled sequencing, and it is done by operators and materials handlers as part of routine execution.

- His rule 6 is to use the kanban system as a means of identifying improvement opportunities. Clearly, this is not on the same level as specifying the circumstances under which a kanban should be detached from a bin.

This chapter concludes the discussion of the information flows' protocol layer, which specifies rules for production operator and logistics personnel to take action without requiring judgment calls. The smoother the protocols work the more responsive the company's logistics network is to what management wants it to do. The following chapters are about principles, methods, and tools to help management at various levels make appropriate decisions.

CHAPTER 14

Scheduling principles

Summary

By regulating flows between production lines, the pull system changes scheduling from a central, plant-wide function to a local one, performed at the level of a cell or line and using methods tailored to local needs. In mixed-flow assembly, leveled sequencing is used to smooth incoming material flows. More generally the lean approach to scheduling separates rate work, which represents the bulk of the volume and is repetitive, from response work, which is non-repetitive and in low volume, but must be performed to provide effective customer service.

Order shuffling and priority games with customers are acceptable only until the work is released to production. Since the production lead time is short, there is little to be gained and much to be lost from expediting WIP. No work should be released for production unless all the needed materials are on hand, and the practice of building "cripples" that are 99% complete but cannot be shipped is disallowed as ineffective, waste inducing, and a threat to quality. In rate work, parts are not pegged to products until actual assembly. Early pegging only occurs with response work.

Emergency response is beyond the scope of pull systems and sequencing protocols, but lean manufacturing and logistics builds a cadre of well-trained managers, engineers, materials handlers, and production operators in the supply chain, who can rise to the occasion and improvise effective ad-hoc countermeasures, as has been demonstrated by Toyota's recovery from the Asin Seiki fire of 1997 or the Mississippi flood of 1993.

Many managers believe that the use of a pull system eliminates the need to schedule the work of production lines. What kanbans provide either to an internal line or to a supplier, is a flow of orders, to which the line has to respond in some fashion. If the line is dedicated to one product, then it may simply respond to the kanbans in first-in–first-out order, but if it is a mixed-flow line, then a more elaborate response is needed, particularly when setups between products are not instantaneous. This chapter examines the principles of the scheduling approach used by lean manufacturers.

Decentralized scheduling

The pull system eliminates the need to direct the work of the entire plant from a central location, as is attempted with MRP/ERP dispatch lists. *Centrally* scheduling hundreds of machines with different setup structures, load sizes, and modes of operation is practically impossible. By regulating the high-level flows between lines, departments, and plants, the pull system reduces the challenge to that of *locally* scheduling tens of units of a few machines or stations each. As long as each of these units delivers the demand expressed by the flow of pull signals, it may have its own, unique approach to scheduling. And because each unit is small, the methods can be better tailored to its needs than if a single method had to apply to the entire plant. In the simplest case of a cell dedicated to one product, picking kanbans first-in–first-out from a box may be all that is needed; at the opposite end, an Advanced Planning and Scheduling (APS) system may be justified to schedule work through the kind of a Flexible Manufacturing System (FMS) that are used to machine components used in aerospace or semiconductor production equipment applications.

The scheduling horizon varies with each industry. It can be one week in aerospace, a shift or a day in the automotive industry, or two hours in computer assembly. For this period of time, the schedule needs to specify the following:

- The sequence of pieces or batches to run in each line.
- The assignment of operators to line positions.
- The issuance of orders to suppliers.

- Adjustments to the volume of work based on fluctuations:
  - Special orders
  - Order cancellations
  - Equipment failures
  - Operator absences
  - Shortages

The Production Control and the Materials organizations focus on the functions that have an external impact. The final assembly schedule, for example, deserves special attention because it determines what can be shipped and drives the requirements for materials in the supply chain. At the other end of the process, the issuance of orders to suppliers involves external business relationships and determines what will be delivered. On the other hand, inside the plant, the scheduling function can often be delegated to first-line management, with production supervisors relying on a technician to work the numbers and maintain the boards and displays needed for communication with the floor.

Leveled sequencing and its purpose

Leveled sequencing, which is described in detail in the next two chapters, is used in mixed-flow assembly to smooth the incoming flow of materials and thereby contain or eliminate the bullwhip effect. It has no *direct* impact on customer experience. Of course, customers eventually benefit, *indirectly*, from improvements to inbound logistics.

Let us assume, for example, that the order fulfillment lead time for a consumer product is five days, that final assembly is sequenced every shift, and that products are shipped directly to consumers by a courier. A customer, will see a consequence if a unit is assembled one day or the next, but not if it is assembled at 9:00 AM or 11:30 AM. Short-interval sequencing does not affect the date and time of delivery into the customer's hands. On the other hand, it does affect the operations of final assembly, internal subassembly lines, and suppliers, particularly those who use body-on-sequence.

There are manufacturing activities for which this objective has little relevance, such as processes that turn a single raw material into multiple products, including casting, stamping, injection molding, and extrusion. As part of the supply chain of an assembler, they produce to their customers' leveled sequences, but they have no need to reshuffle the work to make it smoother for suppliers.

Rate work and response work

The view of the demand that is embodied in the lean approach to planning and scheduling is as a main body of repetitive work supplemented by exceptions. The repetitive work, or "rate work," is based on takt time, and a time budget is set aside to deal with exceptions, or "response work."

In practice, the distinction between rate and response work is based on the Product-Quantity analysis described in Lean Assembly.[1] Rate work is comprised of the A and B products, which have dedicated lines, As for individual items and Bs for families. Response work is the production to order of C items.

Order shuffling

Let us assume for a moment that you are running a lean line with no slack-capacity. The approach to accommodating rush orders from favored customers is to shuffle the orders *prior to releasing them to the shop floor.* Once released, no shuffling is possible, and they should be thought of like passengers on a chair lift.

The orders may be broken up into small lots or individual pieces to make their way through one-piece flow lines and FIFO buffers to come back

---

1. *Lean Assembly: The Nuts and Bolts of Making Assembly Operations Flow,* Michel Baudin, Productivity Press, p.17

together as a customer order when finished. The hand of production control is not allowed to disrupt the flow of materials on the shop floor, which has been engineered to be fast.

This works because the flow time through the shop floor is short. The only reason you have expediters switching jobs around in traditional shops is that the lead times are long. If it takes three months to put three hours of work on a part, then moving it to the head of the line at each station may cut this down. On the other hand, if it takes one shift to do it for every part going through, then there is not much at stake in switching them around on the floor. If the plant is running at full capacity, orders may have to wait, but the only place they are allowed to wait is before release, like skiers in front of the chair lift.

At that point, they are normally data only, and can be shuffled to suit the needs of the sales department, within the constraints of part availability and line capacity.

Don't build cripples!

A common practice in factories with long production lead times is to start production on products for which some components are currently not on hand, and may not even be expected to be on hand by the time the product reaches the point in the process where they are needed. Units that are "99% complete" but cannot be shipped wait in a "final check" area until the missing components arrive. Management's expectation is that, as a result, the units will be completed and shipped earlier than if they had not been released for production until all the components were available. As in the previous section, any possible advantage that might have been gained is negligible once lean manufacturing has reduced production lead times from weeks to hours. On the other hand, the following disadvantages of this approach remain:

1. It increases production lead time and WIP.

2. It commits common parts early, preventing them from being used on units of other products that could have been shipped, sometimes

resulting in deadlocks where two incomplete units each contain the parts that would enable the other one to be finished.

3. It complicates logistics, causing the same parts to be delivered for the same use either to production or to the "final check" area.

4. It causes production work to be performed in repair mode, away from the controlled environment of the production line, with its instructions, fixtures, and tools. As a result, not only is the work done inefficiently, but its quality is jeopardized.

With very few exceptions, the practice is not allowed in a lean environment. When faced with the dilemma illustrated in Figure 14-1, the clear choice is to wait until all parts are available.

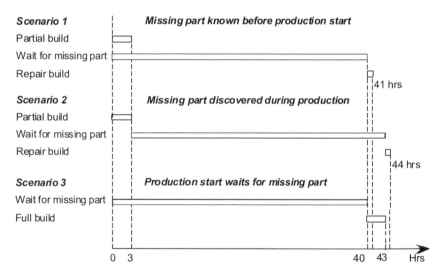

FIGURE 14-1. Building cripples versus waiting for full part availability

Figure 14-1 shows three possible scenarios, in all of which the time needed to complete the product unit is dominated by the 40-hour waiting time for the missing part. The fastest completion is Scenario 1, with the shortage known ahead of production start, where the combination of partial build, waiting, and repair build results is shown as finishing the product two hours earlier than the alternative, after a 40-hour wait for the part. It is unlikely to affect customer experience and not worth pursuing, in light of the problems listed above.

Scenario 2, however, is more common in factories that choose to do partial builds with missing parts, as faulty bills of materials and inaccurate inventory data often cause shortages to be discovered only when assemblers reach for a part and fail to find it. In this case, the wait for the missing part does not start until the partial build is finished, and the product is eventually completed later than in Scenario 3, where production start is postponed until all parts are available.

The few exceptions to the prohibition of partial builds include the car factories do not stop production because of delivery glitches on easily accessible, non-safety-related parts like ornaments or door panels. On the other hand, production is immediately stopped in response to shortages of parts like proportioning valves, which allocate brake fluid between the front and the rear of the car and are inside the structure.

Late pegging of goods to orders

In shops that use MRP/ERP dispatching, it is common to see generic parts in process that are already assigned the serial number of a unit of final product it may not go into for weeks. This is done just so the part can be assigned a due date.

In rate work, parts are not assigned to a unit of final product until they are mounted on it, and the serial number mapping serves strictly for traceability. Since there is no advance pegging of WIP to finished goods, the units of WIP have no due date, and due dates cannot be used to sequence them. The approach to scheduling rate work described in the coming chapters is to reserve resources—a dedicated line or a time slot on a shared line—for each product in a plan that is repeated every shift, every day, or every week. Pull signals then serve to confirm these reservations.

Response work usually accounts for no more than 5% of production volume, but is key to the manufacturer reputation for... *responsiveness.* In this kind of work, the manufacturer buys or makes parts to fill a specific order, and they are automatically pegged to it. The parts are usually kitted into a job that has a traveler attached to it.

When discussing tunnel kanbans in Chapter 11, we saw an example of how this kind of activity can be managed by having a separate shop for it. It is not an option, then time can be set aside for response work in the lines normally used for rate work, for example, in the form of a three-hour block at the end of swing shift every day.

Emergency response

Part of logistics is responding to contingencies. Contrary to the beliefs of many managers during initial implementation, lean manufacturing is not a fair weather strategy. When the Aisin Seiki plant making 99% of all proportioning valves for Toyota in Japan burned to the ground in February '97, it idled all Japanese Toyota plants within four hours, but they were back in production at the normal level of 14,000 cars/day within six weeks.

Toyota accomplished that by mobilizing its supplier network into what the *Wall Street Journal* later called the "equivalent of an Amish barn raising," and this experience is viewed by the company as a validation of TPS/lean manufacturing. Likewise, stateside, by reserving all the trucking available from Chicago to California ahead of the Mississippi flood of 1993, Toyota was able to keep supplying parts from the Midwest to NUMMI in California for weeks while the normally used railroad tracks were under water.

Where you use a pull system, self-adjustments in the rotation speed of signals can absorb volume changes of up to 25% in a month. A spike in demand for items made as *rate work* qualifies as *response work*, and the time set aside for response work also provides surge capacity. These situations are not emergencies.

Emergencies are changes in volume of greater magnitude, such as are caused by fires, floods, earthquakes, or stock market crashes. Emergency response is neither protocol execution nor routine decision making but intelligent *improvisation* by well-trained individuals with steady nerves. Lean manufacturing and logistics provides no stock answers to these situations, but builds a cadre of well-trained managers, engineers, materials handlers, and production operators who can rise to the occasion.

After stating general principles in this chapter, the next two describe specific methods used to schedule mixed flows of products through production lines, first with setup constraints between products, and then without such constraints.

CHAPTER 15

Scheduling lines with setups between products

Summary

Setups constrain scheduling, and setup time reduction gradually relaxes theses constraints. Meanwhile, production lines, cells, and sometimes individual machines need to be scheduled for the smallest batch sizes compatible with the demand and current setup conditions. The sequencing of products is further constrained by such structures as minor setups within product families/major setups between families, or setup matrices with times that are specific to every from/to pair of products.

One approach to use a sequence of products that minimizes total setup time while being responsive to changes in demand is to establish a fixed, repeating pattern for rate work and treat the corresponding assignments as reservations, to be confirmed through pull signals.

In many cases, mixed-flow lines can be scheduled by placing kanbans on a variety of boards on the shop floor with case-specific rules for withdrawing them, without requiring any information technology support. In other cases, such as automated production systems making hundreds of different items, simulation tools can be used to establish a fixed repeating pattern of reservations.

The best way to ship daily to a customer is to make every day what goes out every day. Long setups, however, make that impossible by forcing production runs to cover multiple days. And the resulting large batches must then be stored in a finished goods warehouse, from which daily shipments are drawn, as shown in Figure 15-1.

One of the key aspects of lean manufacturing, however, is the refusal to accept long setups as inevitable. By improving this activity, SMED projects reduce 8-hour setups to 30-min. or even 6-min., which enable the more desirable sequencing pattern shown at the bottom of Figure 15-1.

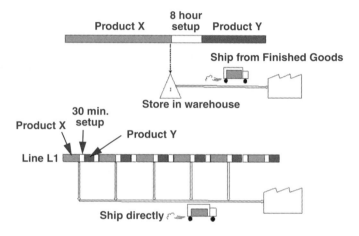

FIGURE 15-1. Quick setups and leveled sequencing

But setup time reduction, however diligently pursued, is not instantaneous. While it is going on, and as long as the setups do not vanish altogether, the problem remains of setting batch sizes and sequencing products.

This chapter examines how scheduling needs to change gradually as setups grow shorter, to take advantage of the gains already achieved and prevent backsliding.

What are the true constraints generated by setups?

The "economic batch quantity" (EBQ) calculations that are traditionally used to set batch sizes are based on assumptions that are not valid for set-ups on production equipment. The EBQ formula is an adaptation of the Economic Order Quantity (EOQ) to a different context. Placing an order has an identifiable variable cost whose main component is freight. If you have to get a third party to bring a truck of materials from a supplier, then there is a cost for this truck that is spread over its content. If it is half full, you will spend twice as much per unit as if it is full.

By contrast, for setups, the main resources are machine and operator time, both of which are already paid for, regardless of whether they are used for production or setups. Quarterly or yearly accounting reports can tally the resources spent on setups and deduce an average cost per setup, but this is not a variable cost that is incurred by doing one more setup this morning.

Where setups become expensive is when they are so frequent they don't leave enough production time to meet the demand and therefore result in lost sales. As shown in Figure 15-2, the marginal setup costs are discontin-uous: negligible as long as you leave enough production time to meet the demand, but unaffordable as soon as you don't.

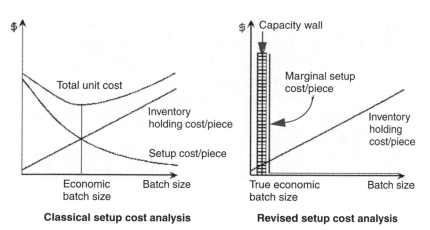

Classical setup cost analysis   **Revised setup cost analysis**

FIGURE 15-2. Marginal cost of setups

For a machine shop supplying an assembly line, the smaller your batches, the lower your WIP and the better balanced it is in mix. Therefore, the best lot size is the one that allows you to do the maximum number of setups that can be done without eating into the required production time. If all the setups are equal, for any given period, it is a simple calculation:

Setup budget = Total available time − Required production time

Number of setups = Setup budget/Setup time

Then you set the batch sizes for your different items to match the needs of assembly. For example, if one unit of the assembled product takes two X's and one Y, then you make the batch size for X twice as large as for Y.

The specific circumstance of each line must of course be considered. For example, if instead of supplying an internal assembly line, a cell makes parts that go directly onto trucks to a customer, in order quantities set by the customer. Then there is no advantage in making batches that are smaller than the quantities going into one truck, since all smaller batches would do is wait.

The constraints imposed on a flexible line by setups can vary as follows:

1. All setups from any item to any other item take the same time. Then the constraint is on the number of setups that can be performed while still leaving enough time for production. This constrains the size of production runs, but not their sequence.

2. There are short setups, requiring, for example, only a die change, and long setups, requiring changes in both the die and the raw material. Then, it also becomes necessary to perform all the short setups possible before a long one.

3. There is a matrix of setup times for every pair of *from* and *to* products. These setups may even be asymmetric, so that going from product X to product Y does not require the same amount of time as from product Y to product X. This happens when setups involve raising or lowering a temperature or changes in paint color, where light to dark is easier than dark to light. Then there is an exact sequence in which to make a run for every product while minimizing the total setup time.

4. The setup time from one product to the next may depend on the entire sequence of products made since the machine started up empty. This can happen on a machining center as a result of inadequate process planning, and needs to be engineered away.

Assume, for example, that we have 816 minutes of work time available on two shifts to make products X, Y, and Z, with required production times as shown in . The time available for setups is 816 − 700 = 116 minutes.

TABLE 15-1. Production time calculation

Product	Quantity	Time / piece	Time required
X	100 pcs.	3.50 min./piece	350 min.
Y	150 pcs.	1.67 min./piece	250 min.
Z	75 pcs.	1.33 min./piece	100 min.
Total			**700 minutes**

If all setups take 15 minutes, then it is possible to do 7 setups everyday, which takes 105 minutes. The sequence in which the products are made is then not constrained by the setup structure. On the other hand, if we have a product family structure such that changing from X to Y or Z takes 60 minutes while changing from Y to Z or Z to Y only takes 10, then there is a strong incentive to cycle through all the products in one family before changing between families, as shown in Figure 15-3.

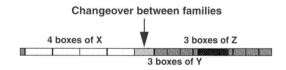

FIGURE 15-3. Changeover within and between families

The more general case of a full setup matrix is illustrated in Figure 15-4. Then the time spent on setups to go through the entire list of products depends on the sequence. In a more general situation, the setups depend on both the "from" and the "to" product and are asymmetrical: going from X to Y doesn't take the same amount of time as Y to X. Examples include the following:

- If one of the setup parameters is a furnace temperature, then the times needed to raise or lower the temperature are different.

- In painting, going from a light color to a dark color is faster than the reverse.

- In detergents, going from a phosphate-free powder to a powder containing phosphate is easier than the reverse, which requires a thorough cleaning.

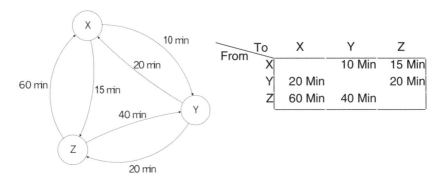

FIGURE 15-4. **Full, asymmetric setup matrix**

In the example of Figure 15-4, the impact of sequencing products differently is as follows:

- X→Y→Z→X→Y: 10 + 20 + 60 +10 = 100 minutes

- X→Y→Z→Y→X: 10 + 20 +40 +20 = 90 minutes

Sequencing setups in this case is akin to solving the traveling salesman problem. Each product is like a city that the machine needs to visit, the setups are one-way roads with different travel times, and we are trying to minimize the total travel time to visit every city.

Chapter 7 discussed the same problem in the context of route planning for supplier milk runs, and the situation is similar. Operations Research software can find an optimal sequence for thousands of products but real situations rarely involve more than ten, or even five, and can easily be solved with the same methods as described in Chapter 7.

Using a fixed repeating sequence

The fixed repeating sequence is particularly useful for rate work, when setup times vary with which products you are changing from and to. This involves two steps:

1. As discussed above, find the sequence with which the line can cycle through all the products with the minimum total setup time.

2. Choose the shortest production run length for the products that is compatible with meeting the demand.

Establishing a fixed repeated sequence is work, but it does not have to be done every day. It pays off in good utilization of the lines doing rate work, and in a mode of operation that is simple and easy for operators to follow. In later sections, this chapter shows how this approach is combined with the pull system to make it responsive to changes and fluctuations.

Scheduling with timetables

Kei Abe[1] designed a system for the repetitive mixed-model production with setups that is based on monthly and weekly timetables that serve as a communication tool between production, production control, sales, purchasing, and suppliers, and are patterned after the school class schedules that anyone with a primary education is familiar with. A version of this system was discussed in Baudin.[2]

---

1. Personal communication

2. *Manufacturing Systems Analysis, with Application to Production Scheduling*, Michel Baudin, Prentice Hall, (1990), pp. 316-320

In the monthly timetable shown in Figure 15-5, routinely made items are listed by decreasing demand and scheduled to be made at regular intervals in production runs intended to be just large enough for setups to be feasible while leaving two hours every day for production in response mode. Grayed items are production runs that have yet to be confirmed by customer orders.

Line 1	May, 2004										
Product	**Mo** 5/2	**Tu** 5/3	**We** 5/4	**Th** 5/5	**Fr** 5/6	**Mo** 5/7	**Tu** 5/8	**We** 5/9	**Th** 5/10	**Fr** 5/11	...
A234Z	100	100	100	100	100	100	100	100	100	100	...
12G94	100		100		100		100		100		...
5PQ23		75		75			75				...
65585		50			50				50		...
ER7FG			50			50			50		...
5S5W6	35				35			35			...
S4D4E			25						25		...
856TG		25									...
LRD45			25								...
WLDOB						25					...
6S4F4V									25		...
...	...	...	...	...	...	...	...	...	...	...	...
Total units	235	250	250	225	235	225	200	210	250	200	...
Rate work min	588	625	625	563	588	563	500	525	625	500	...
Setup budget min	93	55	55	118	93	118	180	155	55	180	...
Response min	120	120	120	120	120	120	120	120	120	120	...
2-shift total	800	800	800	800	800	800	800	800	800	800	...

FIGURE 15-5. Monthly timetable

If such a monthly timetable is sufficient to effectively direct production and logistics, then nothing more is needed. On the other hand, if setups depend on the sequence of the different products, then a table in which they appear in order of decreasing demand does not map correctly to the schedule the production line should follow.

In this case, the monthly timetable needs to be refined within production into weekly timetables that contain the details of timing, sequencing, and setups. While this could be presented in Gantt chart form, Figure 15-6 uses instead a column format that is more similar to that used in personal day planners and school schedules.

	Line 1			Date 5/2/2004	
	Monday	**Tuesday**	**Wednesday**	**Thursday**	**Friday**
	5/2/2004	5/3/2004	5/4/2004	5/5/2004	5/6/2004
7:00	A234Z	A234Z	A234Z	A234Z	A234Z
8:00					
9:00					
10:00					
11:00	Setup		Setup		Setup
12:00	12G94	5PQ23		5PQ23	12G94
13:00			12G94		
14:00					
15:00				S4D4E	
16:00		65585			
17:00	5S5W6		ER7FG		
18:00					5S5W6
19:00		856TG		LRD45	
20:00					
21:00	Reserved for response work				
22:00					
23:00					

FIGURE 15-6. **Weekly timetable**

As described here, the timetable planning system does not use kanbans. Besides being already familiar to all from daily life, it is also more concise than Gantt charts when showing tasks that are started and completed within one day, because it uses *two* dimensions to represent time. On a Gantt chart, date and time are all on the horizontal axis, and they are most useful when tasks span several days and overlap, as happens for example in heavy machining for aerospace applications.

There are several implementation issues with this approach:

- *Update frequency.* The list of products considered "rate work" changes over time. Some are promoted from response to rate work while others are demoted, and the frequency with which this happens varies by industry. Doing it once every three months is not a problem, but if it has to happen every week, the plant is out of the range of applicability of timetable planning.

- *Distribution of timetables.* The most common approach is for production control and line schedules to generate timetables on an electronic spreadsheet, print, and post them in every production line. Alternatively, they can be displayed on computer monitors. The repetitive part of the schedule does not need a real-time update capability, but the more response work there is, the easier it is to justify the use of monitors.

- *Confirmation mechanism.* In Figure 15-5, production runs are confirmed by turning spreadsheet cell backgrounds from gray to white. But if the spreadsheet is a printout on the shop floor, there is more to it than a mouse click. Periodically reprinting and redistributing timetables, or replacing the printouts with monitors are feasible solutions, but the kanban system offers another: it generates a timetable with no confirmations in a sufficiently large format, and attaches incoming kanbans as confirmations. This results in the kanban boards described in the next section.

- *Process involving multiple lines.* If a product is made from start to finish in a single production line, then timetable planning is straightforward, but it becomes complex when multiple production lines are used for different segments of the process, with setup structures that may be different. While there are multiple ways of synchronizing them, kanbans are an effective one that we will focus on.

Using kanban boards

As indicated in Chapter 11, kanbans have the advantage that they can be moved, sorted, arranged, and posted in ways that bins or fixtures cannot, and this section reviews ways different companies have chosen to take advantage of these capabilities to sequence their work.

Example 1: Kanban boards at Wiremold

Figure 15-7 shows one of the kanban boards used at Wiremold to sequence work in a cell that assembles electrical products. With vertical slots, tens of different items can be accommodated in a single level of a

4-ft. shelf but, unlike card pocket systems, this approach does not make the top of each card visible. This is why a label bearing the item number is visible above each slot, and each slot is dedicated to an item.

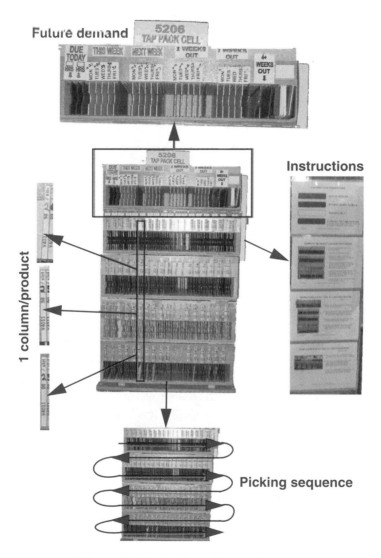

FIGURE 15-7. Wiremold Kanban board example

The concept of this board is that vertically aligned slots are for the same item and that these item-columns are filled from the bottom. As shown at the bottom of Figure 15-7, is done left to right and top to bottom. This has two consequences:

1. The items with the most kanbans pending get picked first. The column for a fast moving item fills up fast and it is frequently picked and conversely, the column for a slow moving item fills up slowly and it is proportionately less frequently picked.

2. Picking left to right prevents long runs for the same item.

3. If there is a setup matrix, the picking sequence can be arranged to minimize the total setup time.

Example 2: Kanban boards at Injex

Figure 15-8 shows a different type of kanban board, used in an injection molding shop at Injex for auto parts going to NUMMI. This is not a cell, but a department with many machines running in parallel. The white cards are preprinted e-kanbans for direct shipment; the brown cards, recirculating kanbans used for parts that are assembled in house.

In Figure 15-8, there is one column for each machine and one row for each product assigned to this machine. The Gantt chart to the right has one row for each machine–product combination and a column per hour. This shop does not have a fixed, repeating schedule. Each day, the scheduler establishes a Gantt chart for each machine, on the basis of doing the shortest jobs first. The scheduler then removes the corresponding kanbans from the board and posts them at the machine for execution and to attach them to completed bins.

One column per machine

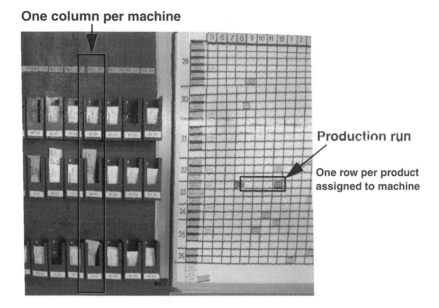

Production run

One row per product
assigned to machine

FIGURE 15-8. Injex kanban board example

How kanban boards work with fixed, repeating schedules

As discussed above, a fixed, repeating schedule can be made responsive to fluctuations in the work by treating it like a set of reservations to be confirmed. In timetable planning, they are confirmed by changing the background color on a spreadsheet cell. The communication of this information to the shop floor, however, may require printing and distribution of hardcopy. This can be avoided by using kanbans for confirmation. Figure 15-9 shows a weekly repeating schedule for a line making the same three products every day.

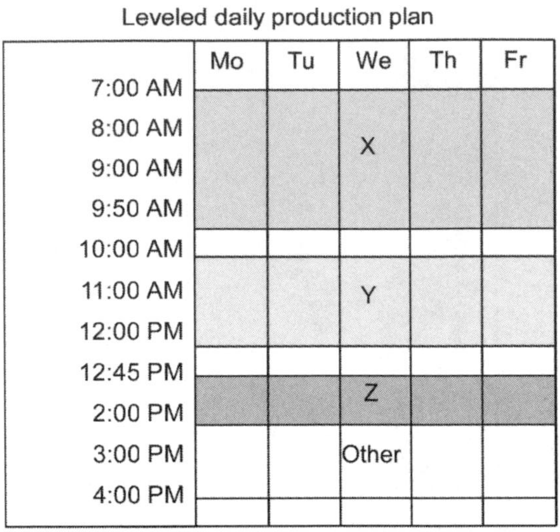

Leveled daily production plan

	Mo	Tu	We	Th	Fr
7:00 AM					
8:00 AM			X		
9:00 AM					
9:50 AM					
10:00 AM					
11:00 AM			Y		
12:00 PM					
12:45 PM					
2:00 PM			Z		
3:00 PM			Other		
4:00 PM					

FIGURE 15-9. Leveled daily production plan

Figure 15-10 shows the flow of confirmation kanbans. Each full pallet carries a card. When the pallet is loaded onto a truck for shipment, the card is pulled out and placed in a collection box. These cards then return to the shop floor and are posted in a card pocket on the scheduling board. With this approach, a simple planning logic can be used without jeopardizing the plant's ability to respond to demand fluctuations.

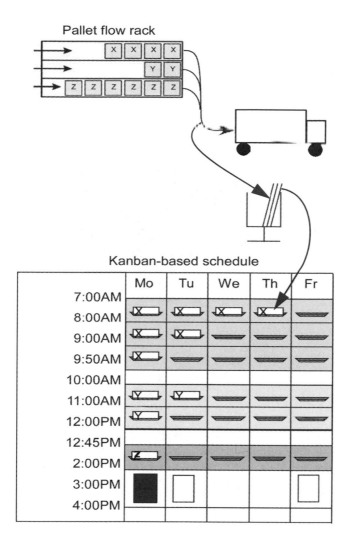

FIGURE 15-10. Schedule confirmation by Kanbans

Scheduling a Flexible Manufacturing System (FMS)

"Flexible Manufacturing Systems" (FMS) are used in machining parts for airplanes, semiconductor production equipment, and other low-volume–high-mix and tight tolerance applications. The key components of an FMS are shown in Figure 15-11.

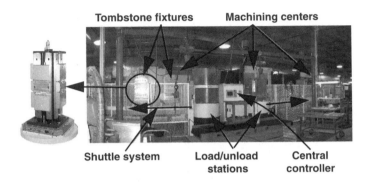

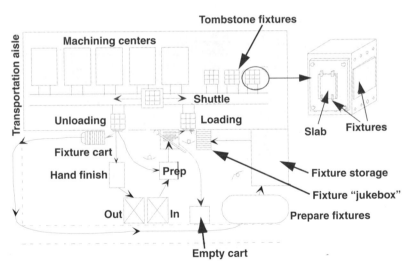

FIGURE 15-11. FMS example

The FMS in Figure 15-11 links five machining centers by a shuttle that routes tombstone pallets through one or more of the centers from a raw slab of metal to a machined part. There are many more items than tombstone faces, and fixtures are dismounted after each use to make room for different ones.

The loading station is like an assembly station. The fixtures are presented to the operator in vertical slots, in a sequence that matches that of the slabs, and oriented so that the operator can pull them from the slot and slide them on the tombstone without turning them. They are light enough to be hand-carried through this short distance, because most of the required strength and rigidity is provided by the tombstone. The raw slabs arrive sequenced and stored vertically in push carts. If they are light enough, the operators can pick them up by hand and mount them onto the fixtures. Otherwise, the preparation of the slab consists of drilling and tapping a tie-down hole at the top, which is then used to attach it to a jib crane at the loading station.

The machining centers all have the same tooling package, and the central controller routes parts automatically through the machining centers. At the unloading station, the parts are all light enough to be hand-carried. Those that require machining on the opposite side return to the loading station, while the others go to a hand-finishing area, where they may be knocked out of what remains of the slab on the periphery, straightened, and deburred. The fixture flow is designed to avoid interference with the part flow. In this case, the amount of WIP in the automatic system is controlled by the number of tombstones, not the number of fixtures. The main issue with fixtures is to have enough to accommodate the variety of items.

Assume the following:

1. This FMS is used to make 200 different items.
2. These items going into 7 products assembled nearby, at takt times ranging from 2 to 5 days.
3. The machining cycle time through the FMS averages 1 hour and ranges from 15 minutes to 3 hours.

The questions then are how to sequence the release of work into the FMS and how to respond to variations and glitches in the assembly process.

Here, a small number of aluminum slabs is transformed into a large number of machined parts, and smoothing the flow of these slabs to the FMS is not the major issue. The objective in this case is to release work into the FMS so that it finishes product sets at rates that match each assembled product's takt time, as shown in Figure 15-12.

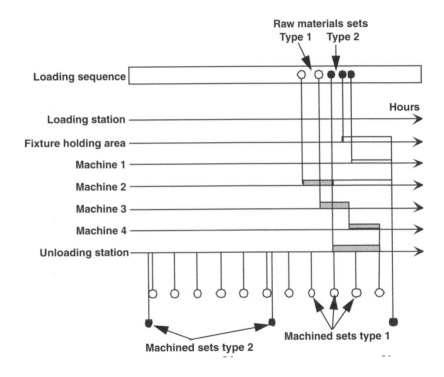

FIGURE 15-12. Objective of FMS release sequencing

Each product set has 20 to 30 parts that we want to finish machining about the same time but that undergo different machining processes. For a few parts, as in Figure 15-12, we can manually draw Gantt charts backwards from the end of the process to determine the start sequence, but it is not practical to do by hand for 200 items going into 7 sets.

First, for each set, we group the parts by process similarity, so that we can load tombstones with matching subsets of parts going into a single set rather than batches of identical parts going into multiple sets. This practice, shown in Figure 15-13, is not currently common among FMS users. It not only supports "one-set flow," but it reduces the problem of sequencing the 30 parts in a product set to 5 or 6 subsets.

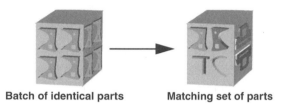

Batch of identical parts   Matching set of parts

FIGURE 15-13. Tombstone with matching set of parts

A solution here is to apply an off-the-shelf production simulator to an imaginary "reverse machining" process, which would be like a movie of the machining process shown backwards. In spirit, the idea is like the backwards explosion of demand done in MRP: starting from the desired result, you calculate what needs to happen before to make it possible. The difference is in the level of detail considered. Instead of the number of parts in the pipeline over time, we follow here each individual part through operation starts and completions, and movements between machines. The idea of reverse machining is illustrated in Figure 15-14.

If we enter sets of parts at takt intervals into the reverse process simulation and "unmachine" them in first-in–first-out (FIFO), then we obtain our start sequence by reversing the resulting sequence of slabs.

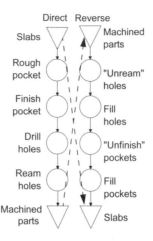

FIGURE 15-14. "Reverse machining" for sequencing

We can then, again, treat the assigned positions in the start sequence as reservations, to be confirmed by kanbans, keeping in minding that parts are pulled from the output buffer of the FMS in product sets but machined in subsets based on process similarity, as shown in Figure 15-15. The word "pitch" here is used with a different meaning than in Chapter 10, to designate the time it takes to cycle through the complete list of subsets in the sequence. The board needs to hold two pitches on sub-boards that can be interchanged when the top pitch is finished.

Through examples, we have seen different ways of scheduling different products through a line that needs to be set up between products in a variety of ways. While this is a common pattern, it is not universal and there are cases where lines, particularly in assembly, can be engineered to be able to switch between products with every unit. The next chapter shows how to take advantage of the opportunities this opens for sequencing and scheduling.

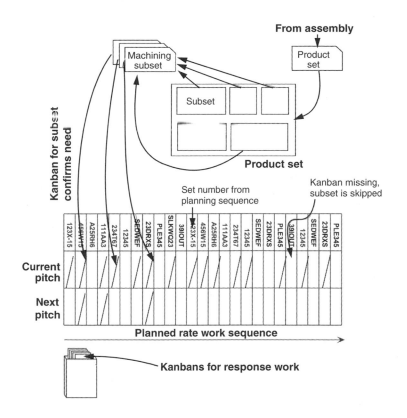

FIGURE 15-15. **FMS kanban board**

CHAPTER 16

Leveled sequencing of mixed-flow assembly

Summary

In mixed-flow assembly, setups between products are instantaneous, and successive units coming down the line can be for different products. Toyota does it for final assembly of cars, by shift, using sequencing algorithms that smooth the flows of thousands of incoming items. The simplest approach is to spread the shift quantity for each product over the length of the shift and drop these patterns onto a common timeline.

Strictly speaking, however, this only smooths the incoming flows if the products have no common parts, and products assembled in a mixed-flow line usually have common parts. Toyota's algorithm builds the sequence incrementally, by selecting for the next unit the product that generates the least deviation from a smooth consumption curve for the parts. While it is clearly as relevant in electronics or aerospace assembly as in the car industry, this method has yet to be implemented outside of Toyota and a few other car makers.

There are production lines, most commonly in final assembly, that can change between products with no downtime, and therefore can have production runs of a single unit. Outside of the automobile industry, manufacturers are just starting to take advantages of the opportunities this creates. This chapter discusses how it can be implemented and the main algorithms used to sequence products.

How leveled sequencing works with the pull system

The most elaborate form of leveled sequencing takes place in mixed-flow assembly when setups are instantaneous, either because the parts for all products are available on the line side at all times or because they have been kitted and sequenced off line. Figure 16-1 shows the high-level materials and information flows associated with this approach. Shown in black, the flows of materials are from the example of an approximation to takt-driven production in Figure 4-4 of *Lean Assembly*, in which the black dots represent single pieces moving to the next operation like clockwork at takt intervals and the other symbols represent the storage, transportation and testing steps the organization has not found a way to eliminate yet.

Production control receives daily demand data in the form of a master schedule from Production Planning, and real time updates on actual production from Final Test. It uses this data to generate a leveled sequence with algorithms that we will describe below. The leveled sequence is passed to the *pacemaker* station, usually the first station of final assembly, which commits itself to each unit in the sequence by actually starting it.

Communication between Production Control and the pacemaker goes both ways. Occasionally, the first station of final assembly does not have the materials needed to start the next unit in the sequence, in which case, consistent with the principle of not building cripples, it skips to the following one. The actual start sequence therefore has small variations from the calculated sequence. This is why body-on-sequence suppliers produce based on the *actual* start sequence. Upstream from the pacemaker, the flow of most components is managed through kanbans, and, as we have seen, this system adjusts automatically for small variations in demand.

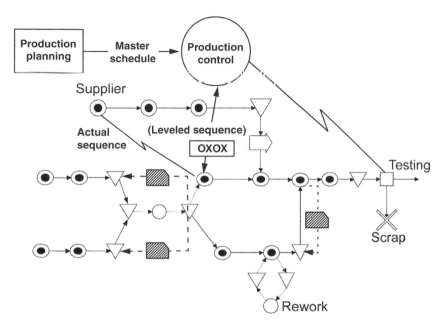

FIGURE 16-1. **Leveled sequencing in mixed-flow assembly**

Leveled sequencing method #1

The concept behind the simplest method for leveled sequencing is shown in Figure 16-2. The demand for a product over one shift, is spread evenly over the shift and then dropped onto the mixed-flow line's common time-line for the shift. It is focused on getting all the products out on their own takt times, and works perfectly *if the products have no common parts.*

If there are common parts, then, from the point of view of such a part, a sequence of units for products it goes into is equivalent to a run of identical units. Since the primary purpose of leveled sequencing is to smooth the flows of materials upstream from final assembly, a more sophisticated method is needed to do it in the presence of common parts.

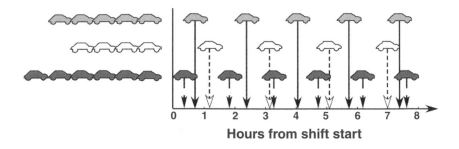

Hours from shift start

FIGURE 16-2. Leveled sequencing method 1 concept

Drawings similar to Figure 16-2 are commonly found in the literature,[1] but it is somewhat misleading because cars assembled on the same line do have many common parts, and this method alone would not yield a smooth consumption of these parts. Method 2, below, addresses these issues.

Suppose you are making three products called "Dot," "Square," and "Star," and that the master schedule is as shown in Table 16-1.

TABLE 16-1. Master schedule

Item	Quantity
Dot	10
Square	5
Star	7

Figure 16-3 shows how to apply method 1 with an electronic spreadsheet. You start with the shift demand by product. Then you list all the units you are going to make, assigning them a sequence number by product. When you divide that sequence number by the demand, it gives you the proportion of the cumulative total demand for each product represented by each unit. We add one to the demand rather than just the demand alone to keep

1. For example, see, "Kanban, Just-In-Time at Toyota," JMA, p. 54, Figure 11.

the last units for all products from scoring 100% and needing a tie breaker. Tie breakers may still be needed if different products have exactly the same demand. Then we sort all rows by increasing values of this ratio, which gives us the leveled sequence.

This simple method is used in some automotive and aerospace assembly applications, Figure 16-4 shows an example at Korry Electronics where the method was coded into internally developed software.

Unit	Rank	Rank/(Demand+1)	Unit	Rank/(Demand+1)
Dot	1	9%	Dot	9%
Dot	2	18%	Star	13%
Dot	3	27%	Square	17%
Dot	4	36%	Dot	18%
Dot	5	45%	Star	25%
Dot	6	55%	Dot	27%
Dot	7	64%	Square	33%
Dot	8	73%	Dot	36%
Dot	9	82%	Star	38%
Dot	10	91%	Dot	45%
Square	1	17%	Square	50%
Square	2	33%	Star	50%
Square	3	50%	Dot	55%
Square	4	67%	Star	63%
Square	5	83%	Dot	64%
Star	1	13%	Square	67%
Star	2	25%	Dot	73%
Star	3	38%	Star	75%
Star	4	50%	Dot	82%
Star	5	63%	Square	83%
Star	6	75%	Star	88%
Star	7	88%	Dot	91%

FIGURE 16-3. Sequencing three products with Excel

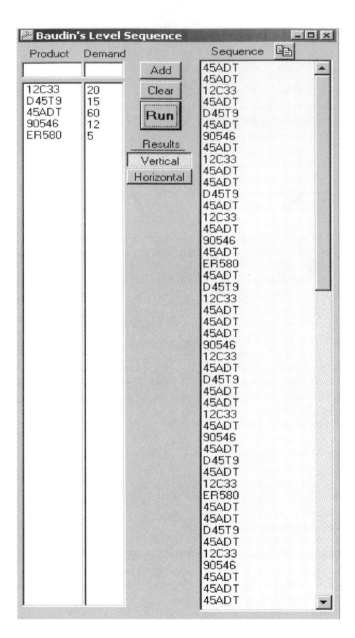

FIGURE 16-4. Leveled sequencing at Korry Electronics

Leveled sequencing method #2

The second method is designed to smooth the consumption of a set of parts. It is iterative. For each part, the diagonal line is the ideal cumulative consumption through the shift, and the purple staircase line is the cumulative consumption of each part based on the sequence already decided and on the impact of each candidate to be the next item.

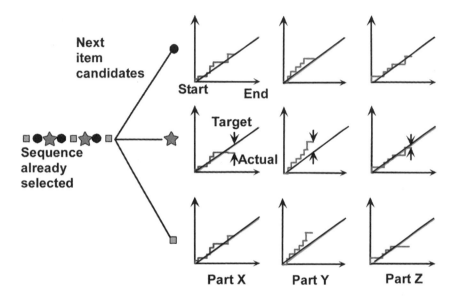

FIGURE 16-5. Leveled sequencing method 2 concept

For each candidate product to be the next item on the list, examine how far it takes the actual cumulative consumption from the straight line ideal for each part in the set. Then select the product giving the least overall deviation.

This algorithm is described in detail in Monden's *The Toyota Production System*. The measure of deviation from the smooth target line to the actual consumption staircase is the square of the difference, summed over all the parts in consideration, and the selected product can be viewed as a least-squares fit. Over time, Toyota has refined this method by adding rules to control the interval between identical vehicles.

Although leveled sequencing is described in the lean manufacturing literature, it is not widely practiced outside of Toyota and a few other car companies. As discussed in Chapter 8 of *Lean Assembly*, assembly managers often see it as a major change whose value they fail to see, because it targets the upstream supply chain rather than their area of responsibility. Leveled sequencing is not addressed in the logistics literature, where the bullwhip effect is described. Toyota's experience, however, shows that it is an effective tool in fighting the bullwhip effect.

The next chapter goes one more level up in the stack of information processing functions, by examining the systems that turn the raw flow of customer orders and market information into master schedules that can be subjected to the detailed sequencing and scheduling described in the last two chapters.

CHAPTER 17

Production planning and forecasting

Summary

Even in a lean plant, the flow of orders needs to be combined with forecasts and filtered into a demand to support leveled sequencing and pull systems. Factories also need to plan shift patterns, staffing levels and overtime, and equipment acquisition, as well as help suppliers anticipate future volumes.

The monthly planning process involves both number crunching and human judgment, for which Tom Wallace has proposed a managerial process called "Sales and Operations Planning" (S&OP) involving iterations and resulting in aggregate plans at the product family level. Toyota generates a master production schedule subject to alterations based on dealer orders up to four days before roll-off, and leveled sequences are calculated two days later.

Forecasting involves not only historical sales data but market intelligence from multiple channels. It is best done at an aggregate level, and requires an objectivity found in goal-driven business organizations. Data analysis should be focused first on visualization techniques, eventually supplemented by forecasting software implementing time-series models.

Customer-supplier agreements in a lean supply chain includes compensation to suppliers when the customer issues forecasts that consistently exceed actual demand. The Sales/ Customer Service organization that receives orders needs to detect patterns that can be used to smooth internal flows, and to negotiate more even delivery schedules with customers.

Chapter 16 was focused on *mix* issues, and on how different items should be sequenced through a production process in order to smooth the flows of materials, assuming a stable aggregate demand. In many plants, however, the flow of customer orders seems chaotic, and first needs to be filtered into a demand placed on production that is sufficiently stable for the combination of leveled sequencing and pull systems to work, while making and keeping promises that are attractive to customers. This chapter describes several approaches used for this purpose.

Planning objectives

Orders from multiple customers for multiple products fluctuate, sometimes exceeding the capacity of the line, and sometimes leaving ample slack time. While lean manufacturing is about responding to customer demand, the approach is not to pass the unfiltered flow of orders straight through to the manufacturing floor. It is a misleading simplification to say that lean manufacturing is producing "to the pull of the customer." Much massaging and filtering of customer demand is needed to schedule final assembly operations in a way that supports pulling parts from the supply chain.

Figure 17-1 shows the intended result. On the right side, firm orders for regularly made items are smoothed into daily rates and supplemented with forecasts for the longer term, with time set aside for "Other" demands.

Generating and updating a leveled production plan with 20 production lines and 500 products and not just for the next four weeks but for the next three to six months is a daunting task, that must be taken on in some fashion in order to support such decisions as:

- Adjusting work time, by adding or cancelling overtime, or changing the shift pattern.
- Acquiring new equipment or setting up new production lines.
- Providing suppliers with input to their own planning process.

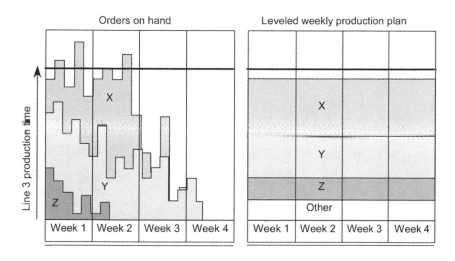

FIGURE 17-1. From flow of orders to leveled plan

Figure 17-2 shows the information ideal flows in production planning and forecasting. It is not a complete picture, particularly because it does not include the exception handling that accounts for much of the information exchange between customers and suppliers. It also does not show planned versus actual reporting or supplier performance monitoring. It is only one of many patterns that may be applicable in a particular manufacturing business. It shows Kanbans being used with suppliers and customers. If they are used in house as well, a complete diagram would also show how Production Control issues and tracks the cards.

Much of Figure 17-2 is similar to what is done in ERP/MRP. In fact, ERP software is used to implement these flows, the major difference with classical MRP implementations being in the way the data is used, for forecasting material requirements rather than to drive operations.

The complexity of the actual processes in hidden in Figure 17-2. "Forecasting," for example, covers both calculations and human judgment. While sales history data can be fed to an algorithm, the other inputs are more complex.

FIGURE 17-2. Planning and forecasting information flows

Customers' product requirement forecasts, for example, are issued by people working for other organizations and with varying skill levels. One dealer may systematically overestimate future demand, while another has the opposite bias and routinely sells more than expected. Market intelligence includes industry forecasts in trade publications, general economic forecasts, monetary policy decisions by the central bank, war and peace, and events like earthquakes, floods or hurricanes that may affect buyer behavior in the near future.

"Complementor" is a term coined by Brandenburger & Nalebuff[1] designating business entities that increase the value of a company's products to its customers. Oil refiners, gas distributors and road builders are complementors to the car industry; software developers, to the computer industry. Companies that are each other's complementors have common interests, and commonly share their assessments of the future. But here again, there is more to interpreting complementors' forecasts than crunching numbers.

After being passed on to Production Control, the resulting demand forecast is subjected to a backwards explosion based on bills of materials and routings, and the resulting information is shown as used in two ways:

- To issue materials requirements forecasts to suppliers.
- To size blanket purchase orders (POs) that provide the commercial framework for ordering from suppliers through kanbans.

In Figure 17-2, this is shown as Forecasting and Purchasing processes using the same output from Production Control. Both of these communications are usually handled by Purchasing, but we separate them to emphasize their differences, particularly in terms of responsibilities with respect to the suppliers. While a blanket PO simply records agreed terms and conditions, a forecast is an input to business decisions that may be costly to the supplier.

On the Sales side, routine processing of customer kanbans and EDI orders can be automated, but the negotiation of terms and conditions and order priorities cannot be. The pull systems, leveled sequencing and the FIFO discipline do not allow priority games to be played with WIP, but it is different *before* orders are released for production.

As discussed in Chapter 14, once an order is on the shop floor, it is no longer just data but involves materials, tooling and people committed to its execution. As long as it is only data, Sales can move it to the back or the front of the queue and negotiate fulfillment lead times or phased deliveries on exceptional orders as it sees fit for the best interest of the company.

Production Control has the most data-intensive role and effectiveness hinges on the maintenance of accurate inventory data through production

---

1. Co-opetition, A. Brandenburger & B. Nalebuff, Doubleday (1996)

transaction processing, supported by visible management and cycle counting, as discussed in Chapter 5, as well as accurate bill of materials and capacity data through engineering.

The kanbans flowing from Customers and to Suppliers are orders that do not need to transit through Sales or Purchasing because they occur within agreed frameworks set in blanket POs.

Drilling down from monthly to daily planning

The pattern in Figure 17-2 is complex, and many factories simply attempt to respond to the daily flow of orders without giving their suppliers any heads up about the future or even anticipating it for themselves. The companies that do simplify the problem by doing the following:

- Consider aggregate volumes for product families.
- Rely on the management structure to provide accurate data.

The question from corporate to the plant may be formulated as, for example, "Can you increase production from 1,000 to 1,200 motors/day?" The plant manager then passes the question on to product line managers, assuming that being responsible for implementing the change will motivate them to provide workable answers. The end result is a series of what-if analyses performed by product line engineers usually on electronic spreadsheets, and occasionally with production simulators.

Tom Wallace[1] has been promoting a specific approach for a periodic planning exercise, which he calls "Sales and Operations Planning" (S&OP). It is typically a monthly review of the business plan in light of new information about the demand and any changes that may have occurred or that need to be made in operations. A monthly meeting of affected managers is the normal venue for this decision-making process. It is based on data, but also reflects the managers' judgment The flows of information in S&OP are shown in Figure 17-3, with the output of the process in red.

---

1. *Sales and Operations Planning*, Tom Wallace, T. Wallace & Co. (1999)

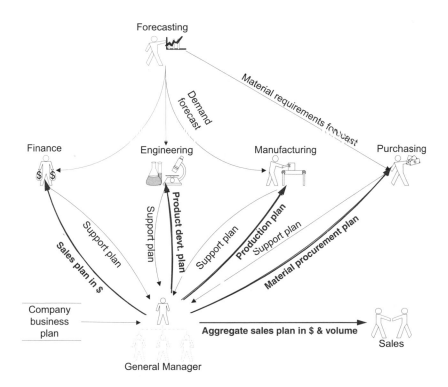

FIGURE 17-3. Sales and Operations Planning overview

S&OP is started by the issuance of a demand forecast. It is reviewed by all the key managers, who propose to the general manager of the business unit their planned response. The general manager reviews these support plans with the approved business plan and budget, and, after possibly several iterations with the managers, convenes a meeting in which the plan is agreed upon and becomes effective.

It is a manual process, conducted at the product family level, that relies on each manager's understanding of the capabilities and capacity of his or her organization, and does not require technology beyond an electronic spreadsheet, as shown in Figure 17-4.

Sales and Operations Plan for October, 2002

Product family: XYZ filters
Target line utilization: 95%

Unit of measure: 1,000 pieces
Target inventory: 10 days

		History			Next six months						Following qrtrs		Year summary:		
													12-mth	Year	Bus.
Sales		Jul	Aug	Sep	Oct	Nov	Dec	Jan	Feb	Mar	Q2	Q3	total	Rev.	plan
	Forecast	50	50	50	50	50	50	50	50	50	150	150	600	$38M	$38M
	Actual sales	51	51	49											
Differences															
	Monthly	1	1	-1											
	Cumulative	1	2	1											
Operations															
	Plan	50	50	50	50	50	50	50	50	50	150	150			
	Actual	49	51	50											
Differences															
	Monthly	-1	1	0											
	Cumulative	-1	0	0											
Inventory															
	Plan	25	25	25	25	25	25	25	25	25	25	25			
	Actual	23	23	24											
	Days on hand	10	10	10	11	11	11	11	11	11	11	11			
	Line utilization	89%	93%	91%											

Demand issues	Supply issues
1. Impact of model change in Oct.	1. New machines installed in Nov.
2. Upturn expected in Europe	2. Labor issues at supplier X
3. ...	3. ...

FIGURE 17-4. Sales and Operations Plan example

Why is the monthly planning process a negotiation between people when, conceptually, it should be a calculation? The scheduling of a cell during a shift is based on hard numbers that are known to production team leaders and supervisors. A machine tool may take one work piece at a time every 53 seconds, a sealant may take 24 hours to cure, and changing these numbers takes a process engineering project.

Logically, the numbers should be usable for monthly planning of an entire product line or even factory, but it would require them to be available in a central database, together with the operating policies of each production team and advanced planning and scheduling software (APS). Not only is it technically difficult, but first line managers prefer to retain local control of detailed capacities and only share with top management a summary in the form of generic units per day or at best a takt time at which they can run a mixed-flow line. As a consequence, the capacity numbers used in monthly planning are *soft*.

It is not uncommon for general managers to ask the managers of production lines that are "100% utilized" to increase production by 20% next month without any additional resources, and for production managers to agree and deliver. On the one side, the general managers want to challenge production with stretch goals; on the other, the production managers anticipate this kind of request by not being completely forthcoming about capacity. This is a context in which sophisticated optimization algorithms are irrelevant. Even though capacity is more visible in a lean manufacturing plant, planning at this level remains a negotiation.

S&OP is not part of monthly planning within the Toyota Production System (TPS), as described by Monden,[1] but the TPS approach is specific to automobile assembly. Like S&OP, it starts from 3-month forecasts that are reviewed by multiple stakeholders, but the outputs are more detailed than in Figure 17-4.

First, forecast quantities for the next month are turned into daily going rates by model and major options, such as body type, engine size, or trim level, which is Toyota's version of a *master production schedule*, and is used as follows:

- As input to the calculation of the materials requirements forecast passed on to suppliers.
- As the basis for short-term capacity adjustments.
- As input to the sizing of stocks of painted bodies and engine/transmission assemblies.

The information in the master production schedule, however, is neither complete nor timely enough to drive production. It is refined through 10-day orders submitted by dealers a week in advance and subject to limited alteration up to 4 days before a car rolls off the assembly line. The final daily quantities with all option details pass from sales to production control 3 days before roll-off, and the leveled sequences are calculated 2 days before roll-off.

On the one hand, we have S&OP, which is a generic process applicable to any manufacturing activity. On the other hand, we have the TPS approach,

---

1. Y. Monden, Toyota Production System, Chapter 5, IIE (1994)

which is specific to car assembly. In a lean manufacturing environment other than car assembly, a reasonable approach is to start from S&OP and add industry specifics consistent with the spirit of the TPS approach but using different quantities and time frames as needed.

Forecasting

Forecasting is not easy, and even the best make mistakes. As of April, 2004, the Toyota Prius in the United States has a waiting list of 3 to 6 months, which means that the company has failed to anticipate the model's popularity. Forecasting is in fact so difficult that many managers won't even try, but they should. We have no choice but to attempt to forecast key business decisions that rely on our expectations for the future and to assist suppliers, who depend on our input for their own forecasts. While forecasting is intrinsically difficult, many practices of mass production companies make it even harder. Being lean does not *guarantee* that you will always read the future correctly, but it gives you better visibility, reduces the effect of your mistakes, and makes them easier to rectify.

Market intelligence

In general, the collection of information about customers is a marketing function, outside the scope of this book. The discussion here is limited to a few examples of techniques that some companies have used to improve market intelligence and grow sales consistently, a benefit that far outweighs the cost reductions achieved concurrently.

Example 1: Using kanbans to boost sales of foreign books in Japan. In 1980, a distributor[1] of foreign books in Japan, having heard of the kanban system, decided to adapt it to his business. Originally, his practice was to order large quantities of books around university semester breaks, when the students of foreign languages would presumably buy the books they needed for the next term. He started sending smaller shipments to bookstores with kanbans inside each book, and reordering continuously the

---

1. Marcel Giuglaris, personal communication, 1980.

books that sold. Within 9 months, his sales volume had doubled, and sales took place at all times, rather than twice a year.

Example 2: Forecasting airline reservations. Today, electronic commerce —be it EDI for business-to-business transactions or online stores for consumers—has created new opportunities for the automatic collection of market intelligence that most manufacturers have yet to exploit. Airlines are not manufacturing companies, but they have been pioneers in this area since the early 80s with their reservation systems, and their accomplishments point the way.

American Airlines' SABRE reservation system, introduced to travel agents in 1975, processed about 100 transactions/second by 1980, and became such an overwhelming competitive advantage that American Airlines was eventually forced to make it "airline neutral" and spin it off as a separate company in 1993. SABRE's success also propelled information systems manager Robert Crandall to the top management of American Airlines. SABRE today is accessible to consumers through on-line services like Travelocity or Expedia. The transaction processing system feeds analytical engines that modify tens of thousands of fares every day with the goal of profitably filling airplanes. Dell is the only major American *manufacturing* company that comes to mind as having achieved anything similar.

Example 3: Toyota's Gazoo internet portal. In 2000, Toyota launched its own internet portal named "Gazoo." This was a major initiative, directly supported by CEO Fujio Cho. Gazoo not only provides information about new Toyota cars, but also about used cars in dealerships throughout Japan, hotels and other travel information, access to shopping for non-automotive products, and finally access to the Internet at large.

Other car makers do not provide on-line information about such topics as *used* car prices. Even Toyota only does this in Japan. What is the motivation? In its early days, Toyota sold cars in Japan *door to door*, and its sales reps knew from neighborhood gossip when a Toyota owner had been promoted and was ready to trade up. This method was later abandoned as too expensive, but it had the advantage of providing much better market intelligence than the dealership system.

Dealers buffer car makers against market fluctuations, but not only do they prevent direct contact with end users but consumers' interactions with dealers are usually limited to haggling. Gazoo is indirect marketing, like the Michelin guides. On-line auctions are to cars as restaurant reviews are to tires: unrelated but nonetheless bonding the consumer to the supplier. Michelin guides, however, are a one-way communication. Gazoo, on the other hand, makes consumers communicate with Toyota by registering and navigating through the site.

Example 4: Homecomings. Homecomings are another method used by manufacturers of products sold through dealers to make *direct* contact with end users. In the United States, this was pioneered by Honda in its motorcycle operations, and later adopted by Saturn for cars. Owners are invited to a party and factory visit which allow product units to "return" where they were made. Honda's homecomings attract about 8,000 bikers to Marysville, OH every year. Saturn attracted about 30,000 drivers in 1994 and 44,500 in 1999. This approach is only possible for products that users are emotional about. Bikers have a bond with their machines and like to congregate; car drivers are less so but can be made to feel that there is something special about their cars. Homecomings would be difficult to imagine for dishwashers or light bulbs.

Homecoming attendees are a self-selected group of users who feel strongly enough about the product to spend vacation time meeting the people who built it. They are not representative of the whole user population. The trend in the number of attendees over time is nonetheless an indication of the rising or waning popularity of the product. User input is also likely to be richer when coming from knowledgeable aficionados than from the general user population.

Analysis issues

Gathering market intelligence is only the first step; you must then extract useful information from this data. Without discussing all the possible analysis techniques, this section describes four general principles on how this activity should be carried out.

Principle 1: Aggregate! The total number of cars and trucks that will be sold in the United States next year is easier to forecast than the number of red coupes with beige seats or the number of 120MB hard disks that will be bought by a particular computer assembler. The larger the number of products in a family and the larger the number of independent buyers, the more laws of large numbers apply and the easier it is to anticipate aggregate demand.

This impacts the structure of the supply chain., allowing the common components of a product family to be made cheaper and with a longer lead time than model and option-specific parts. A mass-customization supplier of messenger bags and briefcases like Timbuk2 Designs buys common components like pen holders and inside pockets from China, but cuts and sews custom, designed-to-order bags in San Francisco. As discussed in Chapter 7, NUMMI receives common parts from a consolidation center in the Chicago area with a 7- to 10-day lead time, and model and option-specific parts from local suppliers with a 220-minute lead time.

Principle 2: Analyze sales history. Past sales numbers are the first source of data. If sales have been increasing on the average of 1%/month for the past two years, it is reasonable to expect that they will do that again next month. If they have dropped by 20% in January every year for the past five years, it is reasonable to expect that they will again next January.

There are of course limits to this extrapolation approach. For example, new products with pent-up demand are characterized by rapid growth in sales followed by a brutal decline once the market is saturated. All sorts of external events, such as wars, floods, stock market crashes, etc. also have an impact on the demand that cannot be anticipated simply from data on past demand. Manufacturing activity is also affected by internal initiatives, such as promotional campaigns, or strategic decisions to terminate products.

Principle 3: Maintain objectivity. Many managers confuse forecasts with goals, and drive their subordinates with statements like "We must sell $15M of widgets next month." The subordinates then have no choice but to produce forecasts with sales adding up to that number. By forcing the numbers to match their needs or wishes, however, the managers are depriving themselves of information they could put to use. The employees who produce forecasts can be rated on the accuracy of these forecasts, but shouldn't be on the basis of whether their forecasts represent good or bad news. Sales reps want the numbers to be high, and so cannot be objective.

Objectivity is the number one requirement for good forecasting, but is harder to come by than one would expect it to be. This is based on an actual example, where the forecast was based on management's insistence that the next month's sales be $1M. Since long-term orders added up to $520K, the only way to make the numbers add up to the figure the boss wanted was to forecast $480K for turns.

Since turns are small orders received from a large base of customers, they lend themselves to trend analysis, as shown in Figure 17-5. In a few minutes, a least-squares fit of a straight line to the past 18 months of data yielded a forecast of $350K ± $50K. The following month, turns came in at $360K. Unsurprisingly, even a crude analysis of historical data outperformed wishful thinking.

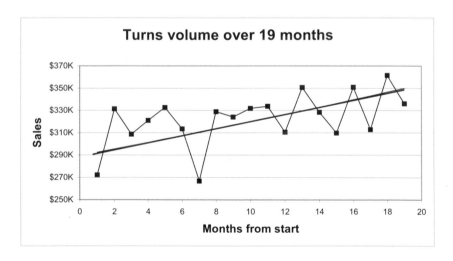

FIGURE 17-5. Trend analysis on turns volume

Principle 4: Use visualizations to identify patterns. The analysis of historical sales data does not always require advanced mathematics. Often, as in

Figure 17-6, a simple time series plot of sales volumes can reveal a pattern that the manufacturer was not aware of. The production manager felt that the demand for this product was unpredictable, but the plot showed sharp peaks occurring like clockwork every two weeks. Further investigation revealed that the peaks were all due to orders placed by the same distributor, while orders from all other customers formed a steady background noise.

There are several possible responses to such a discovery. The supplier can offer the distributor a price reduction in exchange for smoothing away the peak by using a different order and delivery pattern, or, if the distributor refuses, make the product to stock in anticipation of the peak.

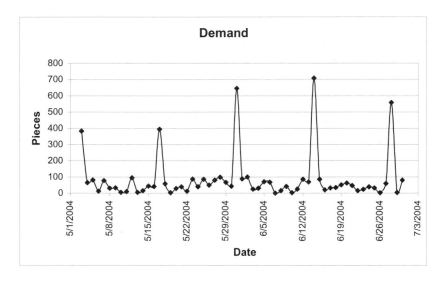

FIGURE 17-6. A demand pattern

Generally, techniques that do not require sophisticated mathematics should be used in priority. With the exception of Edward Tufte,[1] academic

---

1. *The visual display of quantitative information*, E. Tufte, Graphics Press (1983) and other works.

statisticians pay little attention to the "descriptive statistics" that do not use probabilistic models.

Forecasting software[1] implementing sophisticated time series analysis is now available to decompose a series of historical sales data into multiple components reflecting the following:

- A long-term trend
- Seasonal variations
- Business cycles
- Fluctuations

These tools clearly have the potential to improve a manufacturing organization's forecasting ability, both short and long term, but they are no substitute for judgment, require training to set up and interpret the output properly, and do not relieve individuals and organizations of responsibility for their final answers.

Communication of forecasts to suppliers

As shown in Figure 17-2, the demand forecast is converted using MRP into a materials requirements forecast for communication to suppliers. In Japan, however, the term used to describe these documents does not translate to "forecast" but to "delivery notification," indicating that, while being less than orders, they are more than just estimates.

These forecasts can be updated daily, but the scope of the allowed changes is restricted by contract between the supplier and the customer to be within bounds such as are shown in Figure 17-7.

A "frozen forecast," however, is a contradiction in terms. A forecast is an estimate of the future, and events occur in the economic environment that can change our estimates of demand over the next two weeks.

---

1. Business forecasting, J. Wilson et al., McGraw Hill, (2002)

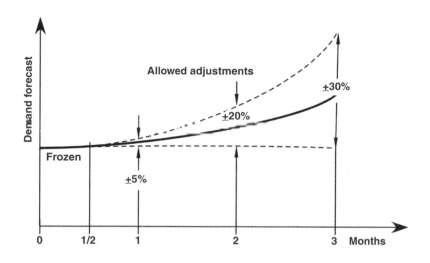

FIGURE 17-7. Example of bounds on forecast updates

Even assuming that the contract has been negotiated so as to allow "thawing" the forecast in response to war, hurricanes, or stock market crashes, the question remains of the nature of the commitment made by the customer when issuing the forecast. Orders come in the form of pull signals, the forecasts are not orders, and the customer is not promising to buy the forecast quantity, even during the frozen period.

In Japan, these contracts typically include sanctions for getting the forecasts consistently wrong. For example, it may stipulate that the customer will not incur a penalty if the forecasts cause the supplier to overproduce for up to two months running, but must buy the overbuild if the forecast is wrong again for a third month. The documents passed on to suppliers are therefore more than just for-your-information estimates with no responsibility assumed, while being less than commercially binding orders.

Involvement of sales and customer service

Figure 17-2 only shows the routine transactions associated with order entry. In many companies, these are executed by a group called "Customer Service" rather than Sales, which is focused on securing new customers and negotiating contracts.

Besides making a manufacturer competitive in price, delivery, and quality, the practice of lean manufacturing also allows suppliers to become "lean certified" by customers who require it and to respond faster to requests for sample quantities of new products, which then lead to new long-term contracts. While thus creating new selling opportunities, lean manufacturing also requires Sales to assist in setting appropriate delivery terms, as in the example of Figure 17-6.

Whether they are OEMs, distributors, dealers, or consumers, customers decide how they order. They may or may not provide any forecasts, and the suppliers' finished goods inventory or capacity utilization status are not their concern. Their expectation is simply that the supplier will promptly deliver whatever product in whatever quantity they ask for and that its quality will be perfect.

The sales reps then have a key role to play in deciding whether the customer can be profitably serviced, and if so, whether to approach his purchasing organization to change delivery terms in a way that is beneficial to both sides. The ability to do this depends of course on leverage: it is easier to be heard from the other side when selling microprocessors to computer assemblers than gaskets to the auto industry, and when working with exclusive dealers than with distributors. As discussed in Chapter 19, it is often practically impossible for customers and suppliers to make changes even though these changes would benefit both.

In many situations, the variability in order volume and timing is due to the bullwhip effect: the underlying demand is stable, but disrupted by idiosyncrasies of the customer's ordering system and of the distribution chain. In Figure 17-6, it is unlikely that the distributor sells nothing for two weeks and then 400 to 600 units in the same day. Instead, the distributor's system only reviews the status of this item every two weeks and orders the quantity required to bring the stock up to a given level.

Figure 17-8 shows this demand pattern over one year, and the finished goods stocks that would result if the production plan were set as follows:

1. Dedicate resources to this product with the capacity to make 100 pieces/day.
2. Allocate storage space for 1600 pieces of finished goods.
3. Build a safety stock of 275 pieces.
4. Set the production rate to the average daily demand of 86.

This policy allows steady production to meet a steady underlying demand, and concentrates the costs due to the largest customer's ordering method in the finished goods stocks. If daily shipments can be set up without driving up shipping costs, the finished goods stock can be reduced by at least 90%. This happens, for example, if the distributor sells many of the manufacturer's products and a full mix-loaded truck can be sent daily, or if the distributor sets up a milk run including a stop at the manufacturer's plant. One way to motivate the distributor is to share the savings generated by the reduction in finished goods stocks.

In other situations the demand that is intrinsically unstable, and its fluctuations are not due to the bullwhip effect. The rapidly growing semiconductor industry is subject to alternations of boom and bust that are amplified in the semiconductor *equipment* industry and its suppliers. It is not uncommon for machine shops making parts for this equipment to see the demand double or vanish overnight. In this case, there is no point in trying to negotiate the ordering pattern with customers. What companies in this predicament do instead is mitigate their risk by diversifying into more stable industries, like automotive or aerospace, and making second-sourcing agreements with competitors to provide surge capacity.

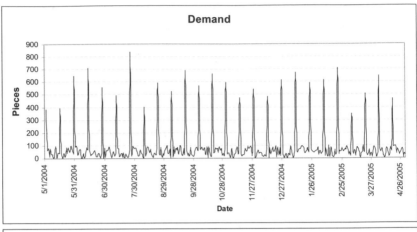

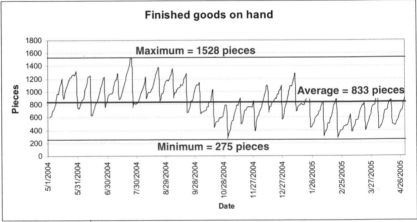

FIGURE 17-8. Constant production response to bimonthly large orders

This chapter concludes the discussion of logistics information flows. The flows of materials and information described in Parts II to IV of this book occur within a framework of supplier–customer relationships, and the upcoming Part V is dedicated to aspects of these business arrangements that are special to the lean enterprise.

PART V

Business relationships in a supply network

Which describes the challenges in outsourcing logistics services and moving supplier–customer relationships from an adversarial model to a collaborative one.

CHAPTER 18

Third-party logistics

Summary

Third-party logistics (3PL) involves the outsourcing of many logistics services beyond transportation, including fleet management, network design, EDI, materials handling, traffic management, and even supplier management. Started as an industry in the United States, 3PL is now used by most manufacturing companies in the United States, Europe, and Asia. Toyota uses it in North America and Europe, but not in Japan.

3PL is a special case of outsourcing, and manufacturers usually turn to it when the objectives of limiting their investments and reducing their costs take priority over control. Political considerations sometimes play a part as well, when a foreign company uses 3PL to engage and transfer know-how to local businesses, and thereby build a reputation for good corporate citizenship.

The availability of 3PL is not a foregone conclusion, particularly in emerging economies. In such cases, manufacturers have been known to either help local transporters grow into 3PL, or to spin off their internal logistics function. 3PL providers can take on most logistics tasks, but should not be used where product knowledge is required, as is the case in kitting parts for assembly, checking quality, or performing last-minute customization.

Defining third-party logistics (3PL)

Third-party logistics (3PL) providers do not make, consume, or sell materials but render logistics services to companies that do.

Perceptions of the scope of 3PL vary greatly. Tanimoto's[1] view is that a 3PL provider plans, manages, and coordinates logistics but does not execute. In this view, 3PL providers have computers, faxes, and phones, but no trucks or warehouses. This is not the way most U.S.-based 3PL providers advertise their services. They present themselves instead as offering logistics services *in addition to* transportation. For example, Transfreight is a 3PL provider to Toyota in the United States and Europe, started in 1989 as a joint venture between the Mitsui general trading company and TNT Logistics, and it advertises the following services:

- *Fleet Management.* Providing and managing vehicles and drivers.
- *Engineering.* Designing logistics services for clients.
- *Material control.* Providing an information system for EDI, exception reporting, and receiving management.
- *Materials handling.* Sequencing, repacking, and consolidation through cross docking.
- *Route and traffic management.* Dispatching drivers on routes, and providing a system for real-time tracking and tracing by customers.
- *Supplier management.* Working with suppliers on pickup times, conformance issues, and requirements for returnable containers and production materials, and training on lean manufacturing as needed.
- *Transportation management.* Transportation services supplement the 3PL's fleet with partner carriers like TST Expedited Services in Canada.

While Transfreight does not include *warehousing* in the list, other 3PL providers do. Kuehne & Nagel, for example, operates 70 distribution centers in the United States that can be used by multiple clients. These 3PL providers have their own resources, and supplement them through partners as needed.

---

1. *Butsu ryu-Logistics no riron to jittai*, Taniichi Tanimoto, Hakutoshobo (2000)

As soon as an acronym like 3PL gained currency, it was only a matter of time before one-upmanship led to the emergence of a "4PL," a term that has been both coined and trademarked by consulting firm Accenture. In Accenture terms, a 4PL provider assembles the resources, capabilities, and technology of its own organization and other organizations to design, build, and run comprehensive supply chain solutions. The difference with what we have been discussing above as 3PL is not obvious, and neither is the need for another middleman.

General Motors is a user and part owner of a 4PL provider called Vector SCM. Vector SCM is allied with 3PL provider Menlo Worldwide Logistics. The differences in activities between these two companies is reflected in Vector SCM's having a few hundred employees, to Menlo Worldwide's thousands.

How 3PL affects lean logistics

As of the end of 2003,[1] 3PL was used to some extent by the majority of manufacturing companies in the United States, Europe, and Asia. 3PL as an industry originated in the United States, but it has successfully spread to the main centers of manufacturing worldwide and is still growing.

3PL is not an original part of the Toyota production system, but, while Toyota still does not use it in Japan, it has embraced it in North America and in Europe, and, in fact, 3PL companies have been started for the specific purpose of serving Toyota in these markets. In all these cases, Toyota has given the 3PL providers special training in lean logistics. In Japan, on the other hand, Toyota relies on suppliers to deliver parts, and on a subsidiary called Toyota Yusou for delivering cars to dealers.

Besides the above-mentioned Transfreight, 3PL providers to Toyota include the following:

---

1. *Third Party Logistics, Results and Findings of the 2003 Eighth Annual Study*, John C. Langley et al., Georgia Tech (2003)

- VASCOR, a joint venture of APL Logistics and Fujitrans Corp. based in Georgetown, KY.

- ALUK (Automotive Logistics UK), a joint venture of Exel Logistics, Frans Maas, Mitsui and Fujuki started in 1988 to support Toyota in the UK and Europe.[1]

3PL: special case of outsourcing

The most common philosophy is that a company should eventually outsource all activities except those based on its "core competencies" or "core technology." What these core competencies are, however, is not always easy to identify.

Some cases are straightforward, such as the following:

- If you are assembling airplanes, then feeding lunch to employees is not a core competency, doing it internally is a distraction, and most companies use catering services instead if available.

- Intel is turning raw silicon into microprocessors, using multibillion dollar wafer fabrication plants, and may well consider that inbound and outbound logistics are not part of its core competency.

- Dell assembles custom computers in high volume with short order fulfillment lead times. Logistics is obviously a core competency for Dell, as is widely recognized.

Others are not so obvious. For example, most automakers count stamping floors, hoods, doors, and other major components of car bodies among their core technologies. But what about the use of small presses on the side to make bracketry? It can be argued that it is an additional application of the same technology and should stay in house, or that it distracts from the focus on large body parts and should be outsourced.

---

1. Distribution (www.dmg.co.uk/distribution), October 1994.

One view of a core technology is that it is an area of the business where no competitor outperforms you. Practically, however, this information may be difficult to obtain. In addition, this view is based on the incorrect assumption that a company could not exist if, for every operation, there were at least one competitor doing it better. You can outperform competitors by integrating the operations better, while underperforming some competitor at every unit operation.

Even if you establish that logistics is a core competency, it does not necessarily follow that you keep it in house. The logistics expertise of Toyota or Dell does not prevent them from outsourcing many logistics-related activities and a substantial part of their expertise is in fact in the management of external providers.

In the absence of a clear definition of a core technology or a core competency, it ends up being whatever management decides to keep in house. In other words, more specific, operational criteria have to be used to make these decisions.

Outsourcing is usually done to avoid investment or to reduce costs. Temporary peaks in activity or emergency response do not justify an investment in permanent resources and are usually addressed by bringing in third parties. More generally, the costs of using third parties are variable, which reduces the company's vulnerability to business cycles and ensures it never has to pay for empty warehouses and idle trucks.

In addition, even in stable businesses, management often concludes that outsourcing is cheaper than in-house production. This is not an easy analysis to make because it involves comparing prices paid to outside providers that are cash outflows with internal costs that include allocations over time for durable assets and among activities for shared resources. Rightly or wrongly, these "make-versus-buy" analyses are carried out and result in decisions to outsource *for the purpose of reducing costs*.

On the other hand, when work is brought in house, the motivation is usually not to get it done cheaper but to control it better. Boeing had been buying machined parts from the Iron Fireman company of Portland, OR for decades when it acquired it in 1974 and turned it into Boeing Portland.

Extending Boeing's benefits to Iron Fireman employees increased costs, but the acquisition enabled Boeing to make sure that the resources of the plant were used exclusively for its benefit.

Compared to the use of one's own trucks and drivers to pick up parts on milk runs to suppliers, the use of 3PL implies a loss of control in several regards, as in the following examples:

- *Returnable container management.* Suppliers using returnable containers with customers report increased occurrences of misrouted or damaged containers when their return is performed by a 3PL provider rather than the customer.

- *Supplier communications.* Every visit by a truck to pick up parts from a supplier is an opportunity for the customer to communicate expectations and receive status information from the supplier, which is lost with 3PL.

Where to use 3PL

For 3PL to be a viable option, it must be desirable for economic or political reasons, businesses offering 3PL must be available in the area, and the outsourced services must not require product knowledge. The following sections elaborate on these three points.

Economic and political issues

Wherever present in the world, for historical reasons, automobile manufacturing pays higher wages than other industries for similar work. In particular, materials handlers working in car assembly factories make substantially more than their counterparts at 3PL providers. The same, however, is not true for every manufacturing industry. If you make food products, cosmetics, or toys, the difference in wage structure may not be nearly as large and may not provide a similar incentive.

Even where there is no major wage difference, another source of cost reduction in the use of 3PL is the sharing of resources with other clients of the 3PL provider. This can be a dominant factor for small manufacturers whose activity could not possibly fill up a fleet of trucks and a network of warehouses or distribution centers.

Finally, even without wage differences and with a sufficiently high volume of activity, management still needs to assess the risks associated with owning and operating its own logistics resources through economic ups and downs. Even if the use of 3PL costs more under a given set of assumptions about the future, it may be prudent to pay a premium for another organization to take on the risk of overinvestment.

When Saturn, Ford, Chrysler, or Mission Foods use Penske Logistics, Schneider Logistics, or Ryder, there is no reason to think that they have any motivation other than economic. When Toyota adopts similar policies in North America and Europe but not in Japan, there may be the added motivation of nurturing a reputation as a good corporate citizen by engaging and training local businesses, thereby defusing any potential nationalistic backlash.

Availability of 3PL services

The availability of 3PL around the factory is not a foregone conclusion. 3PL as well as other outsourcing efforts are often limited by the surrounding infrastructure. Manufacturers who locate plants in isolated areas to take advantage of cheap real estate and tax incentives may place themselves in the position of having to perform all sorts of peripheral services themselves. The operator of a mine in the Andes must take care of providing panettone cakes to workers for Christmas as well as shipping out ore. On the other hand, a plant located in an area with a 100-year history of manufacturing can count on the availability of the services he may want to outsource.

Where road and communication networks are poor, and where there are many borders to cross and tariffs to pay, 3PL services may be difficult to obtain but extremely valuable, and several U.S.-based 3PL providers have made an effort to reach remote places in Latin America.

Even in industrialized areas, 3PL services may be only partially available. For example, there may be trucking companies offering no other services.

A manufacturer with sufficient clout can then encourage the formation of new ventures and train them to meet all 3PL requirements. This is the strategy that Toyota has followed in North America and Europe.

Product knowledge requirements

3PL providers being specialized in logistics cannot be expected to know their clients' products beyond handling requirements. They can transport parts in trucks, handle them on pallets, store and retrieve them in warehouses, and even transfer them between different types of containers without knowing anything more than outer dimensions, weight, need for refrigeration, orientation, or fragility.

On the other hand, some tasks that are usually considered part of logistics are better not entrusted to third parties because they require a deeper level of product knowledge, such as the following:

- *Kitting.* Kitting done by a 3PL provider is done too early, possibly days in advance of assembly, and subject to errors due to pickers not knowing the product. By contrast, kitting by water spiders is done a few minutes before assembly, next to the line, and by an operator who knows the product.

- *Quality checking.* The best time to check the quality of a supplier's parts is when picking them up in the supplier's shipping area. A driver working for the customer can be trained to recognize when a part has been mislabeled, but the most that can be expected of a 3PL driver is to check the paperwork and count bins or pallets.

- *Customizing.* Some suppliers provide last-minute customization services in or near customer plants. Since this is actually modifying the product, it is, strictly speaking, production and not logistics, and it is also the last production operation before the customer sees the product, which does not make it a good candidate for outsourcing.

3PL is an innovative type of business arrangement, used by companies that practice lean manufacturing as well as companies that don't. The practices described in the following two chapters, by contrast, are specific to lean organizations.

CHAPTER 19

Supplier–customer relationships

Summary

In the lean supply chain, the traditionally adversarial, arm's length relationship between supplier and customer makes way for a collaborative approach, centered on long-term single-sourcing agreements, and extensive exchanges of business information and technical know-how. This approach increases the total payoff of the relationship, but transitioning to it is difficult because it requires behavior changes on both sides.

Sustaining it over time also requires management to consistently forego the short-term windfalls that can be reaped through a unilateral return to the adversarial approach. That supplier and customer should collaborate to increase the total payoff does not prevent each one from negotiating aggressively with the other on sharing this payoff.

Supplier–customer relationships versus in-plant logistics

Chapter 1 pointed out that inbound/outbound logistics differed from in-plant logistics in that it is ruled by the interaction of multiple, independent economic agents. This chapter examines the implications of this fact in one specific and frequently occurring situation: a customer and a supplier negotiating the price of a part.

A lean supply chain is characterized by relationships between suppliers and customers that last for the life of a product, with single-sourcing, extensive communication of business and technical information, and collaborative problem solving. The agreements include a schedule of price reductions, to be enabled by quality and productivity improvements in the supplier's plants. The customer assists in these improvements through a variety of supplier support activities. By contrast, the traditional relationship between suppliers and customers is at arm's length, adversarial, and based on short-term contracts.

In negotiating their relationship, a customer and a supplier independently decide how they want to play. To simplify the discussion, we assume here that their only two choices are to be either "adversarial" or "collaborative," and we examine the implications of the choice made by each side.

Two ways to run a supplier–customer relationship

This is a simplified rendition of a situation that commonly occurs in reality. A customer and a supplier are negotiating the renewal of a contract for a part. The customer is a large company that assembles consumer goods from components delivered by about 200 small to medium-size suppliers. Selling this part to this customer provides 20% of the supplier's revenue, who can therefore ill afford to lose it. The customer could switch to another supplier, but it would require a lengthy and costly qualification process and would involve additional risk. Failing to agree is therefore undesirable for both sides.

This kind of situation is common in the automobile or large appliance industry. The PC industry, by contrast, is dominated by suppliers of key components, like Intel, that are in a position of strength with respect to assemblers like Dell or HP. Real negotiations involve many terms and conditions beyond price, which we will assume to have been settled already. The parties are therefore just negotiating the unit price to be paid for the part over a year, for volumes that are already agreed upon.

The supplier's sales rep and the customer's purchasing agent both have limits they are not authorized to cross:

- The *customer's upper limit* is the price above which the customer will not buy. This may be the price paid to date for the part.
- The *supplier's lower limit* is the price below which the supplier will not sell.

While each party usually does not voluntarily reveal its limit to the other, we can assume that the following holds:

$$Supplier\ Lower\ Limit \leq Customer\ Upper\ Limit$$

Otherwise, the parties would not be talking. The goal of the negotiation is to agree on a price between these limits, and the payoffs for both sides are as follows:

- *Customer payoff = Customer Upper Limit − Price*
- *Supplier payoff = Price − Supplier Lower Limit*

This is summarized in Figure 19-1.

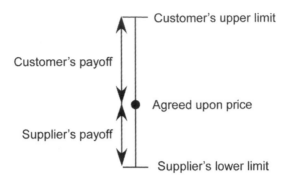

FIGURE 19-1. **Negotiation parameters**

1. The adversarial model

This is to date the dominant model of customer–supplier relationship in the United States. Each side is a "black box" to the other. As shown in Figure 19-2, the customer issues requirements specifications, orders, and quality problem reports; the supplier, lead times, advance shipping notices, and solutions to quality problems. The customer monitors the supplier's delivery and quality performance; the supplier, the customer's promptness in paying bills. They otherwise exchange no business or technical information. The customer maintains at least two sources for each component, both to ensure availability when one supplier fails, and to have leverage over the suppliers in negotiations.

FIGURE 19-2. **Information exchange in adversarial mode**

Neither side's limit can be moved, and the payoff for one side can only be increased through decreasing the other's by the same amount. Equally skilled and patient negotiators will eventually arrive at a price that is equally satisfying—or frustrating—for both sides. Since they do not know each other's limit, they do not know where the agreed upon price falls between them, but they are in fact unlikely to split the difference at the midpoint between the upper and lower limit, because each dollar of payoff is not worth the same for both sides.

For the supplier, if the part is worth $10, an additional $1 in price represents another 10 percentage points of profit, and since the part is 20% of the supplier's business, another 2 percentage points of profit for the entire company. If the customer assembles a part that goes into a $1,000 product, then a $1 reduction in price only represents a 0.1% cost reduction for the product, and is worth less for the customer than the supplier. Equal satisfaction in this case is achieved by a price that is closer to the supplier's limit than to the customer's.

2. The collaborative model

The collaborative approach to customer–supplier relations is in many ways the opposite. Instead of maintaining multiple sources and renewing contracts yearly, the customer commits to a single source for the life of the product, and then works with the chosen supplier to make sure it is successful.

Instead of collecting bids for contract manufacturing of a part designed by the customer, the part is designed by the supplier's engineers, who may know of cheaper ways to meet the customer's requirements. The supplier's engineering and manufacturing capabilities are visible to the customer.

The customer and the supplier share business plans and forecasts, as well as technical information on production processes. The supplier may keep a representative in the customer plant observing assembly operations, and providing feedback on opportunities to make the part easier to assemble or less likely to be confused with other parts. Collaboration may also reveal that a tight tolerance the supplier cannot meet consistently is in fact not necessary and can be relaxed. The customer provides "supplier support," as described in Chapter 20, including training on EDI systems, and technical support on quality problem solving and productivity improvement. Kevin Hop[1] summarized the differences between the two modes of operation in Table 19-1.

TABLE 19-1. **Differences between adversarial and collaborative approach**

Organization	Adversarial approach	Collaborative approach
Top management Customer side	Not involved	Meets with supplier top management on strategy
Top management Supplier side	Ceremonial meeting with customer middle management	Meets with customer top management on strategy
Quality Customer side	Inspects at Receiving and issues problem reports	Eliminates receiving inspection, rates suppliers, audits supplier processes, works with supplier on quality improvements
Quality Supplier side	Replaces defectives and fills out problem reports. Little or no face-to-face interaction with customer.	Works with customer quality on process improvements, communicates issues freely, performs or pays for all inspections and repairs at customer site.

---

1. Personal communication (2004)

TABLE 19-1. **Differences between adversarial and collaborative approach** (continued)

Manufacturing engineering—Customer side	Not involved	Experts from customer plant migrate to supplier development group or are used on loan to support improving supplier processes in the area of quality, productivity and cost to supplier. Improvements in cost. Savings are usually shared 50/50 with supplier.
Product engineering —Customer side	Designs products and issues specs. Gives little support to design change requests.	Issues performance and functional specs to supplier, who designs the product. Open to design changes that benefit both parties.
Product engineering —Supplier side	Weak or non-existent function. Maintains customer specs but has no input on improvements.	Strong function, with autonomous design capability, in partnership with the customer's product design group.

The result of this collaboration is that customer and supplier have a bigger total payoff to share. Supplier quality improvements reduce the need for incoming inspection and testing, and thereby make the parts more valuable to the customer. At the same time, improvements in the part's design and in the supplier's production process reduce the supplier's costs. The customer's upper limit goes up and the supplier's lower limit goes down, and *both* participants can have a larger payoff than with the adversarial approach, as shown in Figure 19-3.

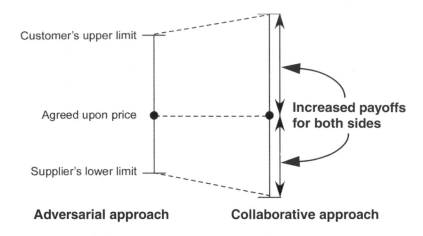

Customer's upper limit

Agreed upon price

Increased payoffs for both sides

Supplier's lower limit

Adversarial approach   **Collaborative approach**

FIGURE 19-3. **Adversarial versus collaborative approach**

Transition to and stability of the collaborative mode

Given that it is beneficial to both sides, one might expect all industrial customers and suppliers to migrate promptly from the adversarial to the collaborative approach. It is not happening, and the collaborative approach that characterizes the Toyota supply chain remains the exception, at least in the United States and in Europe.

Inertia is one explanation. The collaborative approach requires much more work to be put into a customer–supplier relationship, and today's buyers and sellers have not been trained to do it. They are heirs to generations that have practiced the adversarial approach and are comfortable with it. There is, however, another, more compelling reason: the switch requires both sides to change. The payoff matrix in Figure 19-4 shows what happens when only one side changes.

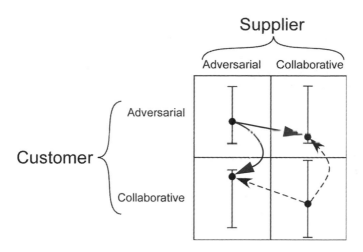

FIGURE 19-4. Payoff matrix

Both sides can choose to be adversarial or collaborative. Assume that both are initially adversarial, then for either side to switch when the other one doesn't is unilateral disarmament. Any business or technical information it shares with the other side is used against it to obtain price concessions. In game theory terms, the situation where both sides are adversarial is a Nash equilibrium, because this strategy is optimal for each side, given what the other one is doing.

The only win–win move is for both sides to change strategies at the same time, and to grant each other a level of trust they did not have before. Since collaboration provides higher payoffs for both sides, one might expect that, once achieved, it is stable. But it is not the case in Figure 19-4. Each side, assuming the other one remains collaborative, has the opportunity to gouge it by unilaterally turning adversarial. Although this move shrinks the total payoff, the side making it catches such a large share that it is advantageous, albeit for a short time: as soon as the other side catches on, we are back to the original mode where both sides are adversarial.

How does this play out in reality? A management change or an acquisition in the customer company may put in charge managers focused on cutting costs. First, they decide that supplier support is a luxury and gut it. Then they turn to suppliers, whom they feel have been coddled, and use all the information available to force them into price concessions.

On the other side, a return to the adversarial mode initiated by a supplier will not take the form of an open attack. Instead, the supplier stops improving, takes advantage of its single-source position to stop investing in new technology, and uses the supplier support group's imperfect knowledge of the supplier's business to deceive it. Some observers in Japan blame Nissan's abuse by suppliers for the difficulties the company experienced in the 1990s, and credit the turnaround in part to the adoption of a tougher, more adversarial stance.

Conclusions

If few companies reap the benefits of collaborative customer–supplier relationships, it is not necessarily because their management does not see the value of it. Moving a customer–supplier relationship from the adversarial to the collaborative mode is difficult because it requires a conscious effort on *both* sides. Furthermore, once it has been achieved, sustaining it over the long haul requires continuity in management on both sides and a determination not to pursue the short-term gains that can be obtained by a unilateral return to the adversarial mode.

Working in a collaborative mode does not mean that price negotiations are a love fest. Collaboration enables the customer and the supplier to increase the total payoff of the relationship, but then they compete for their share of it in the price negotiation. Brandenburger and Nalebuff[1] call this behavior "co-opetition." In spirit, it is no different from collocating furniture stores to attract consumers to a "furniture district," and then competing for their patronage, or agreeing on telecommunication protocols and then competing in the market thus created for devices using these protocols.

---

1. *Co-opetition*, A. Brandenburger & B. Nalebuff, Doubleday (1996)

The desire to work in this mode affects the way companies choose who they do business with. In selecting a supplier, for example, the customer may look more for openness and commitment to improve than for immediate performance. If, during the evaluation, a customer employee asks the supplier's manufacturing manager, "How do you solve your production problems?" "We don't have any production problems." is the wrong answer. It is defensive, not credible, and tells the customer that problems will be hidden. Every manufacturer has production problems, and what the evaluator wants to know is that the supplier will immediately notify the customer, and take short-term countermeasures while pursuing a lasting solution.

The next chapter examines one particular type of collaboration, in which the customer provides "free" consulting to help the supplier increase productivity and improve quality in exchange for price cuts.

CHAPTER 20

Supplier support

Summary

Most manufacturers are new to the idea of supporting suppliers. Since 1970, Toyota has undertaken to help its suppliers implement lean manufacturing. Since 1976, the main vehicle has been autonomous study groups ("jishuken") that evolved in focus from information sharing to implementation of improvements and led to the development of "Kaizen events" in the United States.

A successful supplier support group is undertaken once the company has a track record of lean manufacturing implementation in house. The group is staffed with experienced engineers who have been key contributors to the in-house effort and make a sincere effort to understand each supplier's business, technology, and people, as opposed to relying on compliance checklists and pushing suppliers to start programs that have no bearing on their specific circumstances.

Supplier support for quality assurance is often provided separately, but, in many cases, the most effective way for a supplier to improve quality is to implement lean manufacturing, and the two support efforts should be coordinated. Support should be provided to the entire business of the supplier, not only to production lines making the customer's products, and with a "bedside manner" that shows respect for the supplier's engineers and managers.

Suppliers benefit most from this support by taking the initiative of visiting customer plants, setting meeting agendas and publishing minutes, taking advantage of training offered through the supplier association, presenting at supplier conferences, and maintaining communication with the customer's purchasing organization.

The different types of supplier support

Most manufacturing companies are used to providing *customer* support but new to the idea that they should in any way support or held develop *suppliers*. In the collaborative mode of operation that is characteristic of lean logistics, customers and suppliers work together in the following areas:

- *Lean manufacturing implementation.* This will be the primary subject of this chapter, which discusses how Toyota supports its suppliers' efforts in this area, how these approaches have been adapted in other companies and industries, and what pitfalls should be avoided.

- *Quality assurance.* While lean manufacturing improves quality, there usually is separate organization in charge of supplier quality. In a collaborative relationship, the customer's quality assurance department does more than issue problem reports and demand additional record keeping and inspection, but also provides technical assistance in problem solving.

Collaboration also extends to other areas that we will not go into, including the following:

- *Product development.* In the system known as "black box" or "design in," customers issue functional requirements and engineers from the supplier and the customer organizations collaborate in the development of components that meet these requirements. This system is described by Fujimoto[1] and by Liker[2] in the automobile parts industry. We know of similar efforts in large semiconductor manufacturers working with suppliers of process equipment.

- *New product introduction.* The new product introduction phase is the ramp-up from production of sample quantities to the target production volume. Customers support suppliers in designing and running experiments to stabilize processes, and in setting up "run-at-rate" exercises in supplier plants, to enable the supplier to match the customer's planned takt time.

---

1. *The evolution of a manufacturing system at Toyota*, T. Fujimoto, Oxford (1999), Chapter 5.
2. *Engineered in Japan*, Ed. J. Liker, Oxford (1994), Chapter 7

- *Information systems and production control.* Suppliers need training in understanding the business logic behind customers' information systems as well as daily transaction processing.

Toyota's supplier support system

Toyota is not the only company in Japan or elsewhere to provide supplier support. Honda, Nissan, GM, Ford, and Chrysler all have organized efforts in this area. But Toyota, while not all aspects of its supplier support are transferable to other companies, industries, or countries, is the reference for lean manufacturing/logistics.

Background of *Jishuken* (Autonomous Study Groups)

Toyota started a systematic effort to propagate knowledge of its production system among suppliers with the creation in 1976 of the "Society for Autonomous Research on the Toyota Production System." Its activities started with "Autonomous Study Groups" (Jishuken) that met to discuss the nature of waste and ways to identify it. The term "jishuken" is still in use in the Toyota organization, with a much broader meaning, not only in Japan but in overseas transplant facilities as well.

The original idea was to bring together participants from non-competing companies to discuss the nature of waste and a means of recognizing it. This fits a pattern earlier established by the Japanese Union of Scientists and Engineers (JUSE) in propagating quality control concepts through study groups whose members could freely communicate because the other participants were non-competitors and the low labor mobility in Japan ensured that they would not join a competitor. Inside companies, quality circles also started as study groups in the early 1960s.

Toyota's study groups rapidly expanded the scope of their activities, first to making proposals for waste elimination and then to actually implement changes on the shop floor or in the support organization. By the mid 1980s, the focus of jishuken activity was to achieve immediate improvements while training eyes to see waste, build teamwork, and improve communications. Today, Toyota sees jishuken as a structure to build the future.

Jishuken activity today

It is intended to involve people in all levels of the hierarchy, as follows:

- *Team leaders and group leaders (first-line managers).* Workshops are held once a month, anyone can participate and is expected to. The team or group leader of the target area defines the problem but does not participate, and Maintenance is on standby to help implement changes.

- *Second-level managers.* Workshops are also held once a month, but the participants rotate between plants.

- *Upper managers.* Higher-level managers rotate between companies, working on larger scale projects focused on innovation and involving multiple meetings over several months. This activity is part of business leadership development.

Of course, not everybody is always enthusiastic about interrupting their normal activities to participate in a jishuken. To accommodate individual needs, the system provides flexibility both in the timing of their participation and in the format of the jishuken itself. The major risk in such a program is for it to degenerate over time into ceremonies where participants go through motions for form's sake.

Jishuken in the Toyota organization

In Japan, high-level support is provided by an organization whose Japanese name, "seisan chosa bu" means "production investigation division," but is usually translated as "Operations Management Consulting Division" (OMCD). The OMCD was established in 1970, prior to the development of the jishuken concept, and was part of the production control department until 1996.

Unlike most other companies' supplier support organizations, the OMCD is not part of Purchasing, but Purchasing still has a role in managing supplier quality.[1] The rationale for separating the OMCD from Purchasing to to allay any fear suppliers might have that data shared with the OMCD

---

1. *Supplier Development at Honda, Nissan and Toyota,* Mari Sako, Oxford University, 10/98.

might be used against them in commercial negotiations. The OMCD's organization structure is shown in Figure 20-1.

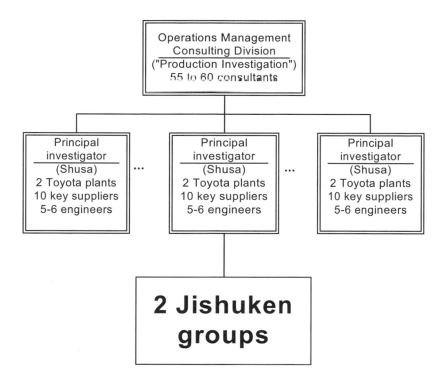

FIGURE 20-1. OMCD organization structure

For a company of Toyota's size, the OMCD is remarkably small. A jishuken group involves 6 to 7 geographically close, non-competing suppliers, with membership renewed every three years, and each member assigns 5 middle managers to the group. According to Sako, jishuken groups involve 56 factories from 52 companies accounting for 80% of Toyota's purchasing budget.

Each member company hosts a two-month project each year, led by a participant from another member and proceeding through weekly meetings, and supported by three visits from the OMCD shusa. In addition to the 30 or so outside participants in the meetings, the host company provides a matching number of its own employees, and the weekly meetings may have up to 60 attendees engaging in problem solving and shop floor improvement.

The OMCD's counterpart in the United States is the Toyota Supplier Support Center (TSSC) which has been spun out as a separate company and provides consulting services outside of Toyota.

Other forms of supplier support

While jishuken is the preferred form of supplier support on the shop floor, it is not the only one. Besides supplier quality management, Purchasing also has a "Kaizen Promotion Office" providing direct consulting support to suppliers through monthly visits.

Supplier associations have also been started at Toyota's initiative in the United States. The Golden State Automotive Manufacturers' Association (GAMA) groups NUMMI suppliers in California, and has a counterpart called BAMA in Kentucky, with "B" for "Bluegrass," grouping suppliers of the Georgetown complex. These supplier associations are vehicles to provide classroom training as needed, and hold regular conferences that are opportunities to exchange technical information between suppliers and provide recognition for achievements.

Supplier support outside of Toyota

From jishuken to kaizen events

In the United States, discussions of lean manufacturing implementation both in house and through supplier support are dominated by the term "kaizen event," which is sometimes also known as "kaizen blitz," "Accelerated Improvement Workshop" (AIW), and sometimes just "kaizen."

Kaizen is a Japanese word, and used by Toyota employees, but not in the sense of kaizen event or blitz, but in the sense of continuous improvement, achieved primarily by "problem-solving circles" that are small groups of volunteer operators, organized like quality circles but with a broader mandate, and meeting for two to three hours per week for months.

In Japan, in everyday life, kaizen[1] means "improvement"; in manufacturing, more specifically it means small improvements to work methods made by the people who do that work. In manufacturing, "kaizen" is opposed to "kaikaku," which means reform or drastic change and is sometimes translated as "innovation." Wrapping foil around the feet of a welding fixture to make it easier to clean is kaizen; redesigning a production line, kaikaku.

Terms like "kaizen event" or "kaizen blitz" were coined in the United States. "Kaizen Blitz" is even a service mark of the Association for Manufacturing Excellence (AME). "Blitz" is German for lightning. "Kaizen blitz," therefore literally means "lightning strike of continuous improvement." A. Laraia, P. Moody, and R. W. Hall[2] describe the birth of the kaizen blitz in 1994 as prompted by the frustration experienced at Critikon, Jacobs Manufacturing, Wiremold, Hamilton Standard, and Pratt & Whitney when trying to use small groups like NUMMI's problem-solving circles as the primary vehicle for lean manufacturing implementation.

Having learned some of the jishuken techniques from Toyota alumni like Chihiro Nakao at Shingijutsu, they adapted it to the American context and the result came to be known as kaizen blitz or event and evolved into the pattern shown in Figure 20-2.

---

1. See *The Idea Generator*, Bunji Tozawa & Norman Bodek, PCS Press (2001)
2. *The Kaizen Blitz*, A. Laraia, P Moody & R. W. Hall, Wiley (1999)

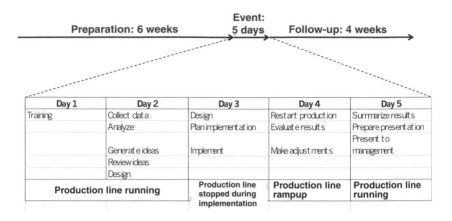

FIGURE 20-2. Kaizen event timeline

Kaizen events are perceived as accelerated improvement, because most of the work is done during one-week of intense activity. From start to finish, however, a kaizen event takes *11 weeks*, not one, including planning upfront and the execution of follow-up action items after the first week. What the kaizen event achieves during its central week is focus, which makes needed resources available; and collocation of the team, which fosters teamwork.

Kaizen events have not only been technically successful, but they have captured the imagination of American manufacturing managers, to the point that many now equate lean manufacturing with kaizen events. But in the Toyota context, the jishukens that were the inspiration for kaizen events are used in conjunction with larger projects such as the two months jishukens conducted at a supplier, with smaller projects executed by small groups on the shop floor in continuous improvement mode, and even individual suggestions.

In many major American companies, supplier support groups do nothing but facilitate kaizen events at suppliers' plants, leaving on the table the opportunities that require other approaches. To be effective, a supplier support organization must have more than that one arrow in its quiver. It must have a well-rounded set of tools that can be applied to the many different challenges faced by suppliers.

Supporting a variety of suppliers

Toyota has hundreds of suppliers, but the OMCD focuses on the top 52, which still is a large number when considering that effective support requires some understanding of each supplier's business, technical, and human issues.

Supplier support groups recruit engineers and managers that have been successful inside the company's operations and know them intimately, but need to broaden their perspectives to be able to help suppliers. The customer may be a car maker with production lines putting out one unit of product every minute, but the supplier may also have divisions that make after-market spare parts, airplane parts for commercial and military use, or components for semiconductor production machinery, all of which have demand patterns that are radically different from car assembly.

In technology, a common occurrence is that the customer is primarily an assembler, while the suppliers do molding, casting, fabrication or machining, all processes with their own dynamics and different from assembly. In particular, issues like process capability, equipment availability, and quick changeovers loom larger while part availability is less of a concern. Supplier support staff with an assembly background also must be careful about concluding that a year's worth of an item is excess inventory before knowing, for example, that it is an exotic alloy from a less-than-reliable monopoly supplier based overseas.

Finally, the labor pools available to the customer and the suppliers may be different. A plant in New England draws labor from a region with a 200-year manufacturing tradition, where multiple generations of the same family have worked in the field, while a maquiladora making parts in Ciudad Juarez uses temporary workers from Mexico's agricultural sector. Even within the same geographical areas, there may be differences by industry. A supplier may have machinists with skills requiring years to hone while the customer only has assembly line jobs that can be learned at a basic level in a few days and mastered in a few months. Or conversely, by offering higher wages, the customer may be able to attract a work force with better training and a higher education level than the supplier who recruits recent immigrants with no manufacturing experience. These differences affect, for example, the types of decisions shop floor teams may reasonably be empowered to make.

In a supplier support situation, each supplier's operations are usually smaller and simpler than the customer's but the variety of issues among different suppliers can bewilder support providers and lead them to the following pitfalls:

1. *Falling back on a process compliance checklist.* Supplier assessment often degenerate, into filling out a 20-page checklist awarding points for having floor markings, cells, andon lights, kanbans, performance charts and other practices, and certifying as "lean" supplies whose score is above a given threshold.

   Supplier support groups do this because they can, not because it's right. It misleads suppliers into thinking that lean manufacturing is process compliance rather than a business strategy to outperform their competition in price, quality, and delivery. Checklists of practices obscure the fact that these practices are moves in a game. The goal is to win the game, not to make all the possible moves.

2. *Limiting their recommendations to universal programs.* When visiting a plant, it is easy to notice that it is cluttered, dirty, and poorly marked, and to identify improvement in this area, through a "5S" program as the first priority.

   For supplier support groups, this recommendation is easy to make, but rarely matches the conclusion they would have reached through a genuine analysis of the supplier's business, technology, and work force. It is also difficult to implement, as evidenced by the failed attempts whose traces can be seen on the shop floors of American factories.

Supplier quality assurance

The need for supplier support in quality assurance

Not all suppliers are equal. Some are outstanding performers in quality; others, on notice that they will be terminated unless they improve. Different policies are needed for different suppliers. The best suppliers probably don't need any incoming inspection, and the whole receiving procedure may be limited to scanning the barcode on a kanban. They may deliver ten times a day, in quantities that can go straight to the assembly line.

At the opposite end of the spectrum are problem suppliers. As long as they are used, the customer needs to check everything they do. Is it the right item? Is it in the right quantity? Do all units work and meet specs? No sampling inspection will do. Every part must be checked. And the incoming materials warehouse should have a zone dedicated to this supplier, to easily monitor all its items. Then, there are levels in between.

If quality issues alone drove the sizing of deliveries, they would be in single units, at intervals matching the takt time of the products they go into. From a strict quality perspective, it would minimize the customer's risk of holding defective parts or parts made obsolete by an engineering change order (ECO), and whenever a supplier would deliver a defective part, feedback about it would arrive before many more are made.

While logistical constraints force customers to receive lots of more than one unit, milk runs keep lot sizes down, and having different policies depending on supplier performance enables you to contain the cost of receiving small lots, since the bad performers requiring attention are few, and either on the mend or on the way out.

Challenges in supplier quality management

Helping suppliers improve quality is difficult, and a customer's efforts to do so can easily degenerate into mandating that the supplier perform activities that have no impact on quality.

An extreme example is the failure analysis of semiconductor chips supplied to car makers. The car maker has developed a problem-solving format that all suppliers are asked to use in response to quality problem reports, and the supplier is expected to do the following:

1. Set up a small team and have the team select a leader.
2. Describe the problem in quantitative and precise terms.
3. Implement and validate immediate countermeasures.
4. Identify and confirm root causes.
5. Verify that the corrective action works and has no undesirable side effects.
6. Implement permanent corrective actions.
7. Prevent recurrence through documentation, training, and mistake-proofing.
8. Congratulate the team and publicize its achievements.

And this process is documented by filling out corresponding forms.

This process was designed for suppliers making parts like pumps or shock absorbers in a few hours, for delivery and assembly in a few days. A team of engineers, technicians, and shop floor operators can huddle around the part, quickly identify what is wrong with it, how it came about, and why it was not detected, and take corrective action.

But semiconductor chips are different: they have undergone a wafer process in the United States for six weeks, and have flown back and forth to Malaysia for assembly and test, prior to delivery to the customer in the midwest. By the time the part arrives at the semiconductor company's failure analysis lab, the event that caused the defect is four months in the past and the operation at which it occurred has undergone three engineering changes.

Failure analysis of a semiconductor chip is not the kind of work that can be effectively done by a team. It is done by an individual engineer, using test equipment, machines to strip thin layers from the chip, and electron microscopes to examine the chip's structure. When successful, the analysis results in a diagnosis that goes into a properly formatted report to the customer but is of no use to the supplier's manufacturing engineers because it is about a process that is no longer in use. To the supplier, complying with this customer mandate is only a cost of doing business.

Another issue is the extent to which a customer should monitor how a supplier produces. Automobile parts suppliers are generally not authorized to change their production processes without going through the customer's Production Part Approval Process (PPAP). Once a process has been proven to yield good parts, customers are wary of changes that may cause a deterioration. The issue is how far this concern should be taken.

For some customers, as long as the physics and chemistry of the operations inside machines are unchanged, suppliers can change the layout of production lines and the means of conveying parts between machines without asking permission. Others, however, demand to review and approve even layout changes that affect neither the technical content of individual operations nor the sequence in which they are performed. By doing this they cross the line from being prudent to being an obstacle to improvement.

Providing genuine support for supplier quality

To avoid burdening suppliers with busy work, the customer's quality assurance group needs to rethink what it can or should require from suppliers, given that it cannot possibly have a deep understanding of the issues faced by hundreds of suppliers working with metals, plastics, glass, ceramics, electronics materials, etc.

Outgoing quality performance can be required, as can traceability and responsiveness in case of emergencies. But it is often counterproductive to prescribe *how* suppliers should go about meeting these requirements. The customer organization has learned tools and techniques that have worked —and not worked—in solving its own quality problems.

Sharing this experience with suppliers is providing genuine support, but the managers and engineers in supplier organizations should be treated as professionals making their own decisions on which methods to use for what purpose in their own plants, and be judged exclusively on the results.

Recommendations on providing supplier support

A supplier support group must be able to show suppliers the results achieved within the customer's plants. All the customer's plants do not have to be lean, but some of them must have production lines that have been sufficiently improved to make supplier support credible. Toyota's reputation gives instant credibility to its supplier support staff, but other companies have to work at building it.

Toyota had been developing its production system for decades before it organized supplier support first within Purchasing for quality in 1965 and then for TPS with the OMCD in 1970. It is not necessary to wait this long, but a customer company's internal lean manufacturing program should have a track record of at least two to three years of success before getting started.

The supplier support group should be staffed internally, with engineers and managers who have been key contributors to the lean manufacturing program in the customer company and are ready to broaden their horizons. Hiring outsiders or engineers right out of school into these positions, as some companies have done, is ill advised.

Professionals with 15 years of experience at suppliers will not take kindly to being "developed" by rookies, no matter how smart or well educated they may be, and they will put forward reason after reason why recommendations won't work. The best possible outcome is that suppliers will train the newcomers, in which case, the result will be more "customer development" than the reverse.

Retention in supplier support groups is also an issue, because their members are attractive recruitment targets for consulting firms. This is one more reason to rotate into these groups individuals with roots and career prospects inside the company.

Supplier support should not target *all* suppliers. It is more effective to have a deep impact on a few key suppliers than a superficial one on many. Toyota's OMCD works with about 50 tier-one suppliers, out of the several hundred Toyota has in Japan. Then the support staff should invest its time in understanding the supplier's unique business rather than apply a one-size-fits-all approach.

Support should be provided to the entire business of the supplier, not only to production lines making the customer's products. This is needed for supplier personnel to trust that supplier support is actually intended to help them, as opposed to finding information to use against them in negotiations. Economically, only the customer receives the agreed price reductions, while cost savings on lines working for competitors add to the supplier's profits.

The suppliers receiving support may already have lean implementation programs in place. Supplier support should leverage, not ignore, these efforts, and show respect to the individuals involved.

While lean manufacturing is an engineering and management discipline applicable anywhere in the world, the methods used to teach, train, and coach, on the other hand, are influenced by national culture. American trainers are expected to provide positive reinforcement and compliment beginners on their early achievements to build up their self-esteem. In Japan, beginning students of traditional disciplines, be it martial arts, sumi-e painting, or sushi making, are made to feel that they are wasting the master's precious time and are bluntly told of their shortcomings. This serves to weed out the half-hearted, so that only those students who are determined enough to take the abuse eventually become disciples.

Many Japanese consultants in the field of lean manufacturing behave the same way, which, in the United States, has earned them the nickname of "insultants," and some members of supplier support groups, trained by these consultants, have adopted the same demeanor in the field. If they have worked directly with Taiichi Ohno for 20 years, they can get away with it. Otherwise, a more culturally sensitive and humble "bedside manner" is more effective. The customer's supplier support group and the supplier's work force are all professionals and fallible human beings working together to solve problems.

Recommendations on receiving supplier support

As lean manufacturing gains momentum, some suppliers are not only offered support but find themselves receiving guidance from multiple customers. The intent of this service, as discussed in Chapter 19, is to enable suppliers to simultaneously lower their prices and increase their profits by improving their manufacturing performance. But on the supplier's shop floor, it is often perceived differently, as unsolicited advice from people who do not know the supplier's business, are not accountable for its performance, and are implicitly threatening to terminate the relationship if the supplier balks.

A common response is to humor the visitors, and focus implementation on projects that will yield the most points on the next audit. This may lead, for example, to mounting andon lights on injection molding machines instead of reducing their setup times. While clearly less useful, it will boost the company's "leanness" score faster.

Some suppliers also receive support from *multiple* customers who may have different ideas of what the supplier should do. One possible response is to accept advice from each customer only on the production lines dedicated to his products, but there are two problems with this approach:

1. It can only function if there is complete separation of production lines by customer. It cannot apply to shared lines or common services.
2. It does not allow for cross-fertilization. Good ideas can come from multiple sources, and the supplier should be able to use them across the board.

Whether working with one or with multiple customers' support groups, the supplier's best response is to take charge of the program. Many dysfunctional responses are possible and do occur, but they can be avoided if management on the supplier side accepts the premise of the supplier support process and does not treat participating in it as just another cost of doing business.

For the supplier as well as for the customer, becoming lean *is* the best available way to secure a prosperous future. Just as Toyota outperforms other car makers, the leanest parts manufacturers also outperform their competition. Even if the customer uses a misleading checklist, a supplier in the driver seat of his own lean conversion does not have to agree to be misled.

The supplier should start a lean conversion program internally and actively manage contributions from the supplier support groups. This involves for example the following:

- Taking the initiative of visiting customer plants in search of ideas.
- Setting the agenda for supplier support visits and publishing minutes.
- Taking advantage of training offered through the customer's supplier association.
- Presenting achievements at the customer's supplier conferences.
- Maintaining communication with the customer's purchasing organization, which funds the supplier support group.

Supplier support, like many of the concepts in this book, is so powerful that it is difficult to envision how a company that does not practice or receive it can compete with one that does. In practice, of course, it requires determination and perseverance in management on both sides to make it work.

Where should you go from here?

Like *Lean Assembly*, this book is more about technical content than implementation methods. As all who have done it know, changing a manufacturing and logistics organization is not only a daunting challenge, but one in which the technical content plays a fundamental role: *how* you implement depends on *what* you implement. The concepts and methods in the preceding chapters were not only intended to be introduced in a logical sequence but also in a sequence in which you can *implement* them.

Because the issues of dock-to-dock logistics inside your plant can be addressed within your own organization, they should be tackled first. Not only do they yield tangible performance improvements for the manufacturing organization as a whole, but they also build you skills base and provide you with a showcase for suppliers, third-party logistics providers, and customers.

This is the basis you need to extend improvement efforts beyond your own walls and involve outside partners. Physical improvements in inbound, in-plant, and outbound logistics together then provide the infrastructure needed for the pull system, leveled sequencing, and lean production planning and forecasting.

That this is the recommended implementation sequence should not be taken to mean that *all* in-plant logistics should be addressed before starting *any* improvement in the supply network, as such an approach would unnecessarily delay progress. The entire plant does not need to have milk runs and an excellent storage and retrieval system in place before approaching suppliers, and not all suppliers need to use returnable containers before kanbans can be introduced. Instead, the timelines should overlap.

Assume, for example, a plant that makes multiple product families, then the usual pattern in lean manufacturing is to have a separate focused factory for each family executing most of the processes with dedicated resources, supported by a common services area in charge of the processes that engineers have not yet been able to distribute among the focused factories.

Then logistics improvement should first focus on one selected product family and, for its focused factory, proceed with in-plant logistics first, then inbound and outbound, and finally the information system. The organization then works its way through the list of product families, applying each time the lessons learned from all the preceding cases.

Finally, while logistics clearly is a key component of lean manufacturing, it is not all of it. Materials managers and logisticians are part of the team that effects the lean transformation of the company, and do their part in cooperation with others.

Bibliography

Books in English

On lean manufacturing and logistics

Toyota Production System, Y. Monden, IIE, ISBN 0-89806-129-6 (1993)

Pull Production for the Shop Floor, The Productivity Press Development Team, Shopfloor Series, Productivity Press, ISBN 1-56327-274-1 (2002)

Supply Chain Development for the Lean Enterprise: Interorganizational Cost Management, Robin Cooper & Regine Slagmulder, FAR/Productivity Press, Portland, OR, ISBN 1-56327-218-0 (1999)

Quick Response Manufacturing, Rajan Suri, Productivity Press, ISBN 1-563-27201-6 (1999)

On logistics and supply chain management

Handbook of Supply Chain Management, James B. Ayers, The St. Lucie Press/ APICS Series on Resource Management, New York, NY, ISBN 1-57444-273-2 (2001)

Supply Chain Strategy, Edward H. Frazelle, McGraw-Hill, New York, NY, ISBN 0-07-137599-6 (2002)

Logistics and Supply Chain Management, Martin Christopher, Prentice Hall/ Pearson Education, London, UK, ISBN 0-273-69049-0 (1998)

Harvard Business Review on Managing the Value Chain, Harvard Business School Press, Boston, MA, ISBN 1-57851-234-4 (2000)

Fundamentals of Logistics Management, Douglas M. Lambert et al., Irwin/ McGraw-Hill, Boston, MA, ISBN 0-256-14117-7 (1998)

Designing and Managing the Supply Chain, David Simchi-Levy et al., Irwin/ McGraw-Hill, Boston, MA, ISBN 0-07-235756-8 (2000)

Logistics, David J. Bloomberg et al., Prentice Hall, Upper Saddle River, NJ ISBN 0-13-010194-X (2002)

Supply Chain Optimization, Charles C. Poirier & Stephen E. Reiter, Berret Kohler Publishers, San Francisco, CA, ISBN 1-881052-93-1 (1996)

Factory Physics, Wallace J. Hopp et al., Irwin, ISBN 0-256-15464-3 (1996)

E-Commerce Logistics and Fulfillment: Delivering the Goods, Deborah L. Bayles, Prentice Hall, Upper Saddle River, NJ, ISBN 0-13-030328-3 (2001)

On supplier support

The evolution of a manufacturing system at Toyota, T. Fujimoto, Oxford, ISBN 0-19-512320-4 (1999)

Engineered in Japan, Ed. J. Liker, Oxford, ISBN 0-19-509555-3 (1994)

On warehouse management

World-Class Warehousing and Material Handling, Edward H. Frazelle, McGraw-Hill, New York, NY, ISBN 0-07-137600-3 (2002)

Warehouse Distribution and Operations Handbook, David E. Mulcahy, McGraw Hill, New York, NY, ISBN 0-07-044002-6 (1994)

Materials Handling Handbook, Raymond A. Kulwiec, Ed., Wiley-Interscience, NY, ISBN 0-471-09782-9 (1985)

Inventory Accuracy, David J. Piasecki, Ops Publishing, Kenosha, WI, ISBN 0-9727631-0-4 (2003)

On military logistics

Lean Logistics: High Velocity Logistics Infrastructure and the C-5 Galaxy, Timothy Ramey, RAND, Santa Monica, CA, ISBN 0-8330-2697-6 (1999)

Moving Mountains: Lessons in Leadership and Logistics from the Gulf War, William G. Pagonis, Harvard Business School Press, Cambridge, MA, ISBN 0-87584-508-8 (1992)

Supplying War: Logistics from Wallenstein to Patton, Martin Van Creveld, Cambridge University Press, Cambridge, UK, ISBN 0-521-29793-1 (1977)

On production control and information systems

ERP: Making it happen, Thomas E. Wallace and Michael H. Kremzar, John Wiley & Sons, New York, NY, ISBN 0-471-39201-4 (2001)

Enterprise Resource Planning, Daniel O'Leary, Cambridge University Press, Cambridge, UK, ISBN 0-521-79152-9 (2000)

Sales and Operations Planning, Thomas E. Wallace, T.F. Wallace & Co., Cincinnatti, OH, ISBN 0-9674884-0-0 (2000)

Integrating Kanban with MRP-II, Raymond S. Louis, Productivity Press, Portland, OR, ISBN 1-56327-182-6 (1997)

On management

The Effective Executive, Peter F. Drucker, Harper Business Essentials, New York, NY, ISBN 0-06-051607-0 (1967)

Co-opetition, A.M. Brandenburger & B. Nalebuff, Doubleday, New York, NY, ISBN 0-385-47949-2 (1996)

Reengineering the Corporation, M. Hammer & J. Champy, Harper Business, New York, NY, ISBN 0-88730-640-3 (1993)

Books in Japanese

Toyota shiki saikyo no keiei, Masaharu Shibata & Hideharu Kaneda, Nihon Keizai Shimbunsha, ISBN 4-532-14923-1 (2001)

Butsuryu. Logistics no riron to jittai, Taniichi Tanimoto, Hakutoshobo K.K., Tokyo, Japan, ISBN 4-561-74134-8 (2000)

Konsai Seisan Shisutemu, Kojo Kanri special issue, March 1991

Kojonai Butsuryu Gyomu Koritsuka no Pointo in Kojo Kanri, Vol. 48 No. 8, 5/2002, pp. 1-55

Toyota Network Bible, T. Nakashima & M. Kakami, Ohmu Sha, Tokyo, ISBN 4-274-94519-7 (1994)

Books in German

Logistik. Wege zur Optimierung des Material- und Informationsflusses, (Logistics. Ways to optimize flows of materials and information) Christof Schulte, Vahlen, Munich, ISBN 3800624540 (1999)

Books in French

La logistique globale, Philippe-Pierre Dornier, Michel Fender, Editions d'Organisation, Paris, ISBN 2708125370 (2001)

Supply chain en action : Stratégie, Logistique, Service clients, de Claude Fiore, Village Mondial; (Les Echos Editions), Paris, ISBN 2842111206 (2001)

Management industriel et logistique 3e ed, Baglin /Bruel /Gareau, Economica, ISBN 2717841768 (2001)

Transport et logistique, Marie-Madeleine Damien, Dunod, Paris, ISBN 2100048325 (2001)

La Logistique, de Hervé Mathé, Daniel Tixier, Presses Universitaires de France - PUF; (Que Sais-Je ?), Paris, ISBN 2130480985 (1998)

Books in Spanish

Logistica y Distribucion Fisica, Gil Gutierrez Casas, McGraw Hill; ISBN 8448113667 (1998)

Manual de Logistica Integral, Jordi Pau Cos, Ricardo de Navascues, Diaz de Santos, ISBN 8479783451 (2000)

Index

APS 41, 272
AS/RS 83, 85, 86
  Control system 85
  Sizing 85
ASN 257
Assembly 9, 10, 11
Assembly line 161, 165
Assembly line balancing 131
Association for Manufacturing
      Excellence 359
Auto-ID 27, 89, 93, 100, 107
Automatic Storage and Retrieval
      Systems 84
Automobile assembly 110
Automobile industry 112, 121, 343
Automobile part 207
Automotive industry 137
Autonomous Study Groups 355
Aviation 10

B

Backflush 188
Backflushing 104
Back-loading truck 144
Bag 164
Baggage claim 86
BAMA 46, 358
Barcode 43, 89, 93, 105, 143, 363
Bill of lading 2
Bill of materials 43, 111
Blanket purchase order 315, 316
Block stacking 83, 85, 90
Blow-molded separator 166
Bluegrass Automotive
      Manufacturers
      Association 46
Body-on-sequence 5, 27, 43, 109,
      110, 111, 121, 162, 273, 304
Boeing 337
Bottom-up 3
Box 164
Boxing 109, 122
B-product 274
Buffer 76
Build manifest 44

Numerics

3PL 6, 333, 334, 338, 339
3rd party logistics 109, 124, 136, 143
4PL 335
5S 38

A

Accelerated Improvement
      Workshop 358
Access 151
Access control 106
Accounting 188
Advanced Planning and
      Scheduling 41, 272
Aerospace industry 137
AGV 85
Air freight 12
Aisin Seiki 41, 278
AIW 358
AME 359
America 172
Andon lights 368
Applied Materials 46, 193
A-product 274

Bullwhip 42
Bullwhip effect 256, 273, 310, 328, 329
Bus 49

C

Capital acquisition request 85
Car assembly 121
Car maker 160
Car rental 10
Carrousel 86
Cart 32, 77
Carton 175
Casting 274
Central aisle 167
Checklist 362
Checkstand 20
Cho, Fujio 321
Chrysler 339
CLM 24
CMC 176
Collapsible 180
Color coding 187
Common carriers 136
Communication technology 43
Complementor 314
Component 109
Compressor 164
Computer systems 27, 38
Consignment 27, 43, 109, 111, 258
Consolidation center 116, 159, 160, 167
  Location 167
  Work 162
Consumer 25, 328
Container
  Disposable 172
Container Management
    Center 176
Container shortage 185
Container standardization 185
Container tracking 187
Containers 172
  Returnable 133, 134
Contamination 174

Continuous improvement 360
Conveyor 49
CONWIP 223
Co-opetition 350
Core competencies 336
Corporate citizenship 333
Corrosion 174
Cosmetics 338
Council for Logistics
    Management 24
Crandall, Robert 321
Crate 164
Cripple 41, 275
Crossdock 4, 74, 78, 140
Customer experience 273
Customer service 1, 311
Customers 14
Customer-supplier relationship 1
Customization 109, 333
  Service center 124
Customization Center 92
Customizing 340
Cycle counting 89, 99, 105, 316

D

Data envelopment analysis 110
Data mining 31, 99
Dead reckoning 105
Dealer 214, 328
Decision 17
Decision making 9
Decision support 4
Dedicated line 199, 207
Deli counter 21
Delivery 109, 136
  Frequency 133
Delivery performance 97
Dell 321, 336
Demand
  Fluctuations 75
Descriptive statistics 326
Design For Manufacturing and
    Assembly 45
Design of experiments 354
DFMA 45

Dispatch list 18
Dispatching 277
Disposable container 172
Distributors 12, 138, 328
Dock 90, 144
Dock number 89
Dock priority 147
Dock-to-dock logistics 12
Double-deep pallet racks 83
Downstream operation 200
Drive-in pallet rack 83
Dry cleaning store 86
Dunnage 169, 175, 179
Dust 174

E

Earthquake 278
ECO 363
Economic agent 342
Economies of scale 109
EDI 5, 27, 43, 251, 315, 321, 333
Effectiveness 28, 30
Efficiency 28, 30
E-kanban 5, 249
Electronic commerce 2
Electronic Data Interchange 43
Electronic document
        interchange 251
Electrostatic discharge 172
Eletronic Data Interchange 5
Email 251
Emergency response 27, 46
Environment 171, 178
Equipment acquisition 311
Equipment failure 273
Equity 160
ERP 18, 41, 99, 190, 277, 313
Escalation procedure 18
ESD 172
Excel 152
Exception handling 18
Excess 76
Excess inventory 76
Expediter 275

Express lane 20
Extrusion 274

F

Fabrication 9, 11, 218
Fastener 10
FAX 251
FAXban 261
FIFO 83, 299, 315
FIFO lane 83
Final assembly 122, 218, 273
Final inspection 109
Finger pincher 181
Finished goods 3, 12, 31, 109, 121
Finished goods inventory 121, 145
Finishing shop 138
Fire 278
First-in–first-out 83, 215, 265, 299
Fixture 37
Fleet management 333, 334
Flexible Manufacturing
        System 272
Flood 278
Flow rack 82, 85, 97, 203
Flow-through 79
FMS 272
Food 338
Ford 43, 187, 339
Forecast 27
Forecasting 5, 11, 19, 42, 320
Forklift 28, 49, 50, 51, 77, 83, 164,
        202, 204
    Driver 90
Fragmentation 102
Frazelle, Edward H. 24
Funds flows 9, 11, 24
Furniture district 350

G

GAMA 46, 358
Game theory 349
Gazoo 321
General Motors 335
Generic queue 20

Georgetown 116
Golden state Automotive
        Manufacturers
        Association 46
Government office 21
Grocery 20

H

Handling equipment 199
Hard disk 101
Headlight 164
High-volume-low-mix 83
Horizontal movement 50
Hot stamp 187
Hotel guest 98
Hub 132
Hunting 102

I

ILVS 255
Inbound logistics 12, 31, 342
Incoming quality assurance 169
Industrial park 148
Information flow 1, 9, 11
Information system 18, 27, 38, 187
Injection molding 274
Injection-molded plastic parts 40
Injex 122, 256
In-line vehicle sequencing 43, 255
In-plant logistics 342
In-plant transportation 3
Insultants 367
Intel 336
Intermodal 140
Internet 27
Inventory 31, 74, 164, 174
    Accuracy 27, 104
    Finished goods 145
    Tracking 104
    Visibility 135
    Water metaphor 75
Inventory accuracy 89
Inventory database 38
Invisible hand 13
Item

Destination 97
Source 97
Volume 97
Item number 96

J

Japan 171, 172
Jishuken 46, 353, 355, 360
Job shop 44
Jones, Dan 213
JUSE 355
Just-in-time sequencing 255

K

Kaizen blitz 358
Kaizen costing 45
Kaizen event 353, 358, 360
Kaizen Promotion Office 358
Kanban 2, 5, 37, 43, 44, 143, 159, 161,
        167, 188, 266, 315, 316, 363
    Central bank 265
    Rule 267
Kanban board 5
Kariya 41
Kitting 168, 333, 340
Korry Electronics 307

L

Label 109
Labeling 122, 187
Labor cost 161
Last-in–first-out 83, 143
Lead time 159, 160
    Predictability 134
    Replenishment 31, 134, 135
Lean Assembly 2
Lean certified supplier 328
Lean engineering 40
Lean manufacturin 18
Lean manufacturing
        implementation 354
Lean Suppliers Association 46
Lean supply chain 311
Less-than-truckload 132
Leveled sequencing 42, 199, 273

Li & Fung 137
LIFO 83, 143
Lift-and-rotate table 159
Lift-and-turn table 166
Line haul 139
Liquids 97
Little's law 199
Local-far milk runs 138
Logistics 9, 10, 11, 194
    Dock-to-dock 12
    Inbound 9, 12, 30
    In-plant 9, 12
    Outbound 9, 12, 31
    Performance 22
    Production boundary 11
Long-distance milk runs 140
Low-volume-high-mix 40
LSA 46

M

Machining 9, 10, 11
Magnet 189
Managing in a lean
        environment 106
Manufacturing 9
Manufacturing density 49
Manufacturing Execution
        System 44, 99
Manufacturing plant 159
MapsOnUs 148
Maquiladora 361
Marked aisle 49
Market intelligence 5, 31
Marketing 320
Master production schedule 311,
        319
Master schedule 5
Material control 334
Material flows 9, 10, 162
Materials handler 5, 201
Materials handling 3, 4, 12, 159, 162,
        200, 333, 334
Materials management 1, 12
Materials organization 201

Materials Requirements
        Planning 42
Meeting
    All-hands 106
    Start-of-shift 106
Mergers and acquisitions 114
MES 44, 99
Middleman 160
Military 3
Milk run 1, 3, 4, 27, 49, 122, 131, 132,
        134, 159, 167, 171, 177, 179,
        209, 266
    Local-far 138
    Remote 142
    Schedule 156
    Supplier 4, 112, 132
Milling machine 25
Mission Foods 339
Mistake-proof 109
Mixed-flow line 207
Mobile rack 82
Monden, Yasuhiro 309
Monthly planning 311
MRP 27, 42, 190, 277, 313, 326
Multiple handling 159

N

Nakao, Chihiro 359
Napoleon 23
Narrow aisle 82
Narrow-aisle truck 51, 77
Nash equilibrium 13, 349
Negotiation 18
Nestable 180
NUMMI 43, 46, 116, 122, 140, 256,
        358

O

OEM 328
Ohno, Taiichi 38, 74, 201, 367
OMCD 356, 361, 366
One-size-fits-all 27
On-line services 148
Order
    Cancellation 273
    Shuffling 274

Order fulfillment 2
Order fulfillment process 31, 39
Order picker 77
Order shuffling 18
Orders
  Replenishment 136
Outbound logistics 12, 27, 31, 342
Output buffer 36
Outsourcing 6, 114, 333
Overseas suppliers 159
Overtime 311

P

Pacemaker 304
Packaging quality 178
Packing material 166
Pagonis, William G. 24
Pallet 50, 74, 134, 159, 165
Pallet jack 49, 52, 77, 166, 202, 203
Pallet rack 32, 51, 52, 85, 89, 97, 202,
        203, 204
  Double-deep 83
  Drive-in 83
  Pushback 83
  Single-deep 82, 94, 102
Pallet stack 52
Palletizing 12
  Automatic 49
  Manual 49
Paradox of stock 31
Parking 102
Part presentation 193
Partial pallet 49
Pay-per-build 43, 111, 162
PC industry 343
Pegging 277
Penske Logistics 339
Physical distribution 1, 12
Pilferage 106
Pit crew 27, 30
Plant Receiving 164
PO 99
POLCA 223
Powders 97
PPAP 365

Priority 17, 18
Problem-solving 46
Procurement 135
Product design 27
Product knowledge
        requirements 340
Production 9, 194
  Performance 19
Production control 1, 4, 5, 265, 273
  Transactions. 189
Production Department 12
Production Part Approval
        Process 365
Production planning 27, 39
Production planning and
        scheduling 9, 11
Production run 5, 203
Production schedule 104
Production scheduling 39
Production supervisor 5
Productivity 29
Product-Quantity analysis 40, 274
Proportioning valve 41
Protocol 9, 17
Protocols 350
Pull 35
Pull signal 37, 204
  Issuing 204
Pull system 4, 27, 35, 41, 42, 104, 199,
        278
Pump 164
Purchase order 99
Purchasing 1, 5
Push cart 52
Pushback pallet rack 83
Pushcart 49
P-valve 41

Q

Quality 109, 136, 143, 333
  Assurance 122
  Packaging 178
  Problem report 97
Quality assurance 188, 195, 354
Quality check 340

R

Rack
 Identification 92
 Orientation 94
Radio taxi 49
Radio terminal 32
Railroad 12
Rate work 40, 274
Raw materials 3, 31, 109
Receiving 1, 3, 10, 18, 95, 133, 143, 146
Recycling 175
Remote milk runs 142
Remote suppliers 4, 137
Reorder point 43, 199, 204
Replenishment 199
Replenishment lead time 31, 134, 135
Replenishment orders 136
Response work 40, 274
Retrieval 10, 30
Returnable container 1, 4, 27, 34, 143, 159, 161, 176, 338
 Frequency of use 178
 Ownership 171
 Tracking 190
Returnable containers 133, 134
 Operating costs 178
 Sorting 176
 Storing 177
Reusable container 164
Reverse machining 300
RFID 89, 93, 100, 105, 107
RFID tag 43, 190
Route 334
Route planning 4, 148
Ryder 339

S

S&OP 311, 316, 317, 319
SABRE 321
Safety stock 76
Sales 5, 328
Sales and Operations
 Planning 311, 316

Saturn 339
Schedule 148
Scheduling 39
Schneider Logistics 339
Sea freigh 12
Seasonality analysis 40
Security 89, 106
Selective pallet rack 82
Semi-automation 49
Semiconductor equipment
 industry 111
Semi-finished goods 109, 120, 233
Semitrailer 143
Sequence Parts Delivery 255
Serial number 99, 104
Service center 109
Setup 5, 145
Setup time reduction 203
Shift 311
Shipping 1, 3, 10, 74
Shop floor operator 18
Shopping mall 101
Shortage 18, 27, 30, 44, 273
Short-interval sequencing 273
Shrinkwrap 28
Shrinkwrapping 109, 122
Shusa 357
Side-loading truck 143
Signage 189
Silo 97
Simulation 5, 199
Single source 27
Single-deep 32
Single-deep pallet rack 82
Single-sourcing 342
Size mismatch 191
Skid 166
sku 96
Slip-seat 139
Slot
 Allocation 96
 Dedicated 77
 Dynamic allocation 77
 Indexing 96
 Manual tracking 98

Separation 94
SMED 203
Smelting 11
SPD 255
Special order 273
Stackable 179
Staffing level 311
Staging area 202, 204
Stamping 274
Stock
    Paradox 31
Stock market crash 278
Stock-keeping unit 96
Storage 10, 30
Storage and retrieval 3, 195
Storage device 82
Subassembly 273
Subway 49
Suggestion systems 360
Sumi-e 367
Supermarket 20, 22, 109, 111
Supplier 12, 14
    Communication 136
    Communications 338
    Domestic 159
    Overseas 4, 159, 160
    Remote 4, 137
    Tier 27
    Warehouses 137
Supplier management 334
Supplier milk run 112, 132
Supplier network 278
Supplier on probation 92
Supplier performance 44
Supplier support 1, 145, 342
Supplier-customer relationship
    Adversarial 342, 344
    Collaborative 342, 345
Supply chain 9, 24, 342
Supply network 135
Sushi 367

T

Taffic management 333

Takt time 299, 354
Target costing 45
The two F's 28
Theft 174
Third-party logistics 6, 333, 334
Time-series 311
Timetable 5
Tool 10
Total Quality Control 215
Tote 50, 74
Touches 49, 50
Toyota 6, 27, 28, 39, 46, 116, 140, 186,
    199, 214, 265, 266, 278, 310,
    311, 333, 334, 339, 348, 353
Toyota Production System 319
Toys 338
TPS 319, 366
Traceability 104
Trading company 168
Traffic 50, 145
Traffic management 334
Trailer 143
Train
    Tow carts 49
Transaction processing 9, 18, 316
Transfers between buildings 51
Transfreight 334
Transportation 4, 10, 30
Transportation management 334
Transportation system
    Performance 50
Traveler 44
Travelocity 321
Truck 28, 143
    Mileage 133
    Side-loading 144
Truck priority 147
Trucking companies 12
Truckload 74
    Full 132
Trusted supplier 89
TSSC 358
Tufte, Edward 325
Tugger train 165

U

US 50, 171
Utilization 29

V

Value
  Presentation 28
  Time 28
Value engineering 45
VE 45
Vector SCM 335
Vehicle 51
Velcro 189
Vendor managed inventory 5, 27,
  43, 257
Vertical movement 49, 50
Victor Fung 137
Video 263
Vigilance 27, 31, 44, 76
Visibility 36, 202
Visible hand 37
Visible management 27, 38, 106,
  187, 316
VMI 5, 27, 257, 258

W

Waiting time 201
Warehouse 1, 2, 3, 4, 49, 109, 164,
  191
  Locations 90
  Management 74
  Manager 81

Saturation point 89
Storage device 82
Tracking 89
Visibility 89, 90
Zone identification 90
Warehouse club 19
Warehouse Management
  System 81
Warehousing 334
Waste
  Seven types 74
Water spider 12, 109, 111, 112, 193
Weather 145
Web-based EDI 251
Webster's 23
WIP 109, 120, 199
WIP tracking 44
Wire basket 188
Wire harness 164
WMS 81, 99, 105
Womack, James 213
Work in process 3, 31, 109
Work station 109
Workpiece 10, 25

X

XML 251

Y

Yanai, Naotake 183